Treasures from the Storeroom

"Then every scribe who has been instructed in the kingdom of heaven is like the head of a household who brings from his storeroom both the new and the old."

Matthew 13:52

Gary Macy

TREASURES FROM THE STOREROOM

Medieval Religion and the Eucharist

A PUEBLO BOOK

The Liturgical Press   Collegeville, Minnesota

A Pueblo Book published by The Liturgical Press.

Design by Frank Kacmarcik, Obl.S.B. Illustration: manuscript detail, *Bishop/Saint Celebrating the Mass*, 11th c., courtesy of The Art Institute of Chicago.

The eight essays of this book have previously been published in:

Gary Macy, *The Theologies of the Eucharist in the Early Scholastic Period* (Oxford: Clarendon Press, 1984) 1–17.

"The Theological Fate of Berengar's Oath of 1059: Interpreting a Blunder Become Tradition," *Interpreting Tradition: The Art of Theological Reflection,* ed. Jane Kopas, Proceedings of the Annual Convention of the College Theology Society, 1983 (Chico, Calif.: Scholars Press, 1984) 27–38.

"Reception of the Eucharist According to the Theologians: A Case of Diversity in the 13th and 14th Centuries," *Theology and the University,* ed. John Apczynski, Proceedings of the Annual Convention of the College Theology Society, 1987 (Lanham, Md.: University Press of America, 1990) 15–36.

"Berengar's Legacy as Heresiarch," *Auctoritas und Ratio: Studien zu Berengar von Tours,* eds. Peter Ganz, R.B.C. Huygens, and Friedrich Niewöhner, Wofenbütteler Mittelalter-Studien (Wiesbaden: Otto Harrassowitz, 1990) 47–67.

"The Dogma of Transubstantiation in the Middle Ages," *Journal of Ecclesiastical History* 45 (1994) 11–41.

"Demythologizing 'the Church' in the Middle Ages," *Journal of Hispanic/Latino Theology* 3 (1995) 23–41.

"Commentaries on the Mass in the Early Scholastic Period," *Medieval Liturgy: A Book of Essays,* Lizette Larson-Miller, ed. (New York and London: Garland Press, 1997) 25–59.

"The Eucharist and Popular Devotion," *Proceedings of the Catholic Theological Society of America* 52, Judith A. Dwyer, ed. (Macon, Ga.: Mercer University Press, 1997) 39–58.

Library of Congress Cataloging-in-Publication Data

Macy, Gary.
    Treasures from the storeroom : medieval religion and the Eucharist
/ Gary Macy.
       p.   cm.
    "A Pueblo book."
    Includes bibliographical references and index.
    ISBN 0-8146-6053-3 (alk. paper)
    1. Lord's Supper—History—Middle Ages, 600-1500.   2. Berengar, of
Tours, ca. 1000–1088.   I. Title.
BV823.M363   1999
234'.163'0902—dc21

98-32330
CIP

Dedicated to my colleagues in the College Theology Society and in the Department of Theological and Religious Studies at the University of San Diego all of whom make up an important part of my experience of the Communion of Saints.

Contents

Preface

Given a work which spans the efforts of nearly two decades, it would be impossible to thank all those who have helped, supported, cajoled, guided, chided me in my research. Surely among the most influential of my mentors include David Luscombe, Keith Egan, Walter Principe, Giles Constable, and Christopher Brooke, all of whom have consistently and patiently, if not always successfully, set me on the right course in my scholarly efforts. Many others have had a major role in shaping one or the other of the essays contained in this volume. Certainly without the aid and insight of Jeffrey Burton Russell, Alan Berstein, Dennis Krouse, Evelyn Kirkley, Roberto Rusconi, Robert Davis, Katherine Tachau, and Robert Swanson, the present set of essays would never have appeared, nor would it have occurred to me to research the questions raised within them. Orlando Espín deserves special thanks, not only for the insights his groundbreaking research has offered me, but also for his unwavering encouragement and support for this project.

I would also like to thank the entire Department of Theological and Religious Studies at the University of San Diego. One and all will recognize their pilfered ideas scattered among the essays. The members of the College Theology Society deserve similar recognition for their ideas, suggestions, support, and correction. I am privileged to work with such fine scholars. The University of San Diego, the Institute for Advanced Study at Princeton and the National Endowment for the Humanities have all provided financial support for one or the other of the research projects presented in this volume. The library of the University of San Diego has also gone far out of its way to track down the odd volumes which I constantly request from them.

Finally, I would like to thank The Liturgical Press for the opportunity of offering these essays to a wider audience.

Introduction

There are four very practical reasons for wishing to reprint the following eight essays in the form of a short book.[1]

First of all, these articles provide an important backdrop to the plenary address, "The Eucharist and Popular Devotion," presented at the 1997 national convention of the Catholic Theological Society of America (CTSA). Several themes raised in that address were actually summaries of the fuller arguments presented in these articles. In two instances the CTSA address borrowed directly from some of the articles in the present volume. Taken as a whole, then, these texts give a much fuller picture of the world of the high Middle Ages—a world I tried to bring to life in the aforementioned CTSA plenary address. Since this address, along with other plenary addresses of Dr. Mary Collins and Dr. John F. Baldovin, occasioned an extended discussion in the journal, *Commonweal,* a fuller presentation of the research underpinning that presentation seemed a useful contribution to the larger issues raised in this discussion.[2]

Secondly, the articles really do constitute a whole, better captured when these texts are themselves considered as a unit. There is frequent interplay of references among the articles as well as an interrelated set of themes which appear in this group of essays. Presenting them as a whole allows for easy intercourse among the references as well as a fuller development of themes raised in the texts.

Thirdly, the essays contained in this volume are not readily available to interested readers or even to fellow scholars. I have had a number of requests for copies, especially of the earlier articles published with the proceedings of the College Theology Society. *Theologies of the Eucharist in the Early Scholastic Period,* the introduction to which is reproduced here, has long been out of print. I have also been told that one of the articles, "Demythologizing the Church in the Middle Ages," is being used as a classroom text, and so I have included it in this volume as a service to those professors who may wish to so use the text.

Finally, bringing the articles together in a single volume permits the author the luxury of explicating themes—presented over the course of a dozen years—in a clearer, more systematic fashion. These six studies are most obviously linked by their subject matter. All of them treat of medieval religion, and all but one specifically of medieval understandings of the Eucharist.

The Introduction to *Theologies of the Eucharist in the Early Scholastic Period* forms a complete essay quite apart from the book in which it originally appeared and contains the clearest statement on the methodology used in all the other essays.

The second of the essays tracks the fate of the ill-conceived but canonically correct condemnation of the teachings of Berengar of Tours, the eleventh-century scholar and heretic. The precise definition of what constitutes "dogma" or "heresy" occupies central place in this article as well in the fifth article which investigates the formal standing of transubstantiation as a dogma in the Middle Ages. Berengar reappears in the fourth article as the heresiarch whose teaching influenced the later popular heresy of the Cathars.

The third essay, "Reception of the Eucharist According to the Theologians" argues that Thomas Aquinas (and his mentor Albert the Great) were intellectual oddities among thirteenth-century theologians of the Eucharist. Their metaphysical approach was largely overshadowed by the symbolic theology of Alexander of Hales and the Franciscan School. This more spiritual approach to the Eucharist had already found a voice in the devotional literature of the commentaries on the Mass. The theology contained in these commentaries is the subject of the seventh of the essays, "Commentaries on the Mass During the Early Scholastic Period."

The studies in the present volume, taken as a whole, attempt to develop similar arguments on several different levels. In this introductory essay, those themes will be explicated on four levels: the historical, the methodological, the theological, and the political.

On the purely historical level, the aim of the essays is twofold. First, an attempt has been made to correct historical errors that have crept into the tradition as well as to introduce new sources to both theologians and historians.

The most obvious contribution to the first of these aims is the essay, "The Dogma of Transubstantiation in the Middle Ages." The article follows up on the studies of Hans Jorissen and James McCue to demonstrate that there was no medieval consensus that transubstantiation was required for belief, much less an attempt to enforce such a belief. The assumption that there was such a consensus is tenacious, however. A recently published textbook, for example, continues to repeat that

"It's [Lateran IV's] members articulated officially for the first time, the doctrine of transubstantiation which declared that the bread and wine of the Eucharist were miraculously changed into the body and blood of Christ at the moment of consecration in the Mass."[3]

Not only is this *not* what transubstantiation means, but no such definition took place at Lateran IV. The question of the role of transubstantiation in medieval belief may be at present much more of a political question than an historical one. The implications of the political issues involved are raised most clearly in the essay "Demythologizing the Church in the Middle Ages"—but more on this later.

"Theologies of Reception" and, to a lesser extent, "Commentaries on the Mass," try to correct the current assumption that medieval eucharistic theology lacked any notion of a true theology of symbol, and that this absence led to a sterile allegorical approach to the liturgy. The argument supporting this view was made most famously by Henri de Lubac in his 1949 book, *Corpus Mysticum*. An evaluation of the limits of Fr. de Lubac's book is included in the "Introduction" to *Theologies of the Eucharist in the Early Scholastic Period*. Father de Lubac, and those who rely upon his book, assume that scholastic theology of the Eucharist was mainly preoccupied with the real presence and thus, ultimately, with transubstantiation. Both the article, "Theologies of Reception," and my earlier book, *Theologies of the Eucharist in the Early Scholastic Period*, argue strongly that this was not so. Again, it is our modern fascination with this question, at least since the time of the Reformation, which scholars appear to be reading back into their medieval predecessors.

Several untapped sources are introduced in the essays. Most notably, the commentaries on the Mass from the early scholastic period are presented in a more favorable light than most recent scholarship has placed them. The essay on this subject includes a list of the commentaries in the hope that others will avail themselves of this rich material. Several of the other studies in the present volume introduce theological figures rarely included in the discussion of medieval eucharistic theology. Special emphasis is placed on the very important Franciscan school of theology and more particularly on the work of Nicholas of Lyra.

Methodologically, the recovery of lost voices will help overcome a nearly unbudgable conviction, shared by most theologians and historians, that all medieval theology can be reduced to "one hefty Dominican." Especially in the essays on the Church in the Middle Ages and in the study on eucharistic reception, the point is most emphatically made that Thomas Aquinas must be understood in his own historical context, as one theologian among many who taught in the mid-thirteenth century. To quote or use Thomas as *the* representative of medieval thought both ascribes to him an authority he never enjoyed in his own era, and condenses centuries of thought into the words of one man. Imagine the outrage of scholars of a later historical period if a historian were to write that Roman Catholic theologians between Trent and Vatican II felt that fideism was essential for Catholicism, with an appropriate footnote to Descartes or Pascal. Theologians of that period would rightly point out that either thinker was but one out of many, and that most Catholic theologians of the time would strongly disagree with their positions. The same applies in the Middle Ages.

This brings up a rather tricky methodological point concerning scholarly languages. Most medieval theologians are not translated and many are not even edited. Does this mean that scholars who wish to refer to medieval theological opinion must learn not only Latin, but also paleography? Of course not; but they certainly must be careful to point out the textual basis for their theories. If the medieval works consulted and used are those by Thomas Aquinas alone, since he is readily available in English, then say so! If the basis is broader than Thomas, based for instance on secondary studies by medievalists who have read more widely, then say that. The important point is to be clear as to sources. Far too many scholars silence the voices of many brilliant medieval women and men by reducing all voices to the one. Not only is such an approach methodologically unacceptable, but also misleads readers into thinking that the theological tradition was much more monolithic than it really was.

This leads to the central theological point made again and again in all the essays, especially in the "Introduction" to *Theologies of the Eucharist in the Early Scholastic Period*. The true tradition of the Church is diversity. Each of these essays, and indeed all of my research, has been directed against what I think of as the "Big Book of Doctrine" school of historical theology. This strange form of authoritarianism, fomented both by the ultramontanism of the late nineteenth-century papacy and by Enlightenment anticlericalism, understands Roman Catholicism as fundamentally an attempt to provide the definitive answers to all questions, usually in one "big book of doctrine," whether it be Thomas's *Summa,* Denzinger's *Enchiridion,* or lately the Roman *Catechism of the Universal Church.*

As the "Introduction" to *Theologies of the Eucharist in the Early Scholastic Period* makes clear, I am very suspicious of any "developmental" historical theology. In addition to the arguments made in that essay, I would add two more. First, any theology that sees a gradual clarification of doctrine in Christian history smacks of incredible egocentrism—"all of human history leads inexorably to . . . us!" We must then be the epitome (so far) of God's creative plan. Late twentieth-century Western society seems already too preoccupied with intense self-absorption and self-adulation. Any theology than encourages this social self-centeredness ought to be avoided. Secondly—and following a similar line of reasoning to that of Terrence Tilley in his excellent study, *The Evil of Theodicy*[4]—developmental theology is just too cruel to those past movements that are not regarded as contributing to present institutions and thought. "Developmental" theology sees anyone or anything that does not prefigure us or our beliefs as either misguided, immature, or heretical. Although I would disagree in general with his world view, I do agree with G. K. Chesterton when he defines tradition:

"Tradition is democracy extended through time. Tradition means giving the vote to that most obscure of all classes, our ancestors. Tradition is the democracy of the dead. Tradition refuses to submit to the small and arrogant oligarchy of those who are walking around."[5]

The theology presumed in the present essays prefers to see each generation of Christians as equally graced by God, each striving to fulfill God's will as they understand it. Each generation failing, misunderstanding, or succeeding as much as we do. If this theological approach is correct, then the past seems not so much a simple path leading (how reassuring!) right to our doorstep, but rather many paths attempting to find their way to God. Perhaps not surprisingly, seen from this perspective, the past may well be more tolerant of diversity than some scholars have led us to believe.

The discovery of such diversity suggests two theological conclusions. First, and at the cost of being repetitious, is the well-founded belief that our true tradition is diversity itself. To be tolerant is a substantial part of our better Christian heritage. If there was diversity in the past, and that diversity was tolerated, then the best way to truly honor the past is to foster such diversity in the present.

Secondly, this understanding of the history of Christianity frees us in the present from a tremendous burden. If the past did not lead ineffably to us, then the future does not absolutely depend upon us "getting it right" either (whatever that might mean to different groups). We are surely called to do and live by, to the best of our ability, what we determine to be God's will (just as those in the past were supposed to do).

"Can it be wrong at any time or place to love God with all your heart and with all your soul and with all your mind and to love your neighbor as yourself?,"[6] asked St. Augustine, paraphrasing the gospel according to Matthew. If we fail, as we often do, God's future will not be destroyed by our failure. Theologians and bishops seem unduly worried that God will not "get it right." The view of history proposed in the present essays frees us to accept our own failures, to accept our inevitable involvement in original sin, without despairing for the future of the Church, of Christianity, or of humankind. Without overstepping the bounds of propriety, I might even suggest that such an approach might allow historians, theologians, bishops, and (dare I say it?) even popes to accept and cherish God's great grace of being able to laugh at themselves.

If theologians and prelates tend to see the past as a mere propaedeutic to their own existence and beliefs, secular historians can be downright defensive about the superiority of the present. The stale odor of social Darwinism wafts too frequently through the latter's works. The essay, "Demythologizing the Church in the Middle Ages" makes the strongest case for the dangers of perpetuating the mythology of a "totalitarian" medieval Church. One need only read Norman Cantor's *Inventing of the Middle Ages*[7] to experience the deep-seated misunderstanding and even hostility many secular academics feel for the medieval "Catholic" Church. When and if this hostility is transferred, in an act of historical confusion, to modern Roman Catholicism, the results can be unintentional bigotry.

I remember being seriously asked by a well known scholar of English literature if Chaucer (or Lydgate, I can't quite recall) was con-

cerned about getting into trouble with the Inquisition for some obscure reference to the Trinity in his work. "What," I was asked, "was
the position of the Church on this issue?" This was hard to answer.
Who did she mean by "the Church"? What made her think that medieval ecclesiastics cared to search poetry for possible Trinitarian heresies? More importantly, did she realize that there never was an
Inquisition in England? I muttered something about the matter really
never having been settled, so Chaucer (or Lydgate) probably never
gave it a thought. She looked at me like an idiot. I was a Roman
Catholic, a scholar of medieval theology, and, by God, I was supposed
to know (and believe) whatever the "Big Book of Doctrine"—which
she knew existed in Rome—said about the Trinity. She almost certainly considered Roman Catholicism superstitious nonsense, but did
agree with ultramontanist Roman Catholics about the existence of
that "Big Book."

There are so many myths surrounding the medieval Church and
medieval theology in particular that, over the years, I have developed
the working hypothesis of being suspicious of everything I read or
hear about the period. To use a common, if silly, example, I have often
heard it said that medievals prized spices, and heavily spiced their
foods, because they used spoiled meat and needed to disguise the
taste. Now, just a moment's thought should call this into doubt—did
the meat go bad the moment it was slaughtered? Was it never fresh?
Or did the medievals deliberately wait for it to go bad before they
cooked it? They knew about salting and pickling meats. Why would
anyone believe that medievals ate bad meat (unless they had to) any
more than any other people who didn't (or don't) have refrigeration?
It just doesn't make sense to believe that people in the Middle Ages
ate spoiled meat and used spices to disguise the bad taste. Couple this
with the fact that medieval cooking recipes (and many actually sur-
vive) are usually from the households of the nobility, and the more
obvious conclusion seems to be that *wealthy* medievals simply liked
fancy, spicy foods when they partied. This is a position, by the way,
with which I have great sympathy.

The equally vibrant myth of a monolithic and autocratic medieval
Church takes little thought to dispel. The long period of time involved resists any generalizations. Even within one particular period
of strong papal control, say that of Innocent III, theologians could no
more be expected to agree with bishops than they do now, nor did
bishops agree with the pope, nor with kings, nor with each other. The

same human motives, for good and evil, prevailed then as now. Finally, even if autocratic control was desired, it would have been extremely difficult to enforce without the modern means of communication and transportation.

The major reason that these erroneous notions persist is political, not historical. In the late nineteenth and twentieth centuries, a truly autocratic notion of Church was propagated with great success and then read back into the rest of Christian Catholic history. On the verge of the twenty-first century we are still wrestling with this terrifically successful campaign of misinformation. The most conservative supporters of the papacy and the papacy's bitterest Enlightenment critics *need* to believe in the totalitarian and monolithic power of the medieval Church. For the former, it gives a sense of tradition and a history to their present understanding of the papacy; to the latter it gives a convenient historical "whipping boy" to blame for the evils of the present.

In these essays I have done my very best to discomfort both camps. "The Dogma of Transubstantiation in the Middle Ages" attempts to meticulously and thoroughly refute the humanist claim that the medieval Church forced transubstantiation down the throats of the faithful. It equally attempts to undermine those Roman Catholics who assume that canonical statements automatically settled debate on theological issues. This latter point is take up directly in "The Theological Fate of Berengar's Oath." Papal statements were not automatically obeyed in the Middle Ages, nor did theologians stop discussing issues just because the pope said they should. The problems with mistaking the medieval Church as monolithic is taken up explicitly in "Demythologizing the Church in the Middle Ages."

In short, the essays contained here are an argument for political as well as theological toleration. To quote from an essay of mine not included in this collection:

"Take, for a moment, one group of distant descendants of the medieval *magistri*. One could analyze the economic structures of academics in the United States (or Europe) and conclude that the entire enterprise is driven by greed and pride. Scholarly publication takes place to advance one's standing in the academic community, and one's salary. Those who do so advance protect their positions by attacking all challengers and by producing loyal graduate students who will advance their positions. Further, those positions are rather narrowly focused, so that only certain approaches are rewarded. Deviance is punished by the inability to get published, resulting in obscurity, reduced salary, and eventually expulsion from the profession."

Now true as this picture may be, it is not the whole picture, nor is it what scholars say, and often believe, they are doing. They will say that they are interested in uncovering the truth; they will say that they are trying to correct errors in understanding the past; they will say they believe that education will advance humankind; and they might even say that they are simply insatiably curious and this is all great fun. At least in their better moments, they will not be lying. Greed, pride, and elitism may play a major role in modern academia, but these are not the ideals of academics, and the actual lives of academics are torn between ideals and temptations. It would be very unfair, not to mention infuriating, to be told that one's ideals were merely clever subterfuges for one's vices. . . . I feel it is worth extending the same courtesy to the medievals that we would wish extended to ourselves as scholars.[8]

You can apply the analogy to your own profession to personalize the point. The people in the past need to be treated with respect as people and not as fodder for the present's political agendas.

Finally, I can only add that I hope the readers of this collection will enjoy them half as much as I enjoyed writing them.

Gary Macy
September 1998

---

1. Notation has been standardized for all the essays as has spelling. Obvious typographical and other errors have been corrected. When possible, references to new critical editions have been made. Otherwise, the essays are produced here as they originally appeared.

2. See the articles by Avery Dulles, Mary Ann Donovan, and Peter Steinfels under the heading, "Disputed Questions: How Catholic is the CTSA? Three Views," in *Commonweal* 125 (March 27, 1998) 13–17. The articles occasioned a heated discussion contained in letters to the editor in the following three issues.

3. Vivian Green, *A New History of Christianity* (New York: Continuum, 1997) 72.

4. *The Evil of Theodicy* (Washington, D.C.: Georgetown University Press, 1991).

5. G. K. Chesterton, *Orthodoxy* (New York: John Lane, 1908) 85.

6. *The Confessions*, l. 3, c. 8 (15), Henry Chadwick, ed. (Oxford: Oxford University Press, 1991) 45–6.

7. Norman F. Cantor, *Inventing the Middle Ages: the Lives, Works and Ideas of the Great Medievalists of the Twentieth Century* (New York: W. Morrow, 1991).

8. "Was there a 'the Church' in the Middle Ages?" *Unity and Diversity in the Church*, Robert Swanson, ed., Studies in Church History 32 (Oxford: Blackwell, 1996) 115.

Abbreviations

DACL *Dictionnaire d'archéologie chrétienne et de liturgie,* Fernand Cabrol, and others, eds., 15 vols. (Paris: Letouzey and Ané, 1924–53).

DDC *Dictionnaire de droit canonique,* 7 vols. (Paris: Letouzey and Ané, 1935–65).

DHGE *Dictionnaire d'histoire et de géographie ecclésiastique,* Alfred Baudrillart and others, eds., 25 vols. to 1995 (Paris: Letouzey and Ané, 1912–).

DMA *Dictionary of the Middle Ages,* Joseph R. Strayer, ed. (N.Y.: Charles Scribners, 1982–89).

DSAM *Dictionnaire de spiritualité ascétique et mystique,* Marcel Viller, and others, eds., 17 vols. (Paris: Beauchesne, 1937–95).

DTC *Dictionnaire de théologie catholique,* A. Vacant, and others, eds., 15 vols. and indexes (Paris: Letouzey and Ané, 1930–67).

LThK *Lexicon für Theologie und Kirche,* Michael Buchberger, ed., 10 vols. and indexes and supplements (Freiburg: Herder, 1957–68).

NCE *New Catholic Encyclopedia,* 18 vols. (N.Y.: McGraw-Hill, 1967–89).

PL Jacques Paul Migne, ed., 217 vols. and indexes, *Patrologiae cursus completus . . . Series latina* (Paris: Garnier Fratres and J. P. Migne, 1878–90).

Chapter 1

Introduction to *The Theologies of the Eucharist in the Early Scholastic Period. A Study of the Salvific Function of the Sacrament According to the Theologians, ca. 1080–ca. 1220*[1]

Over fifty years have passed since Joseph de Ghellinck provided a guide to the wealth of the twelfth-century literature dealing with the early scholastic theology of the Eucharist.[2] Yet this same article, itself essentially a propaedeutic to further study, remains the only general introduction to the early scholastic theology of the sacrament.[3] Although articles regularly appear dealing with the eucharistic theology of individual early scholastic theologians, only a very few scholars have attempted to deal with this material as a whole.

One of the main reasons why the abundance of materials dealing with the Eucharist during this period remains largely ignored by modern scholarship may well be the rather dismal place to which the more general modern studies on the sacrament have condemned the early scholastic period. These studies, beginning with the de Ghellinck article, refer to the early scholastic theology of the Eucharist as fumbling attempts to anticipate the teaching of Lateran IV and of Thomas Aquinas in the thirteenth century by means of a logical and mechanical refinement of the teaching of Lanfranc in the eleventh century.

De Ghellinck certainly viewed the period in these terms. The introduction to his discussion of the eucharistic theology of the twelfth century begins:

"For the history of the theology of the Eucharist, the twelfth century constitutes a period of transition during which the intrinsic value of the works cannot be measured by the interest which they arouse in our own time. They wrote much, they discussed no less. But the writings and discussion scarcely rise above the level of trial studies or tentative advances: imprecision of language, inexactitude of expression, tentativeness of research, vacillation of thought; all of these things place their achievements well short of the perfection of the following century."[4]

For de Ghellinck, the twelfth-century study of the Eucharist had value only in the light of its contribution to the terminology of the Fourth Lateran Council and later thirteenth-century writers, and he leaves little doubt that the particular terminology to which he refers centers on the question of "transubstantiation."[5]

A. J. MacDonald, in his study of the Berengarian controversy, reiterates the approach of de Ghellinck when he treats of the twelfth-century writers:

"The idea of 'the thing of the sacrament' as a real presence, and the doctrine of Transubstantiation as the mode of the sacramental change, were admitted to be the orthodox interpretations of the Eucharist before the end of the eleventh century. . . . The eleventh century was occupied with the philosophic or scientific definition of the doctrine. The twelfth century conducted its theological grounding or foundation."[6]

MacDonald, like de Ghellinck, sees Lateran IV as the climax of twelfth-century eucharistic theology.[7] Both give the impression in their works that the twelfth century was a kind of incubation period between the Berengarian controversy and the statement on "transubstantiation" made by Lateran IV in which scholars painstakingly worked toward an orthodox interpretation of the eucharistic change. De Ghellinck, as a Roman Catholic, saw the conciliar statement as a significant advance in dogma, while the Anglican MacDonald decried the same statement as the outcome of the mistaken identification of the body of Christ born of Mary and the body present on the altar made by most eleventh- and twelfth-century theologians.

The general attitude of de Ghellinck remains the most common stance adopted by contemporary authors who speak of the early scholastic theology of the Eucharist. Jean de Montclos, in his recent study of Berengar and Lanfranc, describes the early scholastic period precisely as the bridge between Lanfranc and Thomas:

"It seems to us that with Lanfranc, Guitmund and Alger the sense of the evolution which will find its completion in the thomistic synthesis clearly manifests itself. One is able to trace a continuous line from Lanfranc to Saint Thomas, passing through Guitmund, Alger, and those who, during the course of the twelfth and thirteenth centuries, will continue the work accomplished by the antiberengarian polemicists with a view to discovering a better formulation of the real presence."[8]

Similar sentiments may be found in B. Neunheuser's discussion of medieval eucharistic theology,[9] and one finds echoes of it in other modern authors who speak of the early scholastic theology of the Eucharist incidentally in their works.[10]

Of the authors who treat of the theology of this period as part of a more general discussion, two authors deserve particular mention. Darwell Stone's monumental *A History of the Doctrine of the Holy Eucharist*, although now quite dated, presents the medieval teaching of the writers in a synoptic form, refraining as the author claims "to enter into controversial arguments or theological reasonings to any extent beyond that which the intelligible treatment of facts necessarily involves."[11] Jaroslav Pelikan includes a section entitled "The Real Presence" in the third volume of his history of doctrines, *The Growth of Medieval Theology (600–1300)*. The section is necessarily brief, and concentrates on the Berengarian controversy, presenting Lateran IV as the settlement of the issues raised therein. Within these limits, however, Pelikan offers what is probably the most complete and accessible presentation of early scholastic theology of the Eucharist.[12] These works, in so far as they refrain from denigrating the early scholastic writers in favor of their successors, offer exceptions to what appears to be a more common stance.

The understanding of the early scholastic period as peripheral to the later scholastic era focuses particularly on the question of the real presence and the use of the term *transsubstantiatio*. In the most important study in recent years on the theology of the Eucharist during the early scholastic period, Hans Jorisson has demonstrated the variety of interpretations which the term *substantia* had during this period and the consequent variety of interpretations of the eucharistic change.[13] Important as this study has been in helping to dissipate the notion of a monolithic evolution of eucharistic thought during this period, the basic approach which Jorisson adopts is similar in many ways to that of de Ghellinck, MacDonald, Montclos, and Neunheuser. Again, he concentrates on the development of the terminology of transubstantiation, particularly investigating the dogmatic value which the twelfth-century theologians placed on such terms.[14] Jorisson's work, while offering a real appreciation of the diversity of early scholastic eucharistic thought, still positions that diversity within a movement towards Lateran IV and Thomas Aquinas.

Another book which attempts to deal with the twelfth-century theologians' approach to the Eucharist is the 1927 monograph of Wilhelm Auer. In what Auer himself has called a "kurzer und nicht wissenschaftlicher Form," the book argues that the development of eucharistic theology during this period found its impetus and locus for discussion in the problems surrounding the continued existence of the "accidents" of the bread and wine after the consecration.[15] The author makes no attempt to relate his thesis to developments in early scholastic philosophy, and the result is more piety than scholarship. The pious Auer, like the scholarly Jorisson, sees the early scholastic period as important especially as it contributed to the terminology used by later theologians to describe the Lord's presence in the Eucharist, or to use Auer's own phrase, the early scholastic theologians were "direct heralds preparing for the golden age of the great Aquinas."[16]

The underlying premises upon which these studies are based will be examined at greater length below. For the moment, let it suffice to say that the early scholastic period has been, and still is, largely seen in terms of the accomplishments of the thirteenth century and continues to be ultimately discerned through the great prism of the Reformation. To underplay the value of using the Reformation as a vantage point for investigating the eucharistic theology of the early scholastic period in these works would be both unrealistic and unfair. Unrealistic, because only three of the works cited above even purport to deal with the early scholastic period as such, and of those, de Ghellinck's article is meant to be merely introductory while Jorisson's research specifically deals with transubstantiation. The others present a more sweeping overview of the period, and the Reformation provides an obvious landmark from which to describe the larger panorama of theological development. Further, the insights gained from such an approach are valuable, if somewhat limited. The development of the terminology surrounding the eucharistic change is important precisely because of the light it sheds on later theological controversy.

The difficulty with such an approach is that it tends to say more about the Reformation controversies and what they saw as central than what the early scholastic period may have felt to be the importance of the Eucharist.

Before proceeding to detail the particular vantage point from which this present study will proceed, a word should be said about three authors who have described the early scholastic theology of the Eucharist from viewpoints slightly different than those discussed above. One of the most important figures in the study of medieval eucharistic theology has been Joseph Geiselmann. Centering his research mainly on the early medieval period, especially the theology of Isidore of Seville, Geiselmann treats of the early scholastic period only in passing.[17] The few suggestions which Geiselmann offers concerning research into that period, however, are worth mentioning. In general, he describes the eucharistic theology of the early Middle Ages as a gradual rise in emphasis of an "Ambrosian" or corporeal understanding of the Eucharist over against an "Augustinian" or more spiritual understanding. The first of these approaches focused on the presence of Christ on the altar, while the second centered rather on a form of Neoplatonic participation in the presence of Christ in the Eucharist. With the Berengarian controversy, Geiselmann sees the most blatant example of the ascendancy of the "Ambrosian" over the "Augustinian" approach to the sacrament.[18] In describing the aftermath of the controversy, however, he points out the continuing use of Augustine's terminology among the early scholastic theologians, particularly Anselm of Laon. Geiselmann suggests that perhaps a new balance between the two general trends of "Augustinian" and "Ambrosian" elements came to exist during this period.[19] In a short article discussing the need for further research into the eucharistic theology of the early scholastics, Geiselmann repeats his views, adding that the rise of popular devotion during this period might provide an important key to its theology.[20] Geiselmann's studies do not deal directly with the early scholastic period, but like Jorisson's later study, they provide an indication that greater diversity existed during that period than is usually accredited to it.

Another scholar who treats of the early scholastic period in terms of a larger historical context is Henri de Lubac in his book *Corpus mysticum*. Treating specifically of the phrase which makes up the title of his book, de Lubac shows that *corpus mysticum* was originally used to differentiate the Body of Christ present on the altar from the body of

Christ born of Mary and present in heaven. Under the influence of medieval theology, the meaning of the phrase changed and gradually came rather to describe the Church as the body of Christ symbolized in the Eucharist.

Like Geiselmann, de Lubac describes the closer and closer identification of the body of Christ present in heaven and the Body of Christ present on the altar culminating in the complete identification of these two forms of Christ's presence by the opponents of Berengar.[21] De Lubac describes how this identification and the resultant insistent defense of the identification causes the term *corpus mysticum* to be transferred to the effect of the sacrament, the Body of Christ which is the Church.[22] Central to this change in terminology stands the figure of Peter Lombard, whom de Lubac sees as the chief advocate in promoting the change.[23] De Lubac has little but scorn for the Lombard and the early scholastic theologians, whose use of dialectic he holds as responsible for the loss of the patristic sense of balance in treating of the sacrament. By overemphasizing the Real Presence and the logical questions raised by that presence, de Lubac feels that the early scholastics lost the notion of symbol essential to the understanding of the Eucharist.[24]

De Lubac's work, while dealing with a different idea from that of de Ghellinck, MacDonald, or Montclos, constitutes a similar approach. The Berengarian controversy marks a kind of watershed after which theologians, for better or worse, emphasized the Real Presence in speaking of the Eucharist. De Lubac's great contribution lies in his delineation of one of the other important concerns of the early scholastic theologians: the relationship of the Eucharist and the Church.[25]

Corpus mysticum remains essentially a textual study and as such has the strengths and weaknesses of a textual study. It demonstrates in a lucid and scholarly manner the change in terminology from the patristic to the medieval periods of the phrase in question. It necessarily does not treat of any particular shorter period of time, nor of other possible changes and problems. De Lubac, however, goes beyond the limits of this textual study in the conclusions he draws. To demonstrate that the early scholastic theologians modified patristic terminology in one area, however unfortunately, cannot serve as a demonstration of the inadequacy of the whole range of early scholastic thought on the Eucharist. Perhaps, because of what *Corpus mysticum* does not treat, de Lubac's sweeping condemnation of the early scholastic period goes beyond the evidence his study provides. The concern to describe

6

the relationship between the Eucharist and the Church was, this study will hope to show, only one of the governing concerns of the early scholastics; a concern which *Corpus mysticum*, because of its focus on the problem of the Real Presence, perhaps overstresses.

Another work, also dealing with the relationship between the Eucharist and the Church as the Mystical Body of Christ, is the doctoral dissertation of Ferdinand Holböck, *Der eucharistische und der mystiche Leib Christi in ihren Beziehungen zueinander nach der Lehre der Früh-scholastik.* Holböck, unlike de Lubac, concentrated specifically on the early scholastic period. His work, mainly a compendium of the teaching of the early scholastic theologians on the Mystical Body, draws far more cautious conclusions than de Lubac. Holböck acknowledges the growing interest which the early scholastic theologians showed in the relationship between the Eucharist and the Church[26] and recognizes that the initial organization of sources by these theologians formed a base for later inquiry.[27] The importance of Holböck's work consists mainly in his thoroughness. He treats of nearly every important theologian from the early scholastic period and manages to include references to several less well-known authors and works. One of the important results of this attention to detail lies in Holböck's recognition of the diversity of the authors whom he treats. In speaking of Durand of Troarn, he points out that this author, unlike later authors, understands the Church to be made up of those individuals united first of all to Christ.[28] He recognizes in the writings of the School of Laon and in Hugh of St. Victor the teaching that the union of the Mystical Body is made up of individuals first joined to God in faith and love.[29] Again Holböck notes that the School of Abelard saw the Eucharist as a sign of the union of the Church formed in baptism, but not as effecting that union.[30] Holböck does no more than point out these variations. His thesis does not demand any overall synthesis nor does he attempt one. Like Geiselmann before him and Jorisson after him, he merely alludes to the richness of thought which might be found in the eucharistic theology of the early scholastics.

Of all the works discussed here, only two, those of Jorisson and Holböck, have attempted to deal exclusively with specific questions raised in the early scholastic theology of the Eucharist. Both studies have indicated an unsuspected richness and diversity. The purpose of this book will be to present, in a schematic fashion, the different understandings of the Eucharist which underlie the variety of teaching on the sacrament during this period.

To suggest such a purpose, however, immediately raises a host of problems which might best be subsumed under the general heading of method. The two most obvious questions to be raised would seem to be: (1) if a schematic presentation is envisaged, what sort of schema will be used, and (2) how can the use of such a method be justified?

To raise large questions of method in the introduction to a book which purports to deal with one of many theological issues dealt with in the relatively short timespan of the early scholastic period is in a sense to open a Pandora's box of debates involving historiography, theological methodology, and epistemology in what might seem entirely inappropriate surroundings. The only justification for such unwarranted temerity would be that a particular approach will be employed here, somewhat different from that of earlier scholars who have dealt with the question, and therefore some explanation and justification for that approach seem to be demanded. Yet to say that is not to say that any attempt will be made, or indeed, ought to be made here to resolve or even present in any kind of depth the complexity of questions involved in the area of historical and theological method. All that will be attempted will be a very basic and perhaps simplistic sketch of the problems involved in choosing and justifying a method for discerning and describing what is after all the real focus of this book, the early scholastic teaching about the Eucharist.

Different assumptions used in handling the medieval sources seem to yield different descriptions of the period in question. To assume, for instance, that bread and wine cannot change into flesh and blood would immediately discredit any literal acceptance of the accounts of the miracle Host at Arras, despite the good historical evidence of several independent and reliable eyewitnesses. That *something* happened at Arras seems indisputable; the description which a historian gives that event (mass hysteria, red fungus, fraud, or miracle) will partially depend on his or her own assumptions about the physical universe. To take a less trivial example, historians differ considerably over their descriptions of the twelfth century and the effect (or lack thereof) of the intellectual and social foment during that century on the development of the recognition of the individual, and the relationship of this development to an interest in "humanism."[31] Part of this divergence is due to choice of subject matter, but it may also in large part be due to the different historians' assumptions about what constitutes humanism and what determines recognitions of individuality and the social status of the individual. Was the twelfth century an ephemeral humanistic "renaissance" or a propaedeutic for the thirteenth or even fifteenth centuries? It seems reasonable to suggest that the answer to this question lies not only, or even mainly, in a closer investigation of the sources, but in a more careful delineation of the assumptions and methods brought to the sources.

The problem compounds itself, or at least becomes more acutely evident, when one enters the area of historical theology. A. J. MacDonald and Jean de Montclos present almost mirror-image reflections in their descriptions of the culmination of the Berengarian controversy, despite their considerable concern for historical sources and detail. MacDonald, an Anglican in the Protestant tradition, describes Gregory VII's condemnation of Berengar as a disastrous error, a chance missed to effect the reformation of the Church which would only come more painfully in the sixteenth century. The theology of Lanfranc, Berengar's opponent, would lead inevitably to Lateran IV, Thomas Aquinas, and Trent, with the understanding that Trent was the embodiment of medieval error. De Montclos sees the theology of Lanfranc as a brilliant contribution to the theology of the Eucharist because it led inexorably to Lateran IV, Thomas Aquinas, and Trent, but Trent here is understood as the definitive enunciation of truth.

There is a particular method at work here, based on a set of historical and theological presuppositions. The major historical presupposition is that the theology and philosophy of Thomas Aquinas were the pinnacle of medieval thought (for good or evil), towards which all earlier thought was groping. This presupposition lies behind, for instance, de Ghellinck's description of the theology of the twelfth century as imprecise, inexact, and tentative. Although this presupposition is shared with some historians of, say, philosophy or culture, and so might be designated a "historical" presupposition, in this particular case, at least, the presupposition is part of a larger theological position. Leaving aside the rather knotty question of the role of Aquinas in the history of medieval thought, it was to Aquinas' theology that the fathers of Trent referred as support for their condemnation of reformed teaching on the Eucharist. If earlier theologians prefigured Thomas, and Trent promulgated Thomas's teaching, then rejection or defense of twelfth- (not to mention thirteenth-) century theology becomes, in a not so subtle way, a rejection or defense of Trent. Thus to see the history of medieval theology is to judge the importance of this history in terms of its relationship to the Reformation.

The approach to Christian history assumed here might be described in more general terms as developmental. Based on the analogy of organic growth, the history of theological thought according to this line of thought, would be described as a movement toward a certain more or less definitive and normative ("mature") expression. For de Montclos, de Ghellinck, and Auer, for instance, such an expression would be Trent, the decrees of which would be normative for understanding the Eucharist. For MacDonald, on the other hand, the normative expression would seem to be the Thirty-nine Articles as presented in the final chapter of his book.[32]

Two further characteristics ought to be delineated in the general theological stance taken by these authors. First, the authors are not explicitly aware of adopting any particular theological stance. What they intend to present is what was taught in the past, simply and directly. Without delving into the thorny problems involved in the interpretations of historical texts, it might at least be noted that such an unstated, and therefore uncritical, adoption of a theological stance would suggest that the authors are unaware of the way in which their presuppositions might affect not only their selections of materials, but also the way in which these presuppositions might predetermine their conclusions.

Secondly, certain dogmatic assumptions tend further to enhance the possibility of a prejudicial presentation of the early scholastic teaching on the Eucharist. The authors discussed here assume that the "mature" expression of the Christian teaching on the Eucharist is normative and hence irreformable at least in the negative sense of proscribing certain theological positions. The implication is that certain normative and usually creedal expressions are revelatory in the sense of an immediate and self-validating disclosure of God in history. The prehistory of that disclosure, the unfolding of revelation as it were, then shares in the normative and revelatory nature of the final definitive expression. Since this final expression of revelation is definitive and irreformable, events leading up to that moment are of historical importance only in so far as they can be seen to contribute toward it. Theology, in both its historical and dogmatic functions, tends to be understood in this approach as attempts directly to describe the Divine's relationship to humanity in order to provide norms for human belief and action. Dogmatic theologians are seen to strive for even more accurate descriptions of all aspects of divine-human relations. Historical theologians relate the success or failure of such attempts in the past by using those expressions of belief which have become canonized as revelatory by a particular Christian community as the criteria by which past events are to be judged.

As already stated, this particular method for doing historical theology should not be underestimated, and the insights gained from such a method are valuable. However, this approach does entail certain drawbacks which suggest that more adequate methods are needed. First of all, areas for research are too easily limited by this model to questions relevant to Reformation disputes. Of the works in question, for instance, nearly all have limited their research to medieval and patristic teaching about the presence of the Lord in the Eucharist. Surely a history of the theology of the Eucharist shaped by this one question offers a very narrow view of the richness of eucharistic thought and practice. Secondly, the expressions of Christian teaching accepted as normative by the authors in question tend to be applied retrospectively to earlier periods and teaching. Those periods in which the discussions of the presence of the Lord in the sacrament received special attention tend to assume major historical importance for this approach. Thus, the works of Paschasius and Ratramnus are deemed to have comprised the first eucharistic controversy, rather than the earlier dispute between Amalarius and Florus. The Berengarian affair receives central attention rather than the ongoing dispute with the Cathars in the twelfth century or the hotly disputed question of the validity of the sacrament contemporaneous with the Berengarian dispute. Medieval teaching, too, becomes subject to the normative expressions accepted by the author. Works which differ from the norm are either heterodox, or "imprecise, inexact, tentative and vacillating." For Geiselmann, for instance, Ratramnus was clearly heterodox, despite the fact that the orthodoxy of his work was never questioned during his lifetime, and MacDonald upholds Berengar's teaching as a courageous proclamation of truth despite its multiple condemnations in the eleventh century. Finally, terms stemming from the Reformation disputes tend to be used to describe positions held by medieval and patristic authors. Geiselmann, for instance, prefers to classify authors as espousing some form of either "spiritualist" or "realist" theology.

By simplifying the theological stance which appears to underlie much of the research done on the eucharistic theology of the early scholastic period, and in the process perhaps overstressing its weaknesses, there is no intention to vilify the work done by these scholars, but merely to point out its limits. Certain unconscious, or at least, inexplicit, dogmatic presuppositions appear to have both limited the areas of research explored in the studies described above, and prejudiced some of the conclusions reached by them. By adopting a somewhat different set of theological assumptions, and by adopting them explicitly, this present study will attempt to broaden the areas of interest for a study of early scholastic eucharistic theology and suggest a different method for schematizing the results of that study.

The major theological premise that this work assumes understands the history of Christianity as the ongoing attempt to live out the Christian message in differing social contexts. The history of Christian thought, then, might be described as the continual attempt to mediate between the lived Christian message and the cultural matrix in which it exists.[33] What is envisaged in abandoning the theological stance of earlier writers is that shift in the understanding of the history of Christianity described by Yves Congar:

"History (is) understood less as continual process of 'development,' that is as progress achieved through a gradual unfolding of what was already implicit, and more as a series of formulations of the one content of faith diversifying and finding expression in different cultural contexts."[34]

To adopt such a theological stance entails the abandonment of the assumption that particular expressions of Christian witness are definitive and irreformable criteria for evaluating the history of Christianity (apart from the quite problematic sense in which Scripture is witness to such an expression in the life and death of Jesus). The normative nature of say Trent or the Thirty-nine Articles would rest in their authoritative proscription of certain forms of religious language in specific historical situations because these usages are felt to misrepresent the relationship between God and humanity embodied in the Christian message. These proscriptions ought not to be applied retrospectively, nor should they be viewed as revelatory in the sense of an immediate and self-validating description of God's actions. They remain revelatory, however, in so far as they fulfill the Christian hope that such proscriptions are signs of God's continued care.

The stance described here raises serious theological questions. How does one know that historically conditioned and therefore changing language remains faithful to the Christian message, or even more basically, how can one know that it is the message of God's love which such historically conditioned language carries? Without attempting to resolve these very important questions, one might at least note that the language of faith has provided a series of metaphors for God by which Christians have lived and died in the hope that these metaphors have a referent, and that this hope comprises a necessary condition for such a life and death. Nicholas Lash appears to be referring to a similar idea in the conclusion of his discussion of the conditions under which theology might be done:

"It is not, I think, simply predictable academic caution that has inhibited me from attempting the further task of specifying the sufficient conditions for such an enterprise (critical theology). It is, rather, the conviction that, in so far as any such further specification were to be possible at all within the limits of historical existence, its grammar would be closer to that of the language of prayer than of theoretical argument."[35]

Without resolving the question of how one judges past (or present) language about God to be truly about *God,* the historian as theologian is faced with the task of recovering and presenting for modern readers earlier attempts to appropriate the Christian message in a particular cultural context. One inevitably faces choices here. What method will be used to uncover and disclose language and actions of the past? Which language and/or actions of the past will be investigated and why? No historian would be capable of investigating or even selecting for investigation any particular period or problem in the past without, implicitly or explicitly, making such decisions. By making explicit, as far as possible, the particular method used in this study, it is hoped that the method and the premises behind it might be more open to correction, revision, or even abandonment.

To mention these options suggests that straightforward criteria exist for choosing and revising the methods used for historical research. Once again, a realistic appraisal of the literature available on methodology suggest at least that the selection of criteria for choosing between methods remains problematic. Without becoming involved in the much discussed problems of what is termed by Bernard Lonergan as dialectic,[36] the criteria employed here might be described as twofold. First, the theological assumptions supporting the method ought to meet the standards demanded of reasonable discourse, and secondly, the method used ought to be suitable for appropriating information from historical sources without contradicting, distorting, or arbitrarily dismissing those sources. What is envisaged here might be described as an appeal to Rudolf Bultmann's distinction between the role of presuppositions and prejudice in historical research.[37] What is desired, without denying the problems inherent in such an attempt, is research based on reasonable presuppositions to the exclusion, as far as possible, of prejudice. The success or failure of that attempt remains more to be judged in the argument of the book than in that of the introduction.

Assuming, as this study does, that the language of faith is a constant attempt to provide metaphors for the inexpressible God in God's relationship to humanity, the method used here will be that of searching out dominant metaphors used in the past, whether reflectively or unreflectively, to describe some aspect of the divine/human relationship. These metaphors would then be used as models to order and interpret the theological endeavors of the past. On this level, the model need not have been used consciously by the theologians under investigation, but need only provide an indication of how their thought might be identified and described in a schematic fashion. The period under investigation may be found to produce one particularly dominant metaphor to describe some particular aspect of religious life, or it may produce several different metaphors, which may themselves be irreconcilable on the level of theoretical models. Particular theologians in the past may display one or more models in their work; even if these models are divergent or conflicting. Certainly in this regard, theologians in the past ought to be accorded the same capacities for confusion, inconsistency, and stupidity as their modern descendants.

The models used here are not meant as descriptions of reality, but only as useful means of appropriating the past in a schematic fashion.[38] A description of each model as well as an explanation of its application to medieval theology occurs in the respective chapters dealing with that model.

The book intends to deal mainly with the work of professional academics rather than with more popular preaching or devotional practices. This is not to say that some attempt will not be made to place the work of the early scholastic theologians within the context of the more popular religious understandings of their time. A presentation of the early scholastic theology of the Eucharist which ignores the cultural setting in which that theology was written inevitably misleads. The *questiones* which appear in the *sententie* and *summe* of this period when presented on their own can frequently give the appearance of recounting opinions solely of academic interest. The authors assumed

14

a whole cultural and social milieu with which they expected their readers to be familiar, and the poor modern reader is often left with the dry skeleton of what was once a vibrant debate. The theology of this period had not yet reached the state of purely academic discussion. It developed in response and sometimes in opposition to the social and cultural movements of the time, answering what were felt to be, not only theological, but also religious and pastoral problems. The discussions of the theologians, then, make sense only in terms of those movements and those problems. Yet, what this study hopes to present is the works of the theologians in their cultural setting rather than a study of popular religious movements.

Further, this study intends to investigate only one of many possible themes in eucharistic theology, that of the salvific function of the sacrament. To put the question under investigation in its simplest form: What use or uses did the educated Christian community in the early scholastic period see in the inherited ceremony of ritual offering and communal eating known as the Eucharist? The question, of course, can be asked of any period in the history of Christianity. It was during this period that, for the first time, the question became of central interest to a great number of professional scholars. The question will, it is hoped, uncover what purpose the theologians of that period themselves saw in the Eucharist and, hence, disclose the major metaphors used by those theologians in speaking of the Eucharist.

Yet, in so narrowing the question under investigation, other important and related questions inevitably suffer short shrift. Certainly, a thorough study of the soteriology of the period would aid in understanding how the early scholastics approached the theology of the Eucharist. Equally, if not more important, would be an investigation of the influence of the developing christology of the medieval thinkers on the understanding of the ritual in which they held Christ to be present. Again, as Henri de Lubac has shown, a theology of the Eucharist nearly always presupposes some particular understanding of the Church. Surely a more thorough investigation of this area would aid in ascertaining the early scholastic theology of the Eucharist. Given the terminology used to describe the mode of the presence of the Lord in the sacrament, the rediscovery of Aristotelian metaphysics could not help but affect the teaching on the Eucharist. Finally, a study of the diversity of liturgical rites used during the period in question would help enflesh a study of a theology ultimately dependent upon those rituals. All these further areas for research will be touched on briefly in this work, but adequately to meet all these demands would require not one, but many studies. One can only hope that by pursuing one study well, one will raise other unanswered questions to entice other and better scholars to pick up where this work leaves off.[39]

The book deals, then, with a particular theological question, and with the answer given that question during the early scholastic period. In doing so, one hopes, it will bring into sharp focus the diversity of the theological thought on the Eucharist. Yet the celebration of the Lord's Supper, then as now, is a living ritual, enacted in community; a mystery which cannot be exhausted by any one theological discussion or question. Ritual, piety, and theology of the Eucharist were, in many ways, seen as more of a unity by the early scholastic writers than by present theologians, and this must be kept in mind when treating of one aspect of the whole complex of relationships present here.

---

1. Originally published by Oxford: Clarendon Press, 1984.

2. Joseph de Ghellinck, "Eucharistie au XIIe siècle en occident," *DTC* 5:1233–1302.

3. See, for instance, ibid., 1234.

4. "Dans l'histoire de la théologie de l'eucharistie, le XIIe siècle constitue une période de transition durant laquelle la valeur intrinsèque des ouvrages ne peut se mesurer à l'intérêt qu'ils sucitent de nos jours. Mais écrits et discussions ne s'élèvant guère au-dessus de travaux d'essais out de tentatives d'approche: imprécisions de language, inexactitudes dans l'expression, tâtonnements dans les recherches, fléchissements dans la pensée, tout cela place ces productions fort en deçà de la perfection du siècle suivant." *DTC* 5:1233–34.

5. Ibid., 1301–02. Cf. ibid., 1234 and 1285.

6. A. J. MacDonald, *Berengar and the Reform of Sacramental Doctrine* (London: Longmans, Green, 1935) 364.

7. See ibid., ch. 22, esp. 404.

8. Jean de Montclos, *Lanfranc et Berengar; La controverse eucharistique du XIe siècle*, Études et documents 37 (Louvain: Spicilegium sacrum Lovaniense, 1971) 470.

9. *L'Eucharistie. II. Au moyen âge et à l'époque moderne,* trans. A. Liefooghe, Histoire des dogme 25 (Paris: Éditions du Cerf, 1966) 57–93, esp. 67.

10. See, e.g., Joseph Powers, *Eucharistic Theology* (N.Y.: Herder and Herder, 1967) 29–31. W. Dugmore and E. L. Mascall, while adopting this general approach, appear open to the possibility of a more diverse interpretation of this period. See Dugmore, *The Mass and the English Reformers* (London: Macmillan,

1958) 39–42, 59; Mascall, *Corpus Christi. Essays on the Church and the Eucharist,* 2nd ed. (London: Longmans, 1965) 185–88; and esp., Dugmore, "The Eucharist in the Reformation Era," *Eucharistic Theology Then and Now,* R. E. Clemens and others, Theological Collections 9 (London: S.P.C.K., 1968) 71–73. See also Tad Guzie, *Jesus and the Eucharist* (Paramus, N.J.: Paulist Press) 64–68.

11. *A History of the Doctrine of the Holy Eucharist* (London: Longmans, Green, 1909) 1:1.

12. *The Growth of Medieval Theology (600–1300),* The Christian Tradition 3 (Chicago: University of Chicago Press, 1978) 184–204.

13. *Die Entfaltung der Transsubstantiationslehre bis zum Beginn der Hochscholastik,* Münsterische Beiträge zur Theologie 28 (1) (Münster: Aschendorff, 1965). See, e.g., 155–56.

14. Ibid., ch. 2. See also 155.

15. *Das Sakrament der Liebe im Mittelalter. Die Entwicklung der Lehre des hl. Altarsakraments in der Zeit von 800–1200* (Mergentheim, 1927) 5.

16. Ibid., 119.

17. The major works by Geiselmann on the Eucharist include *Die Eucharistielehre der Vorscholastik,* Forschungen zur christlichen Literatur- und Dogmengeschichte 15 (1–3) (Paderborn: F. Schoningh, 1926) and *Die Abendmahleslehre an der Wende der christlichen Spätantike zum Frühmittelalter. Isidor von Seville und das Sakrament der Eucharisitie* (Munich: Max Hueber, 1933).

18. Geiselmann, *Die Eucharistielehre der Vorscholastik,* 290–406.

19. Ibid., 431–41. See also 448: "So war um 1100 inhaltliche wie formell im einzelnen so Reiches erarbeitet, daß, es zur Synthese drängte. Sie war das Werk der Schule Anselms von Laon, die damit den Auftrakt für die frühscholastichen Eucharistietraktate gab."

20. "Zur Eucharistielehre der Frühscholastik," *Theologische Revue* 29 (1930) 1–12. Geiselmann reviews here *Das Sakrament der Liebe im Mittelalter,* of which he gives an extremely unfavorable estimation.

21. *Corpus mysticum: L'Eucharistie et l'église au moyen âge. Étude historique,* 2nd ed., Théologie. Études publiées sous le direction de la Faculté de Théologie S. J. de Lyon-Fourvière 3 (Paris: Aubier, 1949) 184–88.

22. Ibid., 288.

23. Ibid., 117–18.

24. Ibid., 252–67, 274–77. See, for instance, 256–57: "Les belles considerations du passé, les symboles ruisselant de richesses doctrinales sont à leur tour relégués au second plan, quoique sans mépris formel. De la dialectique insidieusement négatrice, à laquelle on ne peut se contenter toujours d'opposer un recours à la Toute-Puissance, seule pourra triompher une autre dialectique. Après une séries de tâtonnements, celle-ci, deux siècles après Bérengar, sera prête."

25. This relationship is also treated in a quite abbreviated form by George Tavard, "The Church as Eucharistic Communion in Medieval Theology,"

Continuity and Discontinuity in Church History, eds. F. Forrestor Church and Timothy George (Leiden: Brill, 1979) 92–103. Tavard seems unaware of de Lubac's work.

26. *Der eucharistische und der mystiche Leib Christi in ihren Beziehungen zueinander nach der Lehre der Frühscholastik* (Dissertatio ad lauream in faculatate theologica pontificiae universitatis Gregorianae, Rome, 1941) 190–91.

27. Ibid., 239.

28. Ibid., 12.

29. Ibid., 63–64, 102–22. See, e.g., Hölbock's discussion of the Summa "Inter cetera alicuius scientie," 121–2: "Hier ist also bei der Beschreibung der Wirking der Eucharistie von keiner Incorporatio durch sie die Rede, sondern nur einer ethischen Angleichung an Christus durch Glaube, Hoffnung und Liebe." On this *summa,* see Gary Macy, *Theologies of the Eucharist in the Early Scholastic Period,* 84, 184–85.

30. Ibid., 126–40. See, e.g., 127: "Der Eingliederung in der mystischen Leib wird nicht durch die Eucharistie oder durch die Taufe in Verbindung mit der Eucharistie bewirkt, sondern nur durch die Taufe allein. Die Eucharistie ist bloss Symbol des durch die Taufe auferbauten mystichen Leibes. Dieses Betonunt der Unwirksamkeit der Eucharistie für die Einverleibung in der mystichen Leib ist der Schule Abalards eigen." On the School of Abelard, see Macy, *Theologies,* 114–18, 203–06.

31. For references to discussions of this question, see Macy, *Theologies,* ch. 3, n. 167.

32. *Berengar and the Reform of Sacramental Doctrine,* 406–14.

33. The premise is taken from Bernard Lonergan, *Method in Theology* (N.Y.: Herder and Herder, 1972) xi.

34. "Church History as a Branch of Theology," *Church History in Future Perspective,* ed. Roger Aubert, Concilium 57 (N.Y.: Herder and Herder, 1970) 87.

35. *Doing Theology on Dover Beach: An Inaugural Address* (Cambridge: Cambridge University Press, 1978) 28.

36. *Method in Theology,* 235–66.

37. "Is Exegesis Without Presuppositions Possible?" *Existence and Faith. Shorter Writings of Rudolf Bultmann* (N.Y.: Meridian Books, 1960) 289–96.

38. It might be well to recall the description of models given by Bernard Lonergan, *Method in Theology,* xii: "By a model is not meant something to be copied or imitated. By a model is not meant a description of reality or a hypothesis about reality. It is simply an intelligible, interlocking set of terms and relations that it may be well to have about when it comes to describing reality or to forming hypotheses. As the proverb, so the model is something worth keeping in mind when one confronts a situation or tackles a job."

39. Shortly before the submission of this text for publication, Professor Walter Principe kindly reviewed an earlier version of the work. Among many excellent suggestions, he remarked that the book makes no mention of the

Eucharist as a reenactment of the sacrifice of Calvary. Again, lack of space makes a study of this important area difficult here. I have treated this matter in an unpublished paper given at the annual convention of the College Theology Society, "Morality and the Eucharist in the Middle Ages," and hope to offer a more detailed study in the near future. [Much of the material from "Morality and the Eucharist in the Middle Ages," is included in the article, "Commentaries on the Mass in the Early Scholastic Period" which is included as the seventh essay in this volume.]

Chapter 2

The Theological Fate of Berengar's Oath of 1059: Interpreting a Blunder Become Tradition[1]

One of the more interesting problems which a theologian can confront when attempting to preserve and interpret his or her own tradition remains that engendered by received, approved, and preserved teachings which are theologically incorrect. I am not referring here to ecclesial statements that now seem inadequate, but which when placed within their social, historical, and cultural setting provide a consistent presentation of the Christian message. What I intend to address in this paper is a different problem, that of true blunders. By this, I mean statements of the official Church that embarrassed theologians when they were written and have haunted their successors down through the centuries. It seems somewhat naive historically to presume that such statements do not exist. A quick review of Denzinger should surely disabuse even a cursory reader of any such notions. It seems equally naive theologically to presume that the Holy Spirit could not allow such statements to be made. If the serious foundational problems entailed in such an assumption were not enough, there would remain the strange picture of an irresponsible Church that believes it can say anything on the grounds that the Holy Spirit will miraculously intervene to close ecclesial mouths before officious feet are placed therein. One might then argue that only those statements which are theologically apt make up the tradition, but this would require a major rewriting of history for our own dogmatic purposes. Besides, one is then faced with the thorny question of who will determine which statements will be the tradition.

The simplest and most straightforward means of handling the problem might be to simply admit that the Church, in certain instances, taught the wrong thing, and be done with it. Problems arise here too, however. Surely no one would object if the synodal proceedings of the fourth-century Council of Elvira were not required for belief, but what about the proceedings of Lateran IV, or the teachings of Paul, or even Jesus? Surely cases have been made that these sources too lack theological clarity.[2] Again the problem seems to be one of choosing, rather than uncovering our tradition.

Fortunately, this is not a new problem. Theologians in the past have also faced such dilemmas, and found methods to minimize the damage done by episcopal or papal gaucherie. This paper will present the history of one such misstep. In many ways, the solemn oath taken by Berengar of Tours at the Council of Rome in 1059 is a classic case of the kind of problem outlined thus far. Adopted in solemn assembly at a valid synod called by a legitimate pope, the oath of Berengar was subsequently included in several canon law collections of the early twelfth century, thus finding its way into Gratian's *Decretum* in the twelfth century.[3] Gratian's work, although unofficial, made up a great part of canon law until a new code was issued in 1917. As might be expected, the ever zealous Denzinger included Berengar's oath in his collection of Church teachings.[4] Nor would the oath simply slip into the natural, dusty death of obscurity. Starting with the Cathars in the twelfth century, the oath has been used right up to the present time to demonstrate that the Roman Church ascribes to some strange sort of cannibalism in the celebration of the Eucharist.[5] Theologians again and again had to address themselves to the difficult task of making some sense of the oath in the face of cogent opposition.

The source of this long discussion is short, and very blunt:

"I agree with the holy Roman Church and the Apostolic See, and I profess with mouth and heart to hold as the faith concerning the sacrament of the Lord's supper what the lord and venerable Pope Nicholas and this holy synod by the authority of the gospels and the apostles have given to be held and have ratified to me: Namely, that the bread and wine which are placed on the altar after the consecration are not only signs *(non solum sacramentum),* but also the true body and blood of our Lord Jesus Christ, and that sensually, not only in sign, but in truth *(non solum sacramento, sed in veritate)* they are handled and broken by the hands of the priest and crushed by the teeth of the faithful, swearing by the holy and one-in-substance Trinity and by the most holy gospel of Christ."[6]

From where did this strange statement come, and why was it written? For ten years before the synod met, Berengar, a teacher at the cathedral school at Tours, had been waging a literary war with his fellow theologians, especially those in Normandy, over the proper understanding of the presence of the Lord in the Eucharist. Berengar had, albeit somewhat clumsily, revived an Augustinian understanding of this presence which insisted on its spiritual nature. The theologians in Normandy, were, like most theologians of this time, heavily influenced by Paschasius Radbertus' teaching on the presence of the Lord in the Eucharist. This ninth-century monk, basing himself on passages from Hilary of Poitiers, insisted that only a natural union between the Body of the risen Lord and the Christian believer could effect salvation. Further, this natural union took place through the reception of the eucharistic species. The followers of Paschasius felt that Berengar's insistence on a spiritual rather than a physical or natural presence of the Lord in the sacrament undermined the very possibility of our salvation.[7]

After much discussion, and several condemnations, Berengar was called to Rome by Pope Nicholas II to defend his position. Unfortunately for Berengar, the papal legate, Humbert, cardinal bishop of Silva-Candida, was chosen to draw up an oath for Berengar to sign. Humbert was in no mood for compromise or even understanding. Five years before, he had laid a writ of excommunication on the high altar of Hagia Sophia in Constantinople, thus initiating what would become a permanent schism between the Christians of the East and those of the West. One of the areas in which Humbert judged the Greeks to be heretical was in their teaching on the Eucharist. Humbert felt that the Greeks, in some obscure way, denied a true presence of the Lord in the sacrament by their use of leavened bread in the Mass. Humbert, not known for his tact in any case, may well have felt that both the Greeks and Berengar could be countered once and for all by a clear, bold and strongly worded insistence on the real, physical presence of the risen Lord in the Eucharist.[8] In many ways, he succeeded. The oath of Berengar is clear, blunt, and forceful. It is also, theologically, a disaster.

By juxtaposing the Real Presence of the Lord in the Eucharist *(in veritate)* with the sacramental presence of the Lord *(in sacramento)* Humbert undermined any understanding of sacramental presence itself as a form of reality. Further, by insisting on a grossly sensual presence of the Lord in the sacrament, Humbert raised serious problems involving the impassibility and locality of the risen Lord. Theologians were not slow to realize the issues, especially since Berengar, having returned home and repudiated his oath, threw the logical conclusions of Humbert's statement in his opponents' faces. Are we to believe, Berengar smirked, that "little chunks" of Christ's Body would be spread about on all the altars in Europe to be savaged by the faithful?[9] Does this mean a little more Jesus is made each day as thousands of Masses are being said?[10] Most blasphemous of all, would not such a presence of the Body of Christ on earth entail the faithful in a kind of cannibalism, to say nothing of the indignity of digestion, or desecration by rot, fire, or animals?[11] How is such a teaching compatible with Christian belief that the risen Lord is now incorruptible and seated at the right hand of the Father? [12]

Berengar was brought to heel once again at the Council of Rome held in 1079. Here he signed yet another, and this time more sophisticated, oath.[13] By 1080, Berengar had retired from the theological scene, but his taunts reappeared in the teachings of the Cathars, that amorphous group of dualists who would come to control most of southern France and northern Italy by the end of the twelfth century.[14] For over a hundred and fifty years, European theologians would not be allowed to forget, or ignore, Humbert's debacle. Their responses make fascinating reading.

The earliest of the tracts directed against Berengar's teachings countered his claims merely by asserting the incorruptibility of the risen Christ, thus denying that any change could affect his body.[15] The first theologian to tackle Berengar's arguments in a more systematic way appears to have been Guitmund, a monk of Bec and student of Lanfranc, Berengar's most gifted foe. In his treatise, *De corporis et sanguinis Christi veritate in eucharistia,* written between 1073 and 1075, Guitmund defended Humbert's wording in a fairly literal fashion.

First, Guitmund argued that the verb, *attero,* to crush, can mean just to touch, or to press, really hard. Since both Thomas and the holy women touched the risen Lord, albeit lightly, surely there is no indignity involved in Humbert's assertion that the Body of Christ (in this reading) is touched very hard by the teeth of the faithful. Besides, teeth are cleaner than hands. Just think, Guitmund mused, of all the filthy things you touch with your hands that you would not dare to put in your mouth. Even Guitmund must have sensed that this line of thought was becoming (literally and figuratively) a bit messy, so he then asserted that even if the Body of Christ were divided by teeth or hands, no indignity would result. Appealing to the omnipotence of God, Guitmund argued that the Body of the risen Lord remained impassible, inviolate, and entire in each portion of the species. Here Guitmund found himself on firmer ground, and he used the same principle to argue that even though Christ is present on a thousand different altars, there is only one Lord simultaneously present in many places.[16]

Responding to Berengar's argument that a substantial presence would involve sacrilege, Guitmund insisted that the true Body and Blood remain even when the bread and wine appear to rot or putrify. Just as our Lord took on the form of a gardener to teach Mary Magdalene and that of a pilgrim to teach the disciples at Emmaus, so he takes the form of putrified bread and wine to admonish us for improper care of the reserved species.[17] If an animal is seen to eat the species, this too is for our edification, nor should we be shocked to think of Christ as descending into the bowels of an animal. After all, Guitmund reminded his readers, Christ had been in worse places, like the tomb.[18] When asked what happens when the host is burned, Guitmund allowed that the "sensible qualities" remain behind, but the true Body ascends back to heaven. He denied, however, that any part of the species can be digested, and that if certain of the Fathers lived on communion alone for many years, this was only by means of a miracle.[19] Few theologians would follow Guitmund in defending this more literal understanding of the Berengarian oath.

Alger, canon of St. Lamberts in Liège, offered a similar theology in his *De sacramentis corporis et sanguinis* written in the second decade of the twelfth century. Going somewhat beyond Guitmund's position, Alger argued that the appearances of bread and wine were sheer illusion, and digestion or putrification of the species cannot naturally occur, since there is no substance left to undergo such a change.[20]

An interesting twist to this particular attempt to explain how the Body of Christ can be "broken" occurred in the teaching of Gilbert of La Porrée, the controversial and influential Scripture scholar. Writing in the 1140s, Gilbert argued that the host only appears to be broken, just as a stick placed in water appears to bend, although the mind recognizes that this is not the case.[21] The anonymous work, the *Summa de sacramentis "Totus homo,"* a work associated with Gilbert's students, made this argument at length.[22] The Body of Christ is not, and cannot be, broken here for each section of the species contains the entire presence of Christ. On the other hand, the substance of the bread and wine are gone, so they cannot be the subject of any change. Therefore fraction does not take place, but only appears to take place.[23]

A number of works connected with the contentious but brilliant theologian Abelard both argued that the breaking of the bread is an illusion, and followed Alger in teaching that abuse of the species is an illusion for edification.[24] These writings added a new note to this teaching, however. They argued that the form of the bread and wine continue to exist after the consecration and they miraculously subsist in the air.[25]

Slowly, but clearly, these theologians were moving away from the meaning of the oath. They still attempted to make some sense out of the statement that claimed the Body of the Lord was not broken in sign alone, by asserting that nothing was broken at all since all was an illusion. The larger claim that the Body of the Lord was really and sensually broken by the hands of the priest and crushed by the teeth of the faithful was denied by these authors, despite the halfhearted attempts by Guitmund to make some sense of out of this strange statement. Far more of the theologians of this time, however, directly or indirectly, simply rejected the intention of the oath.

A set of commentaries on 1 Corinthians, dating from the end of the eleventh century, stated that although the true Body of Christ is present under the species of bread, it is the species alone that is crushed, divided in parts, consumed or eaten by mice, while the Body of Christ remains in truth incorruptible and indivisible.[26] This teaching was copied into a collection of *sententiae* used at the famous cathedral school of Laon; not too surprisingly, the teaching appeared in the writings of its graduates.[27] The clearest example of this influence is contained in the writing of Guibert, abbot of Nogent-sous-Coucy near Laon from 1104 to 1124. In a discussion of how sacrilege might affect the Lord present in the Eucharist, Guibert recorded the opinion of Guitmund. He concluded, "I do not know if these arguments (of Guitmund) would ever be satisfactory to myself or to many others. This, however, we know, that it is thought to be subject to these sort of so-called misfortunes from that part, which are species. . . ."[28] Guibert rejected not only the teaching contained in the oath, but even the milder interpretation given to it by Guitmund.

Hugh of St. Victor, the famous Parisian master, himself influenced by teachings of Laon, preferred to gently remove any thoughts of sensual involvement by the Lord in the sacrament from the minds of his students. "Do not think, when you see the parts in the sacrament of the altar, that the Body of Christ has, as it were, been divided or separated from itself or as if torn limb from limb. He Himself remains whole in himself; neither is He divided nor parted. Therefore, He shows you the external appearance *(speciem)*, by which your sense is instructed, and He preserves the internal incorruption of His body, in which his unity is not divided."[29] Hugh's teaching completely contradicted the Berengarian oath, and his teaching on this matter appeared in the writings of several other twelfth-century theologians.[30]

It was Peter Lombard, the Parisian master whose *Sententiae*, written between 1153 and 1155, would become the standard textbook of the scholastic period, who first directly repudiated the oath of 1059. He first treated the whole issue in his commentary on 1 Corinthians, and came to no conclusion on the matter.[31] In the *Sententiae*, however, Peter took a firm stand. After discussing the opinions of Guitmund, Gilbert, and the School of Abelard, he tackled the oath itself, from which he quoted. His commentary reads: "From this it is given to be understood that the breaking, and parts which here seem to be made, are being done in sign *(in sacramento)*, that is in the visible species. And for this reason those words of Berengar that the Body of Christ is said to be handled by the hands of the priest, truly broken and crushed by teeth, not sensually in the mode of a sign *(non modo in sacramento)*, but in truth, are to be distinguished; something truly (is done), but in sign alone *(in sacramentum tantum)*."[32] Peter Lombard made sense of the Berengarian oath by completely reversing its meaning. Since the Body of Christ is certainly now risen and immune to all division, the words of the oath, for the Lombard, must mean the opposite of what they appear to mean. The Lombard had thus simply explained the oath away, and, what is more, this understanding was to become the standard interpretation of the oath by the beginning of the thirteenth century.

Not that the opinion of the Lombard went unchallenged. Walter of St. Victor, the arch-conservative Parisian master writing ca. 1178, accused Peter of being another Berengar, and demanded a return to the literal meaning of the oath.[33] A certain unidentified Abbot Abbaudus, also writing in the twelfth century, railed against those who denied that the Lord's Body was broken in the Eucharist, claiming that "whoever does not truly accept the body of Christ to have been broken, breaks the entire faith in such sacraments, in so far as it exists."[34] Writing about the time of the Lombard, Zachary, the *scholasticus* of Besançon, claimed, "The body of Christ is incorruptible, but on the

other hand, the body of Christ is crushed by teeth and gulped down."
Read, Zachary insisted, "the faith of Berengar, which the Church declared under Pope Nicholas, and you will find it to be so."[35] Zachary
went on to lament, "There are not a few, perhaps rather I should say
many, but they would be difficult to recognize, who feel the same as
the damned Berengar, however they might damn him with the
Church. They damn him in this because, casting away the literal
meaning of the words of the Church, the scandal is removed from the
simplicity of the language."[36] Zachary was quite correct in his perceptions. Most theologians in the twelfth century did not accept the literal meaning of the oath of 1059. They either put forward teachings
which implicitly denied the oath, or like Peter Lombard, reinterpreted
the oath in such a way as to practically reverse its meaning. Yet
Walter, Abbaudus, and Zachary were voices in the wilderness. There
was to be no return to the simple, clear theological ineptitude of
Humbert of Silva-Candida.

Theologians adopted the language of the School of Laon, or of
Hugh of St. Victor, or of the Lombard. When the words of the oath
were mentioned, theologians fell back on the interpretation of the
Lombard.[37] One of the most complete discussions of the oath occurs in
an anonymous commentary on 1 Corinthians written sometime before 1180. "It is customary to ask," the author began,

"concerning the fraction, in what thing it might be, that is, what here
is broken and what the parts of the fraction might signify. Some say
that only the sign (*solum sacramentum*) is broken here, for the reason
that the Body of Christ is impassible and would accept no fraction, no
divisions of parts. But how then will that confession of Berengar be
true which at Rome before Pope Nicholas with thirteen bishops present was prepared and ratified? It is confessed 'that the bread and
wine which are laid on the altar are after consecration not only a
sacrament but also the true Body and Blood of Christ, and they are
sensually taken up and broken in the hands of the priest and crushed
by the teeth of the faithful, not only sacramentally, but in truth.'
Clearly the oath says that the Body of Christ in truth is broken, in
truth crushed by the teeth of the faithful. For the same reason, in the
same manner, in truth, it is seen not only with the eyes of the heart,
but also those of the Body. The error of Berengar was that after the
consecration of the bread, bread remained and the sign alone of the
Body of Christ not His true Body remained here. His confession of

faith expressed the truth, saying he had believed the Body of Christ in truth to be present, not just a sign of the breaking of what first was present. The Body of Christ is in truth what is seen, what is broken, and what is crushed by the teeth of the faithful. But how, you ask, is the impassible broken, how is the undivided divided? I answer; how was God able to die if He was immortal, how is He to be understood if He is incomprehensible? You say according to one in one way, another in another way, yet it is one and same. Thus one and same Body is impassible and still broken, according to one in one way, another in another way and yet both in truth. What it is according to itself and in itself, is impassible; in sign it is divided, in sign seen and crushed by the teeth of the faithful. All of this is done in truth, however, and nothing in mere illusion."[38]

The anonymous author had a good sense of the theological problem involved here. He realized that the Berengarian oath was intended to affirm the Real Presence, and so he interpreted it. Yet he also realized that the oath as it was written asserted the impossible, that the Body of the risen Lord was subject to change and suffering. Like all good academics, he distinguished. In truth, the Body of the Lord is present, and is impassible. Equally in truth, the signs *(sacramenta)* are here handled, broken and crushed. Thus, this is how the oath must be understood.

William of Auxerre, Albert the Great, Thomas Aquinas, and Bonaventure all followed the twelfth-century theologians in affirming the impassibility of the Body of Christ, and in teaching that any changes that occur, occur in the species alone. Albert and Thomas both interpreted the oath of 1059 in the same manner as the Lombard and the commentator on 1 Corinthians.[39] Within one hundred years after the oath had been written, Peter Lombard had effectively reversed the literal meaning of the oath through reinterpretation. Within another hundred years, this reinterpretation had become the standard and accepted theological understanding of the oath. In sum, within two hundred years, theologians had effectively defused the potentially dangerous and certainly unfortunate language of an accepted, and clearly valid, magisterial pronouncement.

Further, throughout most of those two hundred years, theologians had simultaneously affirmed the condemnation of Berengar and rejected the language of the 1059 oath. In this Zachary of Besançon was quite correct. This, then, is how medieval theologians handled at least one instance of inept magisterial teaching. They just "distinguished" it away. Without confrontation, without refutation, they slowly changed the understanding of the offensive document.

What conclusions, then, can be drawn from this example? First, and probably most obviously, the Berengarian oath of 1059, by its very existence, refutes the claim that the Holy Spirit could not allow the magisterium to promulgate theological blunders, nor allow such blunders to become part of the received teaching of the Church. The oath indeed was such a blunder, and it was so received. The point made here may seem obvious or even trivial, since most practicing theologians would not seriously entertain such an understanding of the magisterium. This notion still does play a role, however, in the thought and practice of lamentably large numbers of both laity and clergy. The point bears repeating.

Once this is said, it becomes more difficult to draw any definite conclusions. Perhaps what this example best provides for the modern theologian is an option, a possibility, a different perspective on the problems involved in recovering the Christian tradition. The medieval authors cited here, with few exceptions, knew quite well the meaning of the Berengarian oath, and, when they found it to be theologically unacceptable, they changed that meaning. They appear to do so deliberately, and without qualm. Reason was accepted as playing an important role in accepting, molding, and, in a real sense, creating the tradition through continuous reinterpretation. The appropriation, modification, and even nullification, on reasonable grounds, of magisterial statements is then clearly one way in which theologians have dealt with official statements of Church teaching.

The problems of the Middle Ages are not our problems and their methods are not our methods, and yet their problems and their methods are part of our tradition. They can provide us with models and options from outside our immediate cultural and intellectual setting. In the words of Maurice Wiles, "whether we recognize it or not the work of the Fathers is an important constitutive part of the background of our own thinking. To ignore them is to cut ourselves off from our heritage; it is to refuse to see the issues of faith today in their proper historical perspective. The problems of contemporary theology are new in form, but they are not wholly new in substance. The Fathers cannot solve them for us. That task remains ours. But we limit unnecessarily the resources with which we attempt it if we believe that it can be done without reference to them."[40] It seems, at least to me, that the medieval authors' assumption that the statements of the magisterium must be reasonable to be true, and that the received tradition is subject to critical reformulation in order to make that tradition compatible with reason, is not only a resource worth recovering, it is an inescapable part of our tradition.

Perhaps, briefly, another point could be made here. None of the authors to which this paper refers (except of course Berengar) were condemned for their theology of the Eucharist—neither Guitmund for his crassness, nor Hugh of St. Victor for his deeply spiritual understanding, nor Peter the Lombard for his contradiction of the oath. All were respected scholars; two became bishops. The Church in which they lived allowed the freedom of thought, the pluralism, if you like, that fostered the kind of appropriation and interpretation of Church teaching embodied in the present example. As Henry Adams once so eloquently put it: "A Church which embraced, with equal sympathy, and within a hundred years, the Virgin, Saint Bernard, William of Champeaux and the School of Saint Victor, Peter the Venerable, Saint Francis of Assisi, Saint Dominic, Saint Thomas Aquinas, and St. Bonaventure, was more liberal than any modern State can afford to be. Radical contradictions the State may perhaps tolerate, though hardly, but never embrace or profess. Such elasticity long ago vanished from human thought."[41] Theologians in particular ought to be made more aware that this kind of pluralism *is* our tradition. Pluralism is not a twentieth-century idea which somehow challenges a monolithic tradition, but rather the history of the Church, and especially the history of the medieval Church, is a history of pluralism. To appeal to tradition is to appeal to the history of the Church, and this history often reveals a pluralism and a respect for reason which make our modern efforts appear timid. Tucked away on the back shelves of Wisdom's great storehouse, many such treasures await discovery.

---

1. Originally published in *Interpreting Traditon: The Art of Theological Reflection,* ed. Jane Kopas, Proceedings of the Annual Convention of the College Theology Society, 1983, 27–38 (Chico, Calif.: Scholars Press, 1984).

2. The decisions of the Fourth Lateran Council are not accepted as valid, by, for example, the Orthodox Churches. The exact importance of the teaching of Paul has been debated at least since the time of Marcion and occasioned lively debate in the Tübingen School of the nineteenth century. The discussion of which of the teachings of Jesus are genuine, and even which of these genu-

ine teachings are necessary for belief, goes back at least as far as the second-century Gnostic Christians and becomes central, for example, in the theology of Rudolf Bultmann.

3. Gratian *Decretum, de con. dist.* 2, c. 42. *Corpus iuris canonici,* ed. E. Friedberg, (Graz: Akademische Druck- u. Verlagsanstalt, 1959) 1:cols. 1328–29. Friedberg gives references to earlier collections which included the oath.

4. *Enchiridion symbolorum* ed. Henry Denzinger, 33rd ed. by Adolf Shönmetzer (Freiburg: Herder, 1965) n. 690.

5. On the use of Berengar's arguments by the Cathars and others in the twelfth century, see chapter three of Gary Macy, *Theologies of the Eucharist in the Early Scholastic Period* (Oxford: Clarendon Press, 1984) 58–59. [A more complete discussion of this issue is contained in Gary Macy, "Berengar's Legacy as Heresiarch," included as the fourth essay in this volume.]

6. The text is recorded by Lanfranc, *Liber de corpore et sanguine domini,* c. 2, *PL* 150: 410D.

7. See Macy, *Theologies,* ch. 3.

8. See Joseph Geiselmann, *Die Abendmahlslehre an der Wende der christlichen Spätantike zum Frühmittelalter* (Munich: Max Hueber, 1933) 73–85, 248–52.

9. *De sacra coena adversus Lanfrancum,* W. H. Beekenkamp, ed., Kerkhistorische studien behoorende bij het Nederlandscharchief voor Kerkgeschiednenis 2 (The Hague: M. Nijhoff, 1941), c. 9 (pp. 13–14), c. 30 (p. 66), and c. 35 (p. 94). [A more recent edition of this work is R.B.C. Huygens, ed., *Rescriptum contra Lanfrannum,* Corpus Christianorum, Continuatio mediaevalis 84 (Turnhout: Brepols, 1988).]

10. Ibid., c. 20 (p. 41), c. 21 (pp. 44–45), c. 30 (pp. 67–68) and c. 37 (p. 109).

11. Ibid., c. 39 (p. 123), c. 42 (p. 141), and c. 46 (pp. 159–60).

12. Ibid., c. 6 (p. 7), c. 37 (p. 58), and c. 30 (p. 67).

13. *Die Registrum Gregory VII,* E. Caspar, ed., Monumenta Germaniae historica, Epistolae selectae, 2, 2 vols. (Berlin: Weidman, 1920–23) 6:17a, Caspar, 2:426–27. *Enchiridion,* n. 700.

14. See Macy, *Theologies,* ch. 3.

15. Durand of Troarn, *De corpore et sanguine domini,* pars 3. *PL* 149: 1382A–B; Hugh of Langres, *Tractatus de corpore et sanguine Christi, PL* 142: 1331B–C; Lanfranc of Bec, *Liber de corpore et sanguine Domini,* c. 18, *PL* 150: 430B–C.

16. Guitmund of Aversa, *De corporis et sanguinis Christi veritate in eucharistia,* 1, *PL* 149: 1432A–1436B.

17. Ibid., l. 2, *PL* 1445C–1448C. Guitmund borrowed the idea that Christ took on different forms in speaking to Mary and the disciples from Lanfranc, *De corpore, PL* 150: 424C, although Lanfranc did not use the example for this purpose.

18. *De veritate,* l. 2, *PL* 149: 1448C–1449C.

19. Ibid., l. 2, *PL* 1450A–B, 1451–1453B.

20. *De sacramentis,* l. 2, c. 1, *PL* 180: 807B–814B.

21. Nicolaus Häring, "Die Sententie magistri gisleberti Pictavensis epis-copi," *Archives d'histoire et littéraire du moyen âge* 46 (1979) 64, *sententia* no. 25. For a discussion of other masters who followed Gilbert in this teaching, see Häring, ibid., 45 (1978) 91, and P. C. Boeren, "Un traite inédit du XII siècle 'Convenientibus vobis in unum* (I Cor. 11.20),'" *Archives d'historie doctrinale et littéraire du moyen âge* 45 (1978) 191 and 201, n. 1.

22. The authorship of this work is disputed, although it is commonly included among the works associated with the school of Gilbert. See Artur Landgraf, *Introduction a l'histoire de la littérature théologique de la scolastique nais-sante*, A.-M. Landry, ed., trans. L. B. Geiger, Publications de Institut d'études médiévales 22 (Montreal: Institut d'études médiévales, 1973) 118, n. 337.

23. *Summa de sacramentis "Totus homo," De eucharistia*, c. 19, Umberto Betti, ed., Spicilegium Ponficii Athenaei Antoniani 7 (Rome: Ponficium Athenaeum Antonianum, 1955) 51–53.

24. The teaching appears in three books of sentences; the *Sententie Floria-nenses*, the *Sententie Parisienses I*, and the *Sententie Hermanni*. On their relation to the School of Abelard, see David Luscombe, *The School of Peter Abelard* (Cambridge: Cambridge University Press, 1969) 153–68. For this teaching, see *Sententie Florianensis*, c. 69–71, Heinrich Ostlender, ed. (Bonn: P. Hanstein, 1929) 31; *Sententie Parisiensis 1*, Artur Landgraf, ed., *Écrit théologique de l'école d'Abelard* (Louvain: Bureaux, 1934) 42, and *Sententie Hermanni, PL* 178: 1741C–43A.

25. *Sententie Florianenses*, c. 70, Ostlender, 31; *Sententie Parisiensis I*, Landgraf, 43 and *Sententie Hermanni, PL* 178: 1743D.

26. The passage is contained in two commentaries, one attributed to Bruno the Carthusian and the other to an unknown author, Gratiadei. On the com-plicated problems of dating and attribution associated with these glosses, see Anselm Stoelen, "Les commentaries scriptuaires attribués à Bruno le Char-treux," *Recherches de théologie ancienne et médiévale* 25 (1958) 177–247, and idem, "Bruno le Chartreux, Jean Gratiadei et la 'Lettre de S. Anselme' sur l'eucharistie," *Recherches de théologie ancienne et médiévale* 34 (1967) 18–83. The passages referred to in the text have been edited by Stoelen, "Bruno le Char-treux," 46–47.

27. "Nec remanere substantiam panis et uini, speciem enim tamen uidemus remanere de hoc quod prius fuerat, scilicet formam, colorem et saporem. Et secundum speciem remanentem quedam ibi fiunt que nullomodo secundum hoc quod est fieri possit, uidelicet quod conteritur, in uno loco concluditur, a mure roditur, in uentrum trahicitur. Ideo uero quod non est apparet, at quod est celatur, quia si quod est uideretur et separetur, homines sumere uereren-tur." *Sententie magistri A.*, Vatican City, Biblioteca Vaticana, Vaticana lat. MS. 4361, fol. 112v1–2. On the influence of this book of *sententie* on the school at Laon, see Nicolaus Häring: The *Sententiae Magistri A* (Vat. MS lat 4361) and the School of Laon," *Medieval Studies* 17 (1955) 1–45, and Heinrich Reinhardt,

"Die Identität der Sententiae Magistri A. mit dem Compilationes Ailmeri und die Frage nach dem Autor dieser frühscholastischen Sentenzensammlung," *Theologie und Philosophie* 50 (1975) 381–403. Students who followed this teaching include William of Champeux in the *sententia* published by Odon Lottin, *Psychologie et morale aux XIIe et XIIIe siècles* 5 (Gembloux: Duculot, 1959) 218, and William of St. Thierry, *De corpore et sanguine domini,* c. 10, PL 180: 358B.

28. *De pignoribus sanctorum,* l. 2, c. 4, *PL* 156: 643B–C.

29. *De sacramentis christianae fidei,* l. 2, pars 8, c. 11, *PL* 176: 469B.

30. Cf. *Summa sententiarum,* tract. 6, c. 8, *PL* 176: 144C–145B; Robert Pullen, *Sententie,* l. 8, c. 5, *PL* 186: 966C–D. *Questiones super epistolam, primam ad Corinthios, PL* 175: 531C–D; Adam of Dryburgh, *De tripartito tabernaculo,* pars 2, c. 10, *PL* 198: 705A–C; Baldwin of Canterbury, *De sacramentis altari.* J. Morson, ed., Sources chretiennes 93–94, 2 vols. (Paris: Editions de Cerf, 1963) 1:126; Gerald of Wales, *Gemma ecclesiastica* 1, c. 11, J. S. Brewer, ed., *Giraldis Cambrensis opera* 2 (London: Longman & Co., 1862) 30; Peter of Vienna, *Summa,* cc. 183–86, *Die Zwettler Summe,* Nicolaus Häring, ed., Beiträge zur Geschichte der Philosophie und Theologie des Mittelalters, n. c., 15 (Münster: Aschendorff, 1977) 174. See also note 37.

31. *PL* 191: 1644C–1645B.

32. "Ex his satis datur intelligi quod fractio et partes quae ibi videntur fieri, in sacramento fiunt, id est, in specie visibili. Ideoque illa Berengarii verba ita distinguenda sunt, ut «sensualiter non modo sacramento, sed in veritate» dicatur corpus Christi «tractori manibus sacerdotum»;«frangi vero et atteri dentibus», vere quidem, sed in sacramento tantum." *Sententiae,* l. 4, dist. 12, *Magistri Petri Lombardi Sententiae in IV libris distinctae,* 3[rd.] ed., 2 vols. Spicilegium Bonaventurianum 4–5, (Grottaferrata: Collegii S. Bonaventurae ad Claras Aquas, 1981) 2:306–07.

33. *Contra quatuor labyrinthos Franciae,* l. 3, c. 11, ed. P. Glorieux, "Le Contra quatuor labyrinthos Franciae de Gauthier de Saint Victor. Edition critique," *Archives d'histoire et littéraire du moyen âge* 19 (1952) 261.

34. "Itaque qui vere frangi corpus Christi non concedit, totam fidem tanti sacramenti, quantum in se est, fregit." *De fractione corporis Christi, PL* 166: 1344C–D.

35. "Corpus Christi incorruptibile est; iterum, corpus Christi dentibus atteritur et tranglutitur. Lege fidem Berengarii, quam sibi firmavit Ecclesia sub Nicolao Papa, et ita esse invenies." *In unum ex quatuor,* l. 4, c. 156, *PL* 186: 508A.

36. "Sunt nonulli imo forsan multi, se sed vix notari possunt, qui cum damnato Berengario idem sentiunt, et tamen eumdem cum Ecclesia damnant. In hoc videlicet damnant eum, qui formum verborum Ecclesiae abjiciens, nuditate sermonis scandalum movebat." Ibid., *PL:* 508B.

37. Cf. Odo of Ourscamp, *Quaestiones,* q. 266, J. P. Pitra, ed., *Analecta novissima Spicilegii Solesmensis* (Paris: Tusculanis, 1888) 2:92–93; Peter of Capua,

Summa "Vestustissima veterum," Vatican City, Biblioteca Apostolica Vaticana, Vaticana lat. MS. 4296, fols. 69v2–70r1; Peter Comestor, *De sacramentis,* c. 23, Raymond Martin, ed., in H. Weisweiler, *Maître Simon et son groupe,* Spicilegium sacrum Lovaniense, Études et documents 17 (Louvain: Bureux, 1937) 54–55; Peter of Poitiers, *Sententie,* l. 5, c. 12, *PL* 211: 1250A; Magister Rolandus, *Sententie,* Ambrose Gietl, ed. (Freiburg im Freisgau: Herder'sche, 1891) 234; Magister Simon, *De sacramentis,* cc. 14, 26, 29, 30, H. Weisweiler, ed., *Maitre Simon,* 31, 38, 39–40. See especially Prepositinus of Cremona, *Summa:* "Item queritur in quo sit fractio que habet fieri an sit in corpore Christi vel tantum in specie. Quod sit in corpore videtur ex confessione Berengarii qui iurare compulsus est quod corpus Christ sensualiter frangitur et dentibus atterituri. . . . Solutio. Magistri nostri dicunt quod fractio ipsa tantum est in specie et non in corpore. . . . Sed quod Berengarius dixit sic est intelligendum, sensualiter frangitur, idest species sub qua ipsum est. Non enim credebat sub illa specie esse corpus Christi. Quod dicit, dentibus atteritur, idest sub specie contrita dentibus sumitur." *Praepositini cancellarii de sacramentis et de novissimis. . . .,* E. Pilarczyk, ed. (Rome, 1964) 85–86. See also the references given in n. 30.

38. "De fractione illa etiam queri solet, cuius rei sit, id est, quid ibi frangatur et quid partes ille significent fractionis. Dicunt quidam solum sacramentum ibi frangi eo quod corpus christi inpassibile sit, et nullam recipiat fractionem, nullam partium diuisionem. Sed quomodo uera tunc erit illa confessio Berengarius que rome coram Papa Nicholao presentibus cum xiii episcopis facta est et scripta? Confessus est enim panem et uinum que in altari ponuntur post consecrationem non solum sacramentum, sed etiam uerum corpus et sanguinem christi esse et sensualiter, non solum sacramentum, sed in ueritate manibus sacerdotum tractari et frangi et fidelium dentibus atteri. Ecce dicit quia corpus christi in ueritate frangitur, in ueritate fidelium dentibus atteritur. Eadem ratione ibidem in ueritate uidetur, non solum oculis cordis, sed corporis. Error Berengarii fuit quod post consecrationem panis, panis remanebat et solum sacramentum corporis christi non uerum corpus eius ibi erat. Sua ergo confessione fidei expressit ueritatem, dicens non solum sacramentum fractioni illi sub esse quod prius crediderat, sed corpus christi in ueritate. Corpus enim christi est in ueritate quod uidetur, quod frangitur, et fidelium dentibus atteribur. Sed quomodo inquis si inpassibile frangitur, quomodo si indiuisibile diuiditur? Responsio. Quomodo deus mori potuit si immortalis fuit; quomodo comprehendi si incomprehensibilis? Secundum aliud et aliud dices, et tamen unus et idem. Sic unum et idem corpus inpassibile et tamen frangitur, sed secundum aliud et aliud utrumque tamen in ueritate. Quod secundum se et in se inpassibile est; in sacramento diuiditur, in sacramento uidetur, et fidelium dentibus atteribur. Hec omnia tamen in ueritate et in fantasmate nichil." Vatican City, Biblioteca Apostolica Vaticana, Ottoboniana lat. MS. 445, fol. 117r1–v1.

39. William of Auxerre, *Summa aurea,* 1.4 (Paris: Nicolaus Vaultier et Durandus Geirlier, 1500, rpt. Frankfurt: Minerva, 1964, fols. 259v2–226or1) [see now the critical edition, *Magistri Guillelmi Altissidorensis Summ aurea,* Jean Ribaillier, ed., 5 vols. (Paris: Centre nationale de la recherche scientifique, Grottaferrata: Collegium S. Bonaventurae ad Claras Aquas, 1980–87)]; Albert the Great, *De sacramentis,* tract. 5, pars 2, q. 3, art. 4, Albert Ohlmeyer, ed., *Opera omnia* 26 (Münster: Aschendorff, 1958) 68; Thomas Aquinas, *Summa Theologiae,* pars 3, q. 77, art. 7, the Order of Preachers, eds., *Opera omnia* 12 (Rome: S. C. Propaganda fide, 1906) 202–03; Bonventure, *Breviloquium,* pars 6, c. 9, A Sepinski, ed., *Opera theologica selecta* 5 (Florence: Collegium S. Bonaventurae, 1964) 142–43.

40. Maurice Wiles, *The Christian Fathers* (N.Y.: Oxford University Press, 1982) 180.

41. Henry Adams, *Mont-Saint-Michel and Chartres* (Boston and New York: Houghton Mifflin Company, 1933) 356.

Chapter 3

Reception of the Eucharist According to the Theologians: A Case of Diversity in the 13th and 14th Centuries [1]

Ever since Paul admonished the Corinthians for their overly enthusiastic celebration of the breaking of the bread, Christian writers have distinguished between worthy and unworthy reception. This admonition gradually moved toward theological clarification and codification during the dispute over the eucharistic teaching of Berengar of Tours in the eleventh century. The majority of the opponents of Berengar held to a theology of the sacrament based on the teaching of the ninth-century monk, Paschasius of Corby. In their understanding of that theology, reception of the Body and Blood of the Lord was necessary in order that the natural Body of the Lord might mingle with the body of the recipient, thus granting immortality.

The question then necessarily arose of why the bodies of sinners or infidels or even animals do not become immortal once in contact with the risen Body of the Lord through reception. Beginning with Lanfranc, the most intelligent of Berengar's foes, it was customary for theologians to speak of two modes of reception in the Eucharist. Basing themselves on Augustine, worthy reception was described as spiritual communion, and unworthy reception became known as either corporeal or sacramental reception. Both forms of reception assumed that the believer actually consumed the consecrated species. It was agreed that all believers, sinners or not, received the true Body and Blood. Only the just, however, received the saving effect of this reception. Theologians disagreed about animals and infidels. Some argued all received the true Body of the Lord, mice and men alike. Others insisted that only believers received; unbelievers and animals ate only the species of bread and wine.[2]

In the twelfth century, works associated with the School of Anselm at Laon introduced a third form of Communion, spiritual reception alone. According to these theologians, one could receive the full benefits of the Eucharist by devotional acts which demonstrated a union with God in faith and love.[3] Thus three forms of reception were imperfectly associated with the three elements of the Eucharist. Sacramental reception entailed reception of both the *sacramentum* (the species alone) and of the *sacramentum et res* (the Body and Blood of Christ), while spiritual communion entailed reception of the *res* only (a union of faith working in love or according to some writers, the Church as Mystical Body). Of course, one could also receive both sacramentally and spiritually when one consumed the species in worthy reception.

By the beginning of the thirteenth century, the question of who might receive the Eucharist, and how he or she might receive it, had been fairly carefully explored and several different theories had been put forward regarding reception by, for instance, animals.[4] The discussion was to undergo one further and significant development, however, during the first half of the thirteenth century.

Basing himself on earlier writers, and especially Pope Innocent III, the secular master and later convert to the Franciscans, Alexander of Hales, argued that reception depended upon the recognition of the sign value of the sacrament by the recipient.[5] In Alexander's commentary on Peter Lombard's *Sentences,* written ca. 1222–23,[6] he explained that since the Body of Christ is spiritual food, only an intellectual nature is capable of receiving it. As Augustine had pointed out, the outward sign leads to the inner reality and only the intellect can so reach beyond the sign to the reality behind it. Animals then receive simply the outer forms, the taste of bread and wine. Only humans can understand symbols, and therefore only humans can access the presence of the Lord underlying the symbol *(sacramentum)* of bread and wine.[7]

Writing between 1220 and 1236 in a work now known as the *Quaestiones disputatae "Antequam esset frater,"* Alexander offered a fuller explanation of this form of sacramental theology. There are three kinds of union possible in the Eucharist according to Alexander. One can be united in thought, in love and in nature to Christ. Those who existed before the coming of Christ could be united in thought and love, but not in nature. Angels, too, having a different nature than Christ, cannot receive him naturally. Then, too, Christ can be received with more or less love, and more or less understanding. This means there are different degrees of reception of Christ. Perfect reception would take place only in heaven, Alexander intimated. Those who receive the sign alone, like Jews and pagans, are united only to the sign, as if it were mere bread. Again there is a union of those who both believe and understand the reason for the sign. Finally, there is the greater union of those who believe and love, and this is spiritual reception.[8]

Alexander discussed the question of whether only rational creatures have the ability to receive this sacrament. It would seem that irrational creatures must be able to receive since, once transubstantiation takes place, the Body of Christ remains as long as the species of bread remains. If an animal receives the species of bread, it ought as well to receive the Body of Christ. If, however, by sacramental reception is meant that the recipient touches the reality behind the sign as well as the sign alone, then neither animals, nor Jews, nor pagans can be said to receive sacramentally. True to the principles established earlier, Alexander asserted that to receive sacramentally, properly speaking, is to be united either in nature or faith or charity with Christ. Certainly animals cannot then receive. Even Jews and pagans, however they might share in the same human nature as Christ, do not receive sacramentally since they do not understand the reality underlying the signs.[9]

Alexander's discussion of reception is extremely important. Not only do I know of no earlier author who had so explicitly argued that reception was dependent on the intentionality of the receiver, but Alexander's theology would be very influential. At least four important theologians of the next generation would directly or indirectly follow Alexander's theology. The Franciscans, William of Militona and St. Bonaventure, and the Dominicans, Guérric of St. Quentin, and Guérric's most famous student, Albert the Great, all followed Alexander in asserting the importance of a true theology of sign in the reception of the Eucharist.

William of Militona, writing ca. 1245–49, followed Alexander in his lengthy and elaborate explanation of reception. Because it is a sign, understood only by reason or faith, only rational creatures are capable of reception of the *sacramentum et res* of the Eucharist. Irrational animals are only capable of receiving the accidents of the species, that is the *sacramentum*.

Humans can actually consume the Body of Christ, although it is not digested. The Body does enter the stomach so long as the species exist. The species when vomited contain only the accidents, although it is possible that the substance of the bread is miraculously returned.[10] Only rational creatures can receive, though, because the content of the sign can only be reached by faith or knowledge. Animals receive only the accidents with no substance, so it cannot even be called eating. Further, William argued that reception by unbelievers is only accidental as well, but with the potential for sacramental reception.[11]

William summarized his thought in the following manner: "Therefore an animal is united with the accidents alone; for unbelievers, who inwardly believe nothing, is added an aptitude for sacramental or spiritual reception; for those having a deformed faith is added a knowledge of that to which they are united; to those having a true faith, in which charity is included, is added a union of love."[12]

The Dominican master, Guérric of St. Quentin, offered a very similar, although much briefer, discussion of reception in his commentary on the *Sentences.* Guérric held the Dominican chair of theology from 1233–45, and so it is possible that William used Guérric's discussion in forming his own thought.[13] Guérric held, as did Alexander and William, that only human beings are capable of receiving the Eucharist, as only they are capable of using signs.[14] Further, some of sort of faith is necessary for sacramental reception.[15] Finally, animals are incapable of reception because they lack the necessary intelligence.[16]

These theologians were not the first to suggest that animals consuming the species receive only the accidents. This had already been the teaching of the authors associated with the School at Loan in the twelfth century.[17] Their contribution was to offer an explanation for this teaching based on intellectual intention. Only humans can understand symbols, and therefore only humans can make contact with the presence of the Lord underlying the symbols *(sacramentum)* of bread and wine.

Bonaventure, perhaps the greatest of the Franciscan theologians, followed his predecessors in emphasizing the importance of the disposition of the recipient in the Eucharist. A long discussion of this issue occurs in his commentary on the *Sentences.* Probably written in the late 1240s or early 1250s, it is possible that he revised the commentary during his teaching career which ended with his election as minister general in 1257.[18] Three conditions are necessary for true reception: first, one must be capable of intending the *res* of the *sacramentum;* secondly, one must believe; thirdly, one must understand the significance of the sacrament in order to receive. It is because mice and angels cannot meet these requirements, that they are incapable of reception.[19]

Bonaventure pointed out that true sacramental reception involves reception of the *sacramentum* (the species) as a true sign. First, this means that the species must be received as food with the intention of eating them as food. Secondly, the recipient must be capable of understanding a sign, and in fact of understanding *this* sign. The recipient must intend to receive the Body and Blood of Christ as the Church believes. Therefore, only humans can receive sacramentally. Bonaventure disagreed slightly with William of Militona over the question of heretics. Bonaventure conceded that a heretic might receive sacramentally if the heretic intended to accept what the Church believes to be present. With this one exception, Bonaventure's presentation is very similar to William's. Bonaventure, however, articulated more clearly the central role which intention plays in accessing the presence of the Lord by the recipient.[20]

Bonaventure also made clear the distinction between *situs* and *actum* in sacraments. If one objects that the species cannot be separated from the substance of the Body and Blood after the consecration, Bonaventure argued that while this might be true as far as *situs*, that is that the Body and Blood are united to the place of the species, the two may be separated *ad actum*, that is to say that whatever happens to the species does not also happen to the Body and Blood contained under the accidents. Just as the species are broken by the priest and nothing happens to the Body and Blood, so too the species can be received by an animal or infidel without touching the Body and Blood which are contained under this sign. Only through the intention of the recipient to receive what is believed to lie under the species can the Body and Blood be attained.[21]

In his commentary on Distinction 13 of Lombard's fourth book, Bonaventure discussed what would happen if a mouse ate the consecrated species. First, he argued that a mouse receives some food, but does not receive sacramentally or spiritually. Secondly, he argued that just as a mouse cannot be baptized, so a mouse cannot receive the Eucharist.[22] Bonaventure then went on to discuss two different opinions as to what a mouse eats in the sacrament. First he describes the thought of those who argue that since the presence of the Body and Blood lasts as long as the species, therefore as long as the species subsist in the stomach of the mouse, the Body and Blood are also present. The mouse is not truly said to eat the Body and Blood in this case, however, for the mouse cannot reach the Body and Blood either in nature, nor through knowledge nor in love. Bonaventure rejects this opinion for it is offense to piety to think that the Body and Blood of the Lord might be in the stomach of a mouse.[23]

Bonaventure next discussed the opinion of those who argue that the mouse could never eat the Body and Blood of the Lord, for Christ is only under the sign in so far as this sign is directed to human use, and since a mouse is incapable of this, the Body and Blood disappear and the substance of the bread returns. Bonaventure called this opinion "more common, more honest and more reasonable."[24] Bonaventure then asked whether the Body and Blood of Christ might descend into the stomach of a human. He clearly states that in so far as the effect of the sacrament is concerned, the Body and Blood never descend into the stomach, but pass into the mind of the believer. Whether the substance of the Body and Blood descends into the stomach is a more doubtful issue, however. Bonaventure cites four different opinions here. The first argues that wherever the species subsist, the substance of the Body and Blood exists, even in the stomach of a mouse. The second opinion states that the Body and Blood descend into the stomach of humans alone, and that the substance remains there as long as the species are suitable for refection. A third opinion also holds that the substance descends into the stomach of a human in so far as that act is part of reception, but the substance does not remain in the stomach of the recipient. The final opinion recorded by Bonaventure describes the presence as lasting as long as any part of the species is sensed. After the species are no longer sensed, the further presence of the Lord is spiritual, not physical.[25]

Bonaventure pointed out that all four opinions have reasons to support them, and that it is difficult to judge between them. He rejected the first opinion again because it would be impious to think of the Body of the Lord in the stomach of a mouse. He also rejected the fourth opinion for it lacks tightness of thought. A human being, after all, can also sense food in his or her stomach. Bonaventure would, however, accept both of the other positions as probable. It is probable, therefore, that the Body and Blood are present only so long as the eating takes place, but that they do not remain in the stomach of the recipient. It seemed to Bonaventure more probable, and more reliable to say, however, that the Body and Blood remain in the stomach of the recipient so long as the species have their proper form and are suitable for human consumption. In opposition to William of Militona, therefore, Bonaventure argues that when the species are vomited up by a sick person, the Body is still present if the species are still recognizable as human food, and so great care must be taken in giving communion to a sick person.[26]

Bonaventure clearly carried on the teaching of both the Franciscans and the Dominican theologians who preceded him. The faith and reason of the recipient determined whether the Body and Blood of the Lord would be present, even in unworthy reception, for that individual recipient.

Bonaventure's contemporary, the Dominican Albert the Great, discussed this question at least twice during his long career. His earliest treatment, that contained in his *De sacramentis,* was written ca. 1240. In this short discussion, he followed the teaching first expounded by Alexander of Hales. He explained that since the Body of Christ is spiritual food, only an intellectual nature is capable of receiving it. As Augustine had pointed out, the outward sign leads to the inner reality and only the intellect can so reach beyond the sign to the reality behind it. Animals then receive only outer forms, the taste of bread and wine. Only humans can understand symbols, and therefore only humans can make contact with the presence of the Lord underlying the symbol *(sacramentum)* of bread and wine.[27]

A much longer and more important discussion of the reception of the Eucharist takes place in Albert's commentary on the *Sentences,* written in 1249.[28] Albert distinguished two ways in which the Eucharist might be said to be received sacramentally, as opposed to spiritually. One could say that in one sense, only the sign is received, with no understanding of what the sign meant. On the other hand, one could receive the sign while understanding its meaning. Infidels can only receive in the first sense.[29] In discussing the requirements for either sacramental or spiritual reception, Albert specified more clearly his concerns in this matter. It is necessary for sacramental reception that some sort of relationship exist between the recipient and thing received. Therefore, at least some sort of faith is required, and so infidels cannot be said to receive. Yet, Albert did not wish to deny that the Body of the Lord must be present wherever the species of the bread and wine exist.[30]

Albert attempted to resolve his dilemma in discussing the further question of whether the Body of the Lord can be said to pass into the stomach in reception. He answered by arguing that there are two ways that the Lord's Body can be said to enter into the stomach. The Body could enter the stomach and be digested like any other food, and this is clearly impossible. Secondly, the Body could be said to merely exist in the place where the bread happens to be, that is, in the stomach. In this case, one might say that the Lord's Body does enter the stomach. Albert's problem here has to do with the metaphysics involved in the change. "I do not see, rationally, how the Body of Christ cannot pass into all places into which the species of bread and wine pass, they being the sign under which the whole Christ is contained, according to the truth of the reality signified *(res)*."[31] In saying this, however, Albert was aware that his opinion ran counter to that of at least some of the other masters, and he was careful to put his ideas forward cautiously. He ended his discussion with the caveat, "And I say this without prejudice, because some masters say the opposite."[32]

Albert made explicit in his commentary that a tension existed between a true sacramental theology and the metaphysics involved in the eucharistic change. If the Eucharist is truly a sign, then only those capable of understanding such a sign can be said to be capable even of unworthy reception of the Body and Blood of the risen Lord. Yet if a true substantial change takes place in the Eucharist, then the Body and Blood must be present wherever the species of bread and wine exist. Albert's solution would seem to be similar to that of Bonaventure. The Body and Blood exist as long as the species can be sensed, but no connection exists between the recipient and the risen Lord except in faith. Albert did go further than any of his predecessors, however, in emphasizing the importance of metaphysics over the theology of sign by insisting that the Body and Blood must be present *everywhere* the species exist. This at least implies that the Body and Blood must be present in the stomach of an animal or infidel, a suggestion Alexander, William and Bonaventure reject. It is no wonder that Albert made this suggestion tentatively.

These tentative suggestions would find a full-fledged defense in the work of the most famous of Albert's students, and indeed the most famous of the Dominicans, Thomas Aquinas. Thomas first tackled the subject of eucharistic reception in his commentary on the Lombard's *Sentences*, thought to reflect his teaching in Paris from 1252 to 1256.[33] Thomas accepted two forms of reception, sacramental and spiritual. Sacramental reception entails reception both of the species and of the Body and Blood. Thomas was aware that some theologians admitted forms of reception that included either reception of the species alone or participation in the Mystical Body alone. He accepted the latter, but the former he rejected as inappropriate to the Eucharist, for this would entail a purely accidental reception.[34]

In discussing whether a sinner can receive the Body of Christ, Thomas abandoned the usual arguments in favor of such a reception based on the faith of the sinner. Instead Thomas firmly insisted that sinners receive because the change of the substance of the bread and wine into the Body and Blood of the Lord, once it takes place, cannot be reversed except by another substantial change. As long as the accidents of bread exist, the Body and Blood of the Lord continue in the sacrament. Only when digestion so changes the species that they are unrecognizable, are the Body and Blood separate from the species. Thomas clearly followed Albert on this point, "As long as the species are not changed, there is no way for the Body of Christ to cease to be here."[35] This principle made Thomas's further discussions of this question awkward, for it would assume then that both animals and infidels receive the sacrament, both difficult positions to maintain.

Thomas answered these problems by distinguishing, as Bonaventure had before him, between reception as understood in terms of the thing received and reception in terms of the receiver. In terms of what is received, anyone who receives the species receives the Body and Blood of Christ. In terms of the receiver, however, only those receive who understand this food to be a visible sign of the spiritual reality underlying it. In this sense, neither infidels nor animals can be said to receive the Body and Blood. Thomas explicitly rejected the opinion of Bonaventure, however, that animals cannot receive the Body and Blood as it exists under the signs of bread and wine. "This reason is not valid because of two things," Thomas insisted. First, the species are not changed immediately in the stomach of the animal, and therefore no change can take place in the substance supporting these accidents. The host could be removed and still be used. Secondly, just because a thing is not used for its intended purpose, it does not cease to exist. Therefore, Thomas explained, the Body and Blood of the Lord are received into the mouth of animals and descend into their stomach.[36]

Even Thomas seemed somewhat uneasy with this rather disgusting conclusion and in one passage Thomas seemed momentarily to forget that he had rejected reception of the accidents alone based on his own metaphysical principles. "Irrational creatures in no way spiritually eat, nor sacramentally, because they neither use this eating as a sign, nor eat the sign for the reason that it is a sign. Therefore infidels are not said to eat sacramentally who intend to receive what the Church receives, but believe nothing to be here. And similarly someone who eats a consecrated host, not knowing that it is consecrated, does not eat sacramentally in that way, because he does not eat the sign except *per accidens.*"[37]

Writing some twenty years later, Thomas, in one of his last writings, would merely repeat his insistence that the metaphysics of the sacrament outweigh the importance of the intentionality of the believer. In the *pars tertia* of the *Summa Theologiae*, Thomas presented virtually a repetition of his arguments in the *Commentary on the Sentences*, and once again, Thomas explicitly rejected Bonaventure's argument against reception by animals.[38]

The significance of this difference has not gone unnoticed by historians. As early as 1939, the brilliant young Jesuit, Yves de Montcheuil, pointed out the significantly different understanding of a sacrament that underlies this divergence between Thomas and Bonaventure. More recently the importance of this disagreement has been pointed out by the great liturgist and historian, Pere Pierre-Marie Gy.[39] In summary, Thomas's theology differs significantly from that of not only Bonaventure, but other thirteenth-century theologians in insisting that any reception of the accidents also includes reception of the Body and Blood. The necessary metaphysical connection between the accidents of the bread and wine and the substance of the Body and Blood overrode the theological understanding of the Eucharist as a true sign. Like his mentor, Albert, however, he was reluctant to speak of reception by animals or infidels as true sacramental reception. It was more precisely, no reception at all. If metaphysically, the connection between the accidents of bread and wine and the substance of the Body and Blood could not be broken by the intention of the recipient, neither could it be said that there was any connection, even a sacrilegious one, between an unintentional recipient and the Body of the risen Lord contained in the sacrament.

Thomas's approach to this question is extremely important. First, his arguments would, of course, carry great weight during and after the Reformation in debates about the Eucharist. Secondly, and more interestingly for historians perhaps, he was outspokenly in disagreement with several prominent predecessors and contemporaries. His was certainly the minority opinion when he taught it, and it seems, remained the minority opinion at least until the end of the thirteenth century, and, outside the Dominican Order, beyond.

At least two thirteenth-century Dominicans who discussed this question either explicitly or implicitly reject Thomas's opinion. Hugh of Strasbourg, a student of Albert writing ca. 1265–70, argued that neither heretics nor infidels nor brute animals can receive the Body and Blood.[40] Nicholas Gorran, the Dominican exegete writing before 1285[41] explicitly rejected Thomas's teaching. "It is known," Nicholas stated, "that the Body of Christ is not consumed by animals. Against this (it is argued) that whoever consumes the species containing (it) consumes as well the Body contained therein. I respond that animals do not consume the species as species, that is, according to the relation that they have to that which they contain, but only as (the species) themselves absolutely."[42]

This is not to say that no Dominican authors defended the teaching of Thomas. Peter of Tarentaise, the later Pope Innocent V, writing between 1256 and 1259 accepted as truer Thomas's opinion that animals receive the Body contained under the accidents of bread and wine while rejecting the opinion of Bonaventure. The rest of Peter's discussion of reception, however, depends fairly heavily on Bonaventure rather than Thomas.[43] With John Quidort of Paris, writing in the 1290s, however, a clear defense of Thomas's theology appears. In discussing whether infidels, children or animals receive, John appears to accept Thomas's argument: "Some have said concerning this matter that sinners do not receive. Rather, however, when (the sinner) touches the species of this sacrament with his lips, he touches the substance because as long as the species remain, so long does the true Body of Christ remain nor is there any way in which the substance of the bread is able to return. Therefore whoever receives the *sacramentum*, ought to receive the *rem*, but not the effect. It follows that an infidel receives the *sacramentum et rem* but not sacramentally because they do not receive the sacrament as a signifier."[44]

John followed Thomas's argument fairly closely. He accepted the teaching of Thomas that it was metaphysically impossible for the species to be separated from the Body and Blood of the Lord without some intervening change in the species, but he was reluctant to follow Thomas further, and remove purely accidental reception as a form of reception.

Meanwhile, Franciscan theologians continued to develop their own theology. John Duns Scotus, surely one of the most famous and influential of the Franciscan masters, taught both in Paris and Oxford. We have reports of the lectures which he gave on the *Sentences* of Peter

Lombard in both universities. In Oxford and later in Paris, Scotus consistently taught what might be called the Franciscan line. He did however add his own clarifications. Debate continues on the dating of Scotus' works, but in all likelihood, the two works considered here took final form in the last years before his death in 1308.[45] In the Oxford lectures, Scotus described four kinds of reception: (1) one can receive the sacrament, but not sacramentally; (2) one can receive sacramentally, but not spiritually; (3) one can receive the sacrament, both sacramentally and spiritually and finally; (4) one can receive spiritually, but not sacramentally. Scotus was the first, to my knowledge, to admit a separate form of reception as *sacramentum, et non sacramentaliter.* It does describe quite neatly what Albert seems to have had in mind, but Scotus is the first to argue for these four ways to receive the Eucharist.

The subtle doctor went further than his predecessors, too, in determining the importance of intentionality in reception. For Scotus, those who receive only the species include all who recognize the host only as common food, including heretics and Christians who hold the Eucharist in contempt. The second form of reception includes all who believe the Body of Christ to be present and wish to be joined in union with Christ, whether good or evil Christians. The faithful can receive spiritually whether they receive the consecrated host or merely desire to do so, and thus the four forms of reception are complete.[46]

In his commentary on the *Sentences* given in Paris, Scotus modified his position to follow more closely that of the earlier Franciscan theologian, Richard of Middleton. Scotus here describes three kinds of reception: (1) *sacramentum et non sacramentaliter* as before; (2) *sacramentum et sacramentaliter;* and (3) *sacramentaliter et spiritualiter.* He dropped here the fourth form of reception, spiritual reception alone. In describing the first two forms of reception, he closely followed Richard. Anyone, man or beast, who receives without faith, receives only the species. On the other hand, all who receive with the intention of receiving the Body of Christ do so, and again Scotus listed the different forms of intentionality which this may take.[47]

Herveus Natalis, writing ca. 1301–02, would be the first Dominican theologian since Thomas to discuss the question of reception at length. His discussion is an interesting and intelligent blend of the teachings of Bonaventure, Thomas, and Albert.[48]

Herveus began his discussion by modifying slightly the by then well-known distinction of Bonaventure. One can distinguish between sacramental reception on the part of the sign and sacramental reception on the part of the recipient. According to the first distinction, all receive sacramentally: mice, dogs, and good and evil persons. According to the second distinction, one can receive in two ways, either with devotion, and hence spiritually, or without devotion and hence merely sacramentally.

Whoever receives the consecrated host, whether he or she accepts it as a sign or not, whether humans or animals, all receive the true Body of Christ because it is impossible that a new substance could come to exist here unless some further change takes place. Even more carefully than Thomas, Herveus laid out the metaphysical reasons why this must be so. He followed Albert, however, in distinguishing between receiving the sacrament sacramentally, and receiving the sacrament but not sacramentally. Herveus argued that this distinction applies only to the Eucharist, where is it possible to receive the sacrament, but not sacramentally.[49] The discussion of reception by Herveus demonstrates the marked tendency on the part of both Franciscan and Dominican theologians to integrate the most valuable insights of earlier theologians into a coherent whole with a wholesome disregard for factionalism. This tendency will become more apparent in later writers.

Peter of La Palu, the Dominican master whose commentary on the *Sentences* dates from 1310–12, seems to have lacked his fellow Dominican's subtlety, at least on this point.[50] Peter began his discussion of the modes of reception by asserting two modes of reception, spiritual and sacramental. He based this distinction on canon law. He then went on, however, to describe four modes of reception. The first, both sacramental and spiritual, describes those who receive worthily. The second, neither sacramental nor spiritual, describes those sinners who do not communicate at all. The third, sacramental but not spiritual, describes the reception of sinners who do communicate. Finally, the fourth form of reception describes those who receive spiritually, but not sacramentally.[51]

Peter absolutely insisted that the Body and Blood persisted in the sacrament as long as the species remained unchanged. Some of the conclusions Peter drew from this probably would have greatly embarrassed Thomas. Peter not only agreed that sinners and animals really receive the true Body of Christ, but that if the species are vomited up, Christ ought to be considered still present. The fact that such things are not really useable by humans does not touch the implacable Peter.[52]

Peter even went so far as to insist that if it is possible, a mouse which has nibbled the sacred species ought to be trapped, burned and the ashes dumped down the piscina.[53] He did not mention whether the offending mouse was given a chance to repent before being taken to the fire. Peter would go further than any thirteenth- or fourteenth-century theologians with whom I am familiar in asserting a nearly corporeal presence of the risen Lord in the Eucharist. He certainly also rejected the notion that the intentionality of the receiver could in any way affect the presence for that recipient, be he mouse or man. Peter seems to have been the exception, however, in his extremely physicalist interpretation of Thomas.

Nicholas of Lyra, the Franciscan exegete, became a master at the University of Paris in 1309. He wrote his famous commentary on Scripture between 1322 and 1339, and died while teaching at Paris in 1349. The commentaries are not the only works ascribed to him, however. A short work entitled *Dicta de sacramento* is also attributed to him. It was published in Cologne in 1480, and then reprinted in 1485, 1490, 1495, and a final time in Paris in 1513. Although the work appears to be genuinely that of Nicholas, little or nothing has been written about it.[54]

The work is a discussion of the conditions necessary for worthy reception of the Eucharist, and clearly relies on the discussion of the Franciscans outlined so far. Nicholas suggested twelve requirements for a worthy reception. One must be a human, a viator (that is still in this life), a believer, an adult, mentally competent, fasting devoutly, without awareness of mortal sin, not guilty of notorious crimes, having a clean body, not prohibited by the appearance of a miracle, having a proper minister, and finally having a right intention.[55]

Fascinating as some of these requirements might be, my discussion will be limited to the two conditions most interesting for this study, that the recipient be a human and that he or she be a believer. The first condition, according to Nicholas, immediately excludes both animals and angels. If one asks what an animal receives when it eats the sacrament, Nicholas responded that some argue that the Body of Christ ceases to be here. This is the opinion of Bonaventure, although Nicholas does not name him. Nicholas rejects this opinion, however, both on the grounds of authority, and because God has made a special pact with the church that as long as the species exist after consecration the Body of Christ will remain united to them. Nicholas then posited that animals receive really but not sacramentally.[56]

Nicholas explained further when he discussed why the recipient must be a believer. If one asks what unbelievers receive in the sacrament, Nicholas responded that they receive as animals do. Here using the terminology of Albert, Herveus and Duns Scotus, Nicholas argued that there is a difference between receiving the sacrament, and receiving sacramentally. To receive sacramentally, one must understand the signified reality under the sign, and this neither unbelievers nor animals can do.[57]

Nicholas is consistent in his use of these distinctions. Children before the age of reason can receive really, but not sacramentally, just like animals and infidels. In the same way, those who are mentally incompetent should only receive if they are capable of giving some sign of devotion, or if they were recently capable of such a sign. In short, there must be some evidence that these people are capable of understanding the signification of the species. If not, they are not capable of sacramental reception.[58]

Nicholas stated the importance of asserting the real presence of the Body and Blood of the Lord in the Eucharist somewhat more strongly than earlier Franciscan theologians. As long as the species exist, so does the Body and Blood, despite what happens to the species. He equally strongly asserts, however, that the presence is only there for those capable of understanding that presence. Neither animals, nor infidels, nor children, nor the mentally incompetent can understand the sign value of the sacrament, and therefore they do not have access to the Real Presence. For them, this might as well be ordinary food.

Nicholas' presentation is a thoughtful integration of the theologically important insight of Bonaventure and others that since the Eucharist is a sign, only those capable of understanding this sign are capable of any form of relationship with the Body of Christ really present under the accidents of bread and wine. On the other hand, he was willing to accept Thomas's philosophical insight that as long as the accidents of bread and wine persist, the substance of the Body and Blood must continue to underlie the species.

A similar integration of Franciscan and Dominican theology appears in the writing of the Dominican Durand of Saint-Pourçian. Three versions of his commentary on the *Sentences* exist, and I have used the third recension completed ca. 1313–27.[59] Durand would go further than any previous Dominican writer to reconcile the insights of both Bonaventure and Thomas. Durand started his discussion of reception by insisting, like Bonaventure, that this sacrament is ordained only to the use of humans. Neither animals, nor even the good angels are capable of reception. Only humans have the capacity and necessity of using temporal signs to reveal veiled spiritual realities, and as the Eucharist functions in just such a way, only humans are capable of reception. Infidels also are incapable of receiving this sacrament *per se* and the same may be said of the faithful who accept the consecrated host as unconsecrated. Only humans who understand this sign are able to receive it as it is meant to be received. Others receive only the accidents of the bread and wine.[60]

So far Durand would seem a staunch advocate of the theology of Alexander of Hales, William of Melitona, and Bonaventure. Durand was, however, also faithful to Thomas's thought. He argued that although animals and infidels only receive *per accidens,* the true Body and Blood remain under the accidents as long as they are recognizable as bread and wine. Like Thomas, Durand clearly rejected Bonaventure's argument that the presence ceases when animals receive.[61]

Durand, like Nicholas of Lyra, seemed to be searching for some way of expressing the theologically important truth that the Eucharist is really a sign, a sacrament. Those who are incapable of understanding that sign do not participate in the saving action of the Church. Metaphysically, however, it was impossible that the substance of the bread and wine underlying the accidents of bread and wine should disappear without some further transmutation taking place. Durand, like his Franciscan contemporary, Nicholas, went a long way in reconciling these two truths. They both suggested, in their own way, that there are two relationships here. The theologically important relationship between the risen Lord and the believer is determined by the intention and faith of the recipient. The metaphysical relationship between the accidents of the bread and wine and the substance of the Body and Blood was not determined by the faith of the recipient, but then, neither had this relationship, in itself, any saving power.

This compromise, reached at least by the middle of the fourteenth century, is important for two reasons. First, and most importantly, it has often been thought (and said and written) that the medieval theologians had lost a true theology of sign, a theology that would only be recovered in the Reformation. This is clearly not the case. Without denying the metaphysical presence of the risen Lord in the sacrament, theologians came to insist that that presence was meaningless unless the recipient understood the signs which pointed to it. This is a true theology of symbols; a theology which focuses not so much on the presence of the Lord in the Eucharist, but rather emphasizes the purpose and function of that presence. Catholics in particular might do well to keep this teaching in mind when in dialogue with their brothers and sisters in the Protestant tradition.

Secondly, the history of the theology of reception rehearsed here would demonstrate once again the toleration for diversity which existed during the central Middle Ages. Thomas and Bonaventure, at least, certainly disagreed about the relative importance of metaphysical and theological concerns in understanding the Real Presence. Yet, the diversity of their opinions was not only tolerated, but, on the whole, accepted and developed by later theologians. Condemnations were hurled by neither ecclesiastical officials nor by the competing theological schools. And this could have easily happened. Dominicans were urged by their superiors to support Thomas's thought, and the magisterium was not loathe to step in to settle theological disputes during these centuries.[62]

If there are lessons to be learned from this theological toleration, they surely must include the insight that the history of theology is at its best a history of toleration and diversity; and even such disputed issues as the Real Presence have a tradition of more breadth than a narrow reading of post-Reformation theology would lead one to believe.

---

1. Originally published in *Theology and the University*, ed. John Apczynski, Proceedings of the Annual Convention of the College Theology Society, 1987 (Lanham, Md.: University Press of America, 1990) 15–36.

2. Gary Macy, *Theologies of the Eucharist in the Early Scholastic Period* (Oxford: Clarendon Press, 1984) 47 passim.

3. Macy, *Theologies*, esp. 86–96.

4. For a discussion of this entire issue, cf. Artur Landgraf, "Die in der Frühscholastik klassische Frage *quid sumit mus*," *Dogmengeschichte in der Frühscholastik* 3 (2) (Regenburg: Friedrich Pustet, 1955) 207–22, and Gary Macy, "Of Mice and Manna: *Quid mus sumit* as a Pastoral Question," *Recherches de théologie anciénne et médiévale* 58 (1991) 157–66.

5. Ideas similar to those espoused by Alexander exist in late twelfth- and early thirteenth-century writers. Cf., for instance, Innocent III, *De sacro altaris mysterio*, l. 4, c. 16 : "Nam in quo similitudo deficeret, in eo sacramentum non esset, sed ibi se proderet, et fidei locum aufferret, neque jam crederetur quod ita fieri non oportet. Itaque quantum ad nos servat per omnia corruptibilis

cibi similitudinem, sed quantum ad se non amittit inviolabilis corporis veritatem." *PL* 215: 867. See also Peter of Capua, *Summa "Uetustissima ueterum"* (1201–02): "Et potest dici quod etiam in ipso sumente manet materiale corpus donec in eo est aliqua forma ipsius panis. Non tamen incorporatur ei quia cibus est anime non corporis ut dicit Augustinus." Vatican City, Biblioteca Vaticana, Vaticana latina MS 4296, fol. 70r1, and Jacques de Vitry, *Historia occidentalis* (ca. 1219–25): "Forma igitur gustatur, sentitur, dentibus atteritur. Corpus autem non in uentrem descendit, sed ob ore ad cor transit. Comeditur sed non consumitur." J. F. Hinnebusch, ed., *The Historia occidentalis of Jacques de Vitry: A Critical Edition*. Spicilegium Friburgense 17 (Fribourg: The University Press, 1972) 231.

6. On the dating of Alexander's works, see Alexander of Hales, *Quaestiones disputatae 'Antequam Esset Frater,'* Collegium S. Bonaventurae, eds., Bibliotheca franciscana scholastica medii aevi 19–21 (Florence: Quaracchi, 1960) 34*–36*.

7. E.g., "Quaestio est propter quid, si corpus Christ ibi est, non sumitur a brutis animalibus. — Responsio est ad hoc, quod differt sensus in brutis et in nobis. Est enim in nobis ordinatus ad rationem, in brutis vero non. Quia ergo corpus Christi sub sacramento non dicit tantum quod ad sensum pertinet, sed quod ad rationem, quod sensus est a brutis sumitur, scilicet species panis; quod in ordine ad rationem est non sumitur, scilicet corpus Christi." Alexander of Hales, *Glossa in quatuor libros sententiarum*, Collegium S. Bonaventurae, eds., Bibliotheca franciscana scholastica medii aevi 15 (Florence: Quaracchi, 1957) 204. Cf. also 161–62.

8. *Quaestiones disputatae*, 966–67 (no. 199), esp. 967: "Item, alia est unio speciei tantum, ut in iis qui manducant secundum quod est sacramentum solum, sicut panem aliquem, ut Iudaei vel pagani. — Item est unio secundum rationem signi, ut in eo qui credit et intelligit; et maior adhuc est eo qui credit et diligit, ut in iis qui spiritualiter accipiunt; et sic secundum quod maior unio, maior manducatio."

9. Ibid., 699–700 (nos. 205–10). E.g.: "Respondeo: manducare sacramentaliter, ut proprie dicitur, est attingere rem sub sacramento; ergo ubi nullo modo attingitur, nec per modum crediti, nec per modum cogniti, nullo modo est manducatio sacramentalis vel sacramentaliter; sed est quodam modo manducatio carnalis, et adhuc, proprie non est ibi manducatio carnalis, quia non est ibi divisio substantiae, cum non sit ibi nisi divisio accidentium solum. . . . Ad hoc quod obicitur de Iudaeo vel pagano, dico quod plus est in hac manducatione quam in manducatione irrationalis creaturae, quia unio est ibi in natura. Tamen quia non est ibi cognitio rei sub specie, et cum manducatio sacramentalis importet accipere species et attingere rem quae est sub sacramento fide, non manducant sacramentaliter."

10. This is the opinion of Pope Innocent III, *De sacro altaris mysterio*, l. 4, c. 16, *PL* 215: 863.

11. William of Militona, *Quaestiones de sacramentis,* C. Piana and G. Gál, eds., Bibliotheca scholastica medii aevi 23 (Florence: Quaracchi, 1961) 695–700. For the dating of this work, see the introduction, 5*–33*.

12. Ibid., 701: "Unde brutum unitur solum accidentibus; infidelis nihil penitus credens superaddit quandam aptitudinem ad sacramentalem vel spiritual manducationem; habens fidem informem superaddit quod unitur cognito, habens formatum credito, in quantum habet caritatem unitur ut dilecto."

13. On the dating for Guérric's reign as master, see James Weisheipl, *Friar Thomas D'Aquino: His Life, Thought & Works* (Washington, D.C.: The Catholic University of America Press, 1974) 65–66.

14. "Respondeo secundum diuinam naturam est cibus angelorum. Secundum utramque Christus est cibus hominum. In Christo enim duplex est natura, humana scilicet et diuina. Et simile in homine duplex, corporalis et spiritualis. Unde homo in ipso plenam inuenit refectionem. Item cibus est hominum secundum duplicem statum uie scilicet comprehensionis. In utraque enim statu uidetur sed differentur quia in statu comprehendoris, fidem sine uelamine. In statu uero uie sub uelamine fides. Enim accepitur sub speculo et enigmate quia uero uiator non cognoscit sine sensu. Oportet quod uelamen subiectum sit sensui quia uero signum eius quod uelatur oportet quod ducat in illud ideo non sumitur nisi a rationalis, scilicet homo. Ideo solum ab homine sumitur." Guérric of St. Quentin, *Sententie,* Paris, Bibliothéque Nationale, nat. lat. 1604, fol. 36r2. Cf. William of Militona, *Quaestiones de sacramentis,* 702–03.

15. "Item altera sunt qui habent fidem formatam, aliqui qui habent fidem informem, aliqui qui neutrum. Si plus accedit ad manducationem secundum susceptionem sacramenti habens fidem formatam quam habens fidem informem. Ergo qui nullo modo habent fidem nullo modo accedunt. Ergo nullo modo accepint non habens fidem formatam uel informem. Ergo tota sumendi est fides non natura. Unde non quia homo uel rationalis sed quia fideles." Ibid. Cf. William, *Quaestiones de sacramentis,* 716.

16. "Quod obiicitur de mure. Dico non commedat quia solum sumatur ad illo qui habet sensum ordinatum ad intelligentiam." ibid., fol. 36v1.

17. Landgraf, "Die in der Frühscholastik klassiche Frage," 207.

18. See, for instance, David Burr, *Eucharistic Presence and Conversion in Late Thirteenth-Century Franciscan Thought,* Transactions of the American Philosophical Society 74 (3) (Philadelphia: The American Philosophical Society, 1984) 8.

19. Bonaventure, *Commentaria in quatuor libros sententiarum* in *Opera Omnia* 4 (Florence: Quaracchi, 1889) 204.

20. Ibid., 204–05.

21. Ibid., 205.

22. Ibid., 307.

23. Ibid., 308.

24. "Et haec opinio communior est et certe honestior et rationabilior." Ibid.

25. Ibid., 310–11.

26. Ibid., 311.

27. *De Sacramentis* in *Opera omnia* 26 (Münster: Aschendorff, 1985) 65A-B, 66A.

28. On the dating of Albert's works, see Burr, *Eucharistic Presence,* 16.

29. *Liber 4, dist. 9, art. 3, Commentarii in Sententiarum* in *Opera omnia,* vol. 29, eds. August and Emil Borgnet (Paris: Vives, 1890–99) 218.

30. Ibid., *art.* 4, Borgnet, 219.

31. ". . . quia non video rationabiliter qualiter corpus Christi non transit ad omnem locum, ad quem transeunt species panis et vini, sub quibus secundum veritatem rei continetur totus Christus." Ibid., *art.* 5, Borgnet, 220.

32. "Et hoc dico sine præjudicio: quia quidam Magistri dicunt oppositum." Ibid.

33. On the dating of Thomas's works, see Weisheipl, *Friar Thomas D'Aquino,* 358 ff.

34. Thomas Aquinas, *Scriptum super sententiis magistri Petri Lombardi,* M. F. Moos, ed. (Paris: P. Lethielleux, 1947) 365–66.

35. Ibid., 368–69. Cf. 369: ". . . ideo quamdiu species non mutatur, nullo modo desinit ibi esse corpus Christi: . . ."

36. Ibid., 370–71.

37. "Ad tertium dicendum quod creatura irrationalis nullo modo spiritualiter manducat, neque sacramentaliter; quia neque utitur manducatio ut sacramento, neque manducat sacramentum dicitur manducare infidelis qui intendit recipere hoc quod recipit Ecclesia, quamvis hoc credat nihil esse. Et similiter etiam ille qui manducaret hostiam consecratam, nesciens eam consecratam esse, non manducaret sacramentaliter aliquo modo, quia non manducaret sacramentum nisi per accidens; nisi quod plus accederet ad sacramentalem manducationem, inquantum est aptus natus sacramentum ut sacramentum manducare: quod bruto non competit. Nec tamen oportet quod sit alius modus manducationis tertius a duobus praedictis; quia hoc quod est per accidens, in divisionem non cadit." Ibid., 371.

38. *Summa theologiae tertia pars,* q. 80, P. Caramello, ed. (Rome: Marietti, 1956) 488–91.

39. Yves de Montcheuil, "La Raison de la Permanence du Christ sous les Espéces Eucharistiques d'après Saint Bonaventure et Saint Thomas," *Mélanges théologiques,* 3rd ed. (Paris: Aubier, 1951) 71–82, and Pierre-Marie Gy, O.P., "La Relation au Christ dans l'Eucharistie Selon S. Bonaventure et S. Thomas d'Aquin," *Sacrements de Jésus Christ,* J. Dore and others, eds. (Paris: Institut Catholique de Paris, 1983) 70–106.

40. "De modis sumendi eucharistiam Cap. xvi: Corpus Christi quatuor modis sumitur. Quidam accipiunt illud spiritualiter tantum vt qui accipiunt esse sacramenti. id est. gratiam et non sacramentum corporis Christi. De hoc

modo sumendi dicit Augustinus Crede et manducasti. id est. corporis Christi mystico incorporatus es. Quidam sacramentaliter tantum vt communicantes in mortali peccato: quia licet Deus sit vbique per essentiam, non tamen per gratiam. Quidam spiritualiter et sacramentaliter, vt qui accipiuntur rem et sacramentum. id est. communicantes in gratia. Quidam neutro modo, vt qui nec rem nec sacramentum accipiunt vt heretici qui nichil conficiunt. Primi non manducantes manducant. Secundi manducantes non manducant. Tercii manducantes manducant. Quarti non manducantes (non) manducant." Hugh of Strasbourg, *Compendium theologice veritatis* (Paris, 1515) fol. 142v. On Hugh's dates, see Burr, *Eucharistic Presence*, 25.

41. On Nicholas' dates, see the *NCE* 10:453.

42. "Item ibidem glossa. Sciendum quod a brutis corpus Christi non sumi-tur. Contra. quicumque sumit species continentes sumit contentum corpus. Respondeo bruta non sumant species ut species, scilicet, secundum ordinem quem habent ad contentum sed secundum se absolute." Nicholas of Gorran, *Commentaria ad I Corinthianos,* Paris, Bibliothéque Mazarine, MS 270, fol. 199r2.

43. Peter of Tarentaise, *Innocentii Qvinti . . . In IV. Librum Sententiarum Commentaria . . .* (Toulouse, 1651; rpt. Ridgewood, N.J.: Gregg Press Inc., 1964) 100–03, 142. Cf. Bonaventure, *Commentaria in quatuor libros sententiarum,* 201–02, 310–11. On the dating of this work, see Burr, *Eucharistic Presence,* 25.

44. "Item juxta hoc utrum infideles, pueri et bruta animalia. Ad hoc dixerunt aliqui quod peccator non suscipit. Immo substantiam cum labiis tangit species huius sacramenti quia quamdiu maneret species tamdiu manet uerum corpus Christi nec est uia quando substantia panis possit redire. Ideo quere recipit sacramentum debet quod recipiat rem sed non effectum. Sequitur infidelis suscepit sacramentum et rem sed non sacramentaliter quia non reficit signum ad signatum." John of Paris, *Sententie,* Paris, Bibliothèque Mazarine 889, fol. 82r1. On the dating of this work, see the introduction to *Jean de Paris (Quidort) O.P, Commentaire sur les Sentences. Reportatio. Livre I,* Jean-Pierre Muller, ed. (Rome: Pontificum Institutum S. Anselmi, 1961) and the *DMA* 7:136–37.

45. On the controversy surrounding the dating of Scotus' works, see Burr, *Eucharistic Presence,* 76.

46. *Opus Oxoniensis* in *Opera omnia* 17 (Paris: Vives, 1894) 75.

47. *Reportatio Parisiensia* in *Opera omnia* 24 (Paris: Vives, 1894) 27–28.

48. On the dating of Herveus' work, see Fredrick J. Roensch, *Early Thomistic School* (Dubuque: Priory Press, 1964) 106–17.

49. Herveus Natalis, *Hervei Natalis Britonis In quatuor Libros sententiarum Commentaria . . .,* (Paris, 1647, rpt. Farnborough, Hants. England: Gregg Press Limited, 1966) 345:1A–2C.

50. On the dating of Peter's work, see Roensch, *Early Thomistic School,* 124–31.

51. "Secunda conclusio est quod est duplex modis manducandi, scilicet spiritualiter et sacramentaliter. *De cons.* d. 3 c. 'Quia passus, etc' et 'Qui manducat cum multis aliis.' Unde aliquis manducat sacramentaliter et spiritualiter vt in fide et charitate communicans. Alius neutro modo nec sacramentaliter nec spiritualiter, sicut peccator non communicans. Tertius sacramentaliter non spiritualiter sicut peccator fidelis communicans. Quartus spiritualiter et non sacramentaliter vt iustus non communicans. Sed si habet actu deuotionem ad sacramentum vt deuote audiens missam tunc magis, si autem desideret communicare aut celebrare nec possit, tunc maxime." *Exactissimi et quorum probati a clarissimi doctoris Petri de Palude predicatorii ordinis . . . quartus sententiarum liber . . .* (Paris, 1514) fol. 35v2.

52. "Secunda conclusio est quod potest istud sacramentum suscipere: quia eius essentia est materie consecratio quam brutum vere sumit quia vere manducat species sub quibus vere est corpus Christi. Et dato quod per hoc reddantur inhabiles ad vsum hominis propter quem sunt: nihilominus non propter hoc desinit ibi esse benedicta: sed per accidens est: sicut si homo comederet hostiam consecratam quam crederet simplicem: quam si brutum manducare non potuit miraculum est: sicut asinus heretici manducare non potuit: sed flexis genibus hostiam adorauit." Ibid.

53. "Respondeo. si mus potest exenterari debet: et mus quidem debet conburi et cinis in piscina periici." Ibid., fol. 36v2.

54. For a recent summary of what is known about Nicholas' life and works, see the *DMA* 9:126.

55. "He sunt conditiones necessaria requisite ad idoneum susceptorem sacramenti eucharistie per quas potest responderi ad plures questiones consuetas fieri. Requiritur enim quod sit homo, viator, fidelis, adultus, mente preditus, ieiunus deuotus, sine conscientia peccati mortalis, crimine non notatus, corpore mundus, apparitione miraculosa non prohibitus, a ministro ydoneo tempore debito, intentione recta." Nicholas of Lyra, *Dicta de sacramentis* (Cologne, 1495). The edition is unfoliated.

56. "Prima conditio est quod sit (homo) per quod statim excluditur omne brutum animal et angelis siue bonus siue malus. Sed si queratur Numquid brutum animal suscipit sacramentum. Dixeratur aliqui quod immediate quando brutum suscepit sacramentum desinit ibi esse corpus Christi. Sed hoc reprobatur a magistro sententiarum in quarto de consecratione. Et similiter in decretis de conse. di.ii.ca. Qui bene non custodierit. Et ideo dicitur ab aliis aliter et melius ut videtur quod quamdiu species ille sacramentales mutare non fuerint per calorem naturalem stomachi: tamdiu remanet ibi corpus Christi. Vnde sicut habemus ex speciali facto diuino quod ad vltimam dispositionem corporis humani deus infundit creando ipsam animam et eam tenet in corpore durante tali dispositionem: sic etiam deus statuit pactum cum ecclesia quod tamdiu esset ipsum corpus Christi sub sacramento quamdiu permanent ille species quam prius afficiebantur et aspiciebant panem sicut

subiectum a quo postea miraculose separantur et manu tenentur et propter illud est ut redderet deus ecclesiam certam quando ibi esset corpus Christi et quando non. Recipit ergo brutum realiter et non sacramentaliter et hoc exponam inferius in tercia conditione." Ibid.

57. "Tertio dixi (fidelis) et intelligo non illum qui de fide solum instructum est sed illum qui iam accepit sacramentum baptismi et factus est per hoc de familia Christi. Ex quo statim patet quod cathecumino quamtamcumque habenti fidem perfectam non debet hoc sacramentum administrari. Sed si queratur Numquid infidelis recipiendo sacramentum recipit corpus Christi dicendum de ipso sicut de bruto supra tactum est quod sumit realiter sed nullo modo sacramentaliter inquantum infidelis. Si queras Numquid idem est sumere sacramentum et sacramentaliter sumere. Dico quod non quia sumere sacramentaliter addit supra sumere sacramentum modum sumendi videlicet quod referat signum in signatum suum credendo et si opus est confidendo ore quod sub illis speciebus veraciter contineatur corpus Christi quod non facit infidelis nec etiam brutum." Ibid.

58. "Nunc autem pueri ante annos discretionis et si possunt eucharistiam realiter sicut quemcumque alium cibum comedere, non tamen possunt hoc sacramentum sacramentaliter manducare nec eo uti ut sacro signo, referendo significandum in signatum sed ut communio signo, et sic propter carentiam discretionis non percipiunt ibi veraciter continere corpus Christi." Ibid. See also: "Si autem sit amentes sic quod non fit furiosus sed tantummodo loquens inania et a vero sensu alienatus. Adhuc distinguendum est, quia vel pretendit actus et signa deuotionis tunc potest ei ministrari, si vero nullum actum aut signum deuotionis pretendit, recurredum est ad tempus precedens passionem quia si tunc petierit et deuotionem pretenderit et obstet aliquid aliud periculum, licite potest sibi dari." Ibid.

59. On the dating of this work, see Weisheipl, 343, *NCE* 4:1114–16, *The Oxford Dictionary of the Christian Church,* 2nd ed. (Oxford: Oxford University Press, 1974) 433–34, and the *DMA* 4:313–14.

60. Durand of Saint-Pourçian, *D. Durandi a Sancto Porciano, . . . in Petri Lombardi Sententias Theologicas Commentariorum libri III* (Venice, 1571; rpt. Ridgewood, N.J.: The Gregg Press Incorporated, 1964) fol. 312vA-B.

61. Ibid.

62. The Dominican General Chapter of Paris in 1279 held that no attack on Thomas's work would be tolerated within the order. For details, see Weisheipl, *Friar Thomas D'Aquino,* 341 ff.

Chapter 4

Berengar's Legacy as Heresiarch[1]

The extent of Berengar's influence on later generations has undergone considerable change in the last one hundred years. The eighteenth- and nineteenth-century scholars Pierre Le Brun, Jules Corblet, and Thomas Simmons described Berengar's influence as extensive. According to these scholars, not only did Berengar's theology continue to be refuted well into the twelfth century, but on a popular level, eucharistic devotions were introduced to counter the influence of his teaching. Miracle stories were told to prove the existence of the risen Lord in the consecrated bread and wine, and even art was enjoined in the struggle to lure the hearts and minds of the masses away from the heresy of Berengar.[2] These scholars just assumed the influence of Berengar, and did not seem to feel the need to demonstrate the extent of his influence.[3]

Most modern scholars, on the other hand, portray Berengar as having very few followers after his death, and describe the Berengarian affair as a purely academic matter, little affecting popular understanding.[4] Few scholars would now argue that Berengar was the founder of a popular movement or even of a school of thought. Although the theory that the Berengarian challenge was responsible for the introduction of popular eucharistic practices still finds adherents, the work of Gerard Grant has gone a long way to weaken this argument.[5] If the modern scholars are correct in understanding Berengar as an academic who had little or no popular appeal, how has it happened that Berengar has been perceived to have been as influential as these earlier scholars once assumed him to be? Why was Berengar dubbed, already in the words of St. Thomas, "the first deviser of this heresy,"[6] rather than, as seems more appropriate, the only perpetrator of his heresy?

The simplest solution to this question would seem to be to find out if anyone really did continue on as Berengar's disciple, expounding his particular form of eucharistic theology. There is no shortage of people so described. Unfortunately, of the people actually named as followers of the heresy of Berengar, few, if any, really taught what Berengar did. Gregory VII was accused of following the teachings of Berengar by the rebellious German bishops meeting at the synod of Brixen in 1080. The motives for this indictment were fairly transparently political, and cannot be taken too seriously.[7] Rupert of Deutz charged the canons of Liège with whom he disputed (including, most likely, Alger of Liège) with reviving the heresy of Berengar.[8] Walter of St. Victor, that old grouch, reproached Peter the Lombard for being another Berengar.[9] Neither Alger nor Peter came close to adopting Berengar's thought, in fact both specifically condemned it, and these remarks can be dismissed as rhetorical thrusts issuing from the heat of controversy.

A more serious allegation was made by Hugh Metel regarding Master Gerland, teaching in Besançon ca. 1131–48. Hugh suspected Gerland of teaching that Christ is present in the Eucharist in figure only, and surely this was Berengar's teaching.[10] Hugh did not describe Gerland as a student or follower of Berengar, however, and the records that do exist concerning Gerland speak of him as a well-respected master of liberal arts.[11] Siegfried, prior of St. Nicholas near Laon, heard of a similar teaching concerning which he consulted Guibert, abbot of Nogent, sometime during or before the year 1119. Almost certainly, though, this reference was to the controversy between Rupert of Deutz and the canons of Liège which occasioned Rupert's tagging Alger and company as followers of Berengar.[12] Master Gerland then stands, rather shakily, as the sole representative of the Berengarian tradition. This obscure reference to a little-known liberal arts professor, coupled with a few vitriolic outbursts, hardly seems basis enough to crown Berengar a heresiarch.

While there seems to be no particular master who expounded Berengar's thought, there are references to anonymous groups called "Berengarians," suggesting that perhaps Berengar's teaching was carried on as a popular movement. Surely, the opponents of Berengar assumed that he was the leader of a whole group of heretics. Durand, the monk of Fécamp and later bishop of Troarn, wrote his tract, *De corpore et sanguine domini* against Berengar ca. 1053–54. In it, he spoke in the plural of "inventors of modern heresies and hatchers of impious dogmas" and bestowed the title of heresiarch on Berengar.[13] Lanfranc of Bec, opposing Berengar ca. 1063, spoke of Berengar's "disciples and followers."[14] Almost certainly Durand and Lanfranc were referring to Berengar's students and supporters. He was, after all, a famous master. Besides his students, Berengar, at least in the early years of the controversy, enjoyed the support of his bishop, Eusebius Bruno of Angers and that of Paulinus, the bishop of Metz.[15] There seems little doubt that Berengar's teaching had quite a reputation, and that fear of its extent and influence were real. The question is whether this influence ever coalesced into either a coherent school or movement.[16]

The best evidence that Berengarianism was widespread seems to come from Guitmund, the later bishop of Aversa, who attacked Berengar and his "followers" ca. 1073–75 while a monk at Bec.[17] Guitmund named at least four different kinds of "Berengarians," who, according to Guitmund, disagreed even among themselves. Some taught that the Body and Blood of the Lord are not present at all, but that the sacraments are only figures. Others seemed to agree with the Church, but actually held a form of impanation. This was held to be the teaching of Berengar himself. Yet others sharply disagreed with Berengar, arguing that the bread and wine are partly changed and partly remain. Finally, there were those who claimed that the Lord is present in the species, but that when the unworthy receive, the species revert back to bread and wine.[18]

Not all of these groups can be identified, but at least two of the groups do not seem to be followers of Berengar at all. Those who denied any presence in the Eucharist sound more like the groups of wandering teachers condemned in Ivois, near Trier, ca. 1122, or those who appeared in Soisson ca. 1114. Similar accusations were made of the preacher Ramihrdrus killed in Cambrai in 1074, and of Tanchelm who taught in Utrecht and Antwerp, ca. 1100–15.[19] It is even more unlikely that the fourth teaching, that the unworthy cannot receive, should be ascribed to Berengar. Guitmund alleged that the followers of this teaching based themselves on a story from the lives of the Fathers in which an old man saw angels removing the host from an unworthy recipient and replacing it with charcoal.[20] This teaching did indeed appear in the work of a late eleventh-century writer, but not Berengar of Tours. It was Honorius Augustodunensis who quite clearly taught what Guitmund attributed to Berengar. In his *Elucidarium*, written between 1098 and 1103,

Honorius contended that those who do not remain in Christ, although they seem to receive, do not. The Body of the Lord is taken to heaven by angels, while the unworthy are given charcoal by the devil.[21] Honorius gave Cyprian of Carthage as his authority for this teaching, referring to a story related by Cyprian of an unworthy recipient who found only ashes in his hands after reception.[22] Is it possible that the "Berengarian" whom Guitmund had in mind was actually Honorius? This seems unlikely as there was a twenty-year gap between the work of Guitmund and that of Honorius. Yet the similarities between the teaching attacked by Guitmund and defended by Honorius are striking. Could Guitmund and Honorius share a common source? The place, if not the time, seems to lend support to this supposition. Honorius may well have picked up this teaching during his stay in England and Guitmund too had important connections there, including his teacher Lanfranc. Guitmund even turned down an offer of an English episcopate offered to him by William the Conqueror. It is just possible, then, that Honorius was recording a teaching of which Guitmund was previously aware, and which he castigated as "Berengarianism."

Both Honorius' and Cyprian's story argued for a form of Donatism, and the teaching that either the unworthy do not receive or, more frequently, that an unworthy minister could not confect the sacrament, was not uncommon in the eleventh and twelfth century. The most famous instance, of course, would be the teaching of the Waldensians.[23] Once again, anyone familiar with Guitmund's work could see in the Waldensians, among others, a revival of a form of what at least Guitmund labeled "Berengarianism."

Moving into the twelfth century, one again finds references to the "heresy of Berengar." William of St. Thierry warned Rupert of Deutz, in a fatherly way, to be careful that Rupert's theology not fall into the heresy of Berengar and his followers.[24] Abelard mentioned in the *Theologia Christiana,* written 1123–24, that the controversy over the Eucharist was not yet over, and Zachary of Besançon remarked in the middle of the century that "There are not a few—indeed they are plentiful, but unobtrusive—who are of the same opinion as the condemned Berengar, yet they condemn him as the Church does."[25] Writing ca. 1140, Peter the Venerable alleged Peter of Bruys and his cohorts to be worse than Berengar. Finally, Gregory, bishop of Bergamo, writing in 1146, directed his tract on the Eucharist against the "new Berengarians."[26]

Most probably, Gregory was referring to the Cathars who would have been active in northern Italy by this time.[27] It is harder to guess whom Zachary has in mind, since, as he says, they kept their mouths shut. I have suggested elsewhere, however, that both he and Walter of St. Victor may have been alarmed by the revival of a more Augustinian and mystical interpretation of the Eucharist which had its beginnings in the School at Laon.[28] William of St. Thierry was clearly concerned about Rupert's theology, not Berengar's; and Abelard could have been alluding to the dispute between Rupert and the canons of Liège since this would have take place shortly before the *Theologia* was written. Then again, Abelard might have had in mind William's criticism of his own teaching on the Eucharist, albeit this did not appear in written form until some twenty years later.[29] These are isolated instances, however, and would hardly indicate a conscious revival of Berengar's teaching.

The allusions by Peter the Venerable and by Gregory of Bergamo are more intriguing, because they suggest that the teachings of Berengar were being continued by heretical groups in the twelfth century. The general beliefs ascribed to Peter of Bruys or the Cathars do not reflect Berengar's actual teaching, but they do share some similar characteristics. Both groups of heretics deny, in one way or another, the Church's teaching on the Eucharist. It is here, I hope to show, that Berengar may have gained his reputation as the father of a continuing heresy. Over the course of time a series of teachings ascribed to Berengar became linked with those heretical groups which denied the orthodox teaching on the Eucharist. The most threatening of these groups would be the Cathars. In so far as medieval or modern writers believed Berengar to be responsible for the teaching of these heretics, they could justly credit him with the title of heresiarch.

To start with, there are certain of Berengar's authentic teachings which these heretical groups are at least accused of adopting. In his *Rescriptum,* for instance, Berengar pointed out that there are many places in Scripture where Jesus is referred to metaphorically. Jesus is called the corner stone, a lion, and a lamb. Berengar claimed that this is the mode of speech used when the priest calls the bread the Body of Christ during the liturgy. Just as the apostle spoke metaphorically when he called Jesus the rock from which water flowed in the desert, so too here, the priest would be speaking only metaphorically. Jesus was not really a rock.[30] This same dictum, including the same reference from Paul, *"Petra Christus erat,"* was accredited to heretics by two different authors. Writing in 1146, Gregory, the bishop of Bergamo, accused the "new Berengarians" of using this argument.[31] The layman, Georgius, writing specifically against the Cathars a hundred years later, also attributed this contention to his opponents, including the proof text from Paul.[32] This is the clearest example of an authentic teaching of Berengar ascribed to later heretics. Of course, the accusations of Gregory and Georgius do not prove that the heretics were familiar with Berengar's writing. It was common practice in the Middle Ages to charge one group of heretics with inculcating errors associated with classic heretical positions. The Cathars were seen as Manicheans, for instance. Augustine's descriptions of the Manicheans of his own time could be applied equally to these new Manichees. The connection between Berengar and later heretical groups, however artificial and even unjust, was made. Once made, future authors might assume a continuity between the former heretic and the opinions they found ascribed to later dissidents.

A second teaching associated with Berengar early on in the dispute concerning the Eucharist was stercoranism, that is, the belief that the Body and Blood of the Lord are eaten, descend into the stomach and are subject to digestion, and finally, as the name of the teaching suggests, undergo defecation.

Since Berengar in his known writing was adamant that the Body of Christ remained in heaven and the risen Lord could in any case suffer no ignominy, what are the grounds for this accusation? First of all, Berengar did hold that, if, as his opponents alleged, the Body of the Lord is actually present in the Eucharist, then this body must necessarily be subject to all forms of desecration, including digestion.[33] His was a *reductio ad absurdum*, however, and clearly intended as sarcasm. Secondly, Jean de Montclos has argued convincingly that Berengar was accused of stercoranism because of his description of the *sacramenta* of bread and wine as perishable. Based on the letter of Berengar to a certain Brother Richard written in 1051, Montclos surmises that it was Ascelin of Chartres who initiated the charge based on discussions with Berengar. The Chartrains, it seems, deliberately disseminated this slander. A letter by Humbert of Silva-Candida written in 1051 to Eusebius Bruno, bishop of Anger and Berengar's ordinary, used the term, *stercorianista*, to describe both Berengar and Eusebius.[34] Humbert based his knowledge of Berengar's teaching on letters he had received from France, and Montclos suggests that these letters came from Chartres.[35] Humbert, interestingly, would be the first to use this term, with which he also besmirched the Greek Church in his response to Nicetas Stethatos written in 1054 during the azimite controversy.[36]

Durand of Troarn reproached Berengar for this abomination in his *De corpore et sanguine domini*. Durand may have been basing his charge on the earlier accusations of Humbert and Ascelin, but this need not necessarily be the case. Durand had his own sources, and in his indictment of Berengar, he was paraphrasing a similar condemnation by his favorite master, Paschasius of Corbie. Quoting "a certain apocryphal book," Paschasius rejected as "frivolous" the notion that the holy mysteries might be mixed in digestion with ordinary food.[37] The passage to which Paschasius alluded occurred in the alleged second letter of Clement contained in the Pseudo-Isidorian collection, and suggests that the eucharistic fast has been mandated to avoid the mixing of the body of the Lord with common food.[38]

Durand, then, could either have been responding to an actual argument made by Berengar against realist claims, or he could have followed Humbert and Ascelin in their accusations, or he may have assumed that any error mentioned by Paschasius could be ascribed to Berengar. In any case, Durand's indictment would hold, and stercoranism would remain associated with Berengar.[39] The accusation occurred again in the letter of Gozechin of Mainz to Berengar written between 1066 and 1070.[40]

Guitmund, unlike Durand, spoke of what he at least purported to be actual instances where Berengar raised stercoranism in defense of his position, using as an authority Matthew 15:17, "Do you not see that whatever goes into the mouth passes into the stomach, and so passes on?"[41] In discussing the stories of saints who lived on the Eucharist alone, Guitmund recounted Berengar's claim to have proved that any defecation that occurred during such fasts must have been caused by the sacrament. Guitmund at least pretended to take Berengar literally, and demanded to know who would dare to perform such experiments. Guitmund than proceeded to refute the results of any such inquiries should they have taken place.[42] It is difficult to take Guitmund too seriously in his suggestion that Berengar and his followers might have undertaken some rather disgusting observations, but once again, and this time more dramatically, stercoranism was coupled with the name of Berengar.

Alger of Liège noted this blasphemy as one of the *varii errores, variaeque haereses* against which he wrote in his *De sacramentis corporis et sanguinis dominici* ca. 1110–15.[43] Alger, unlike Durand and Guitmund, did not specifically name Berengar as one of the targets of his work and in fact, Alger's immediate occasion for the tract seems to have been the dispute between Rupert of Deutz with the canons of Liège.[44] He did, however, charge the *dialectici* of raising this particular issue and he could easily have had Berengar in mind, as he appeared to be copying Durand on this point.[45] He certainly reviled Berengar as a heretic, and quoted the oath of 1059 in his discussion of the fraction of the host.[46] He also included the Greek Church among the *Stercoranistae*, and here he may have been following the lead of Humbert of Silva-Candida.[47] Alger added to Durand's sources, however, a tract of Heriger, the tenth-century abbot of Lobbes. Heriger was concerned that a letter by the Carolingian scholar, Rhaban Maur, allowed that the Body of the Lord was subject to digestion.[48] Alger copied Heriger, again noting that the heretics appealed to the passage from Matthew to give their argument the illusion of authority.[49] Alger, like Guitmund before him, held that the heretics argued that one could live on the sacred species, and that natural functions would continue uninterrupted.[50] This particular argument would be found among the reported teachings of several heretical groups.

The most widespread and influential of these groups were the Cathars. Alan of Lille, in his *Contra haereticos*, written between 1185 and 1200, recorded the teaching, reporting that the heretics used Matthew 15:17 in their defense.[51] Ébrard of Béthune in his *Liber contra waldenes vel antihaeresis*, written shortly before 1212, contended that the Cathars performed the same experiments with the sacrament which Guitmund once attributed to Berengar.[52] Georgius also made the accusation of stercoranism in his *Disputatio inter catholicum et paterinum haereticum* ca. 1240–50. The Cathars were again described as using Matthew 15:17 as a proof text, the objection that Alger and Alan had noted.[53]

The Cathars were not alone in being accused of stercoranism, however. Hugo Speroni, teaching a form of spiritualized Christianity in Piacenza ca. 1177–85, was also charged with using the stercoranist argument to support his denial of the Real Presence.[54] Garnerius of Rochefort, writing ca. 1208–10, noted that the spiritualist followers of Amalric of Bène raised this objection to the reception of Christ in the sacrament.[55] Jacques de Vitry included a complete discussion of the Eucharist in his *Historia occidentalis*, written between 1219 and 1225. He recorded many opinions and objections which he considered heretical, and his witness is of particular interest since he spent time in the Midi preaching against the Cathars.[56] In his response to the heretics concerning the continued existence of the species, Jacques included the story of an experiment which disproved stercoranism. A doubting priest consumed the Eucharist in great quantities and, after fasting from all food for several days, became extremely weak.[57]

Berengar almost certainly did not teach stercoranism, but Durand and Guitmund said that he did. So, when later writers were faced with other heretics who denied the Church's teaching on the Eucharist, they could have turned to Durand and Guitmund and Alger for help. The temptation to accuse their opponents of the most disgusting beliefs would be great, and stercoranism certainly met that requirement. Later writers could have simply assumed that what had been said of Berengar could be said of any other eucharistic heretic. There always remains the possibility as well that groups like the Cathars, or Amauricians, who denied the value of any material entity, did indeed attempt to prove their point by demonstrating the absurdity of the real presence. But whether actually taught by the heretics or not, it was Berengar who was first accused of stercoranism, and once later heretics were also so indicted, that connection between the two would be readily available.

Guitmund of Aversa also accused the "Berengarians" of the rather sarcastic teaching that if the Body of Christ were actually present on all the thousands of altars upon which the Mass were said from the beginning of time, then the Body of Christ, even if it were the size of a mountain, must be devoured by now.[58] It is possible that Berengar may have made such a remark. In his *Rescriptum*, he did argue, firstly, that it would be impossible for the body of Christ, now impassible and in heaven, to be either augmented or diminished.[59] Later on in the same work, Berengar adamantly denied that the Lord could be rushing back and forth from heaven to all the thousands of earthly altars upon which the liturgy was occurring.[60] The two positions might well have been pulled together in heated debate to produce the kind of snide comment which Guitmund records. Peter the Venerable, writing against Peter of Bruys, recorded the same teaching. Peter, however, specifically attributed it to Berengar. Peter both quoted the words used, and the circumstances under which they were uttered.[61] Interestingly enough, Peter was not quoting from Guitmund here and so appears to have heard the story from an independent source.

The comment, whether Berengar of Tours made it or not, again became closely associated with the Cathars. According to Walter Wakefield, "It was a favored quip (of the Cathar preachers) to say that if the body of Christ was really in the bread in quantity as great as a mountain, priests would long ago have eaten it all up."[62] The teaching was recorded by Durand of Huesca, the converted Waldensian in his *Liber antiheresis*, written ca. 1190–94,[63] as well as by Moneta of Cremona, writing ca. 1241–44.[64] Moneta's reference was later copied by Georgius in the *Disputatio inter catholicum et paterinum haereticum*.[65] The most precise of such references, however, came from Eckbert of Schönau in his *Sermones contra catharos* delivered in 1163.[66] According to Eckbert, "A certain man of our times who was accused of having tasted of our Cathars, when asked on his deathbed whether he wished to be given the body of the Lord, was remembered to have said that even if the body of the Lord existed in such quantity that it were the size of the Hermelstein, from that time when it first began to be eaten it certainly must have been consumed by now."[67] The reference to a particular mountain gives the story the ring of truth, and so it may well be that the Cathars did use this teaching. Peter of Vaux-Cernay, in his *Historia Albigensis* described the heretics as instilling this blasphemy into the ears of the simple in order to prove that the Body of Christ was no different than simple bread.[68] Did the Cathars actually borrow this teaching from Berengar? It seems unlikely, as Berengar's written work had a very limited distribution. Much more likely the Cathars had read Guitmund or Peter the Venerable to good effect. There is yet another possible explanation. Guitmund's "Berengarians" might have, in fact, been Cathars, and Peter's story may have attached the Cathar teaching to a story about Berengar sometime after the death of the master. From the earliest instance, that of Guitmund, the objects of this attack could then be seen as Cathars, misnamed Berengarians by Guitmund. Berengar, in this interpretation, never had anything to do with this teaching. Whatever the explanation, however, the connection between Berengar and later heretical groups would seem clear to anyone familiar with the literature.

Yet another teaching ascribed to Berengar which would enjoy an heretical reputation was the teaching that if the Lord were actually present, then animals could receive the Body of the Lord. Again this is the kind of sarcastic response of which Berengar was capable, and in one passage in the *Rescriptum*, Berengar remarked that if the "little pieces" of the Body and Blood of the Lord were present on the altar, they would be subject not only to desecration by humans, but also by animals, birds, fire, and putrefaction.[69] Wolfhelm, abbot of Brauweiler, wrote to Meginhard, abbot of Gladbach, sometime in the 1070s to warn against Berengar's teaching. Wolfhelm reported Berengar to have argued that if mice eat the Body of Christ, they cannot have Christ in them, nor can they have eternal life, therefore the Body of Christ cannot be in the consecrated bread.[70] If Wolfhelm can be trusted, then Berengar did indeed use this argument to ridicule the teaching of his opponents.

Guitmund also accused Berengar of teaching that the Body and Blood of the Lord descend into the stomachs of mice or other animals.[71] Guitmund went on to respond as well to those who claimed to have seen animals eat the consecrated species, and then later to have found the remains in their bodies. Even Guitmund found this testimony unlikely, however.[72] John of Mantua, writing between 1081–83, warned his patroness, Matilda, Countess of Tuscany, against the heresy of Berengar.[73] Included in his short treatise on the Eucharist John mentioned the problem of animals touching the Body of Christ.[74] It seems reasonable to assume that John was responding to what he felt was an objection raised by the great heretic. Alger of Liège, following Guitmund's lead, also accused the heretics not only of pointing out the different indignities which the Body of Christ might undergo if really present, but again responded to the heretics' claim to have found the species in the stomach of a mouse.[75]

The question of what the church mouse eats if it gets its little paws on the reserved species would remain a bedeviling and fascinating question for medieval theologians.[76] The question was not just an interesting riddle, however. A number of theologians continued to raise the question specifically in the context of the challenge of heresy. Alan of Lille included a sophisticated presentation of the problem of animals savaging the species in his *Contra haereticos*.[77] Durand of Huesca offered what he purported to be a quotation from a Cathar who used this argument to refute orthodox teaching: "This is not to be believed, for a mouse truly eats the host, or a dog or pig, if they find it, or even an adulterer or murderer eats this host."[78] Jacques de Vitry also included as heretical the teaching that animals might desecrate the species.[79] Jacques realized, he explained, that many of these discussions would be pointless and excessive if it were not necessary to respond to the relentlessness of the heretics.[80]

In conclusion then, one can find a whole series of teachings, some originally put forward by Berengar and others attributed to him, which survived to be later associated with heretical groups, especially the Cathars. When A. J. MacDonald wrote that Berengar's teaching had been associated with that of the Petrobrusiani, Albigenses, Cathari, and Waldenses, he was quite correct. When he added that no historical connection between Berengar and these sectaries can be established, he was only partly correct.[81] Berengar was not a forerunner of the Cathars, or indeed of any other heretical group. His students did not appear to carry on his teaching about the Eucharist, nor did any popular movement espouse Berengar as their figurehead. Berengar did leave a legacy as a heresiarch, however.

A twofold process seems to have placed him in the ranks of Arius and Nestorius. First, during his life or shortly thereafter, he was accused of teaching things he didn't teach, or at least his teachings were wildly exaggerated. Secondly, some of his teachings, as well as several of those foisted upon him, were also associated with heretical groups to which Berengar had no historical or theological link. Perhaps groups like the Cathars did use some of Berengar's alleged teachings to frustrate their orthodox foes. The texts were ready to hand in the works of Durand, Guitmund, and Alger. The fact that the sources speak of specific instances and groups who used these teachings suggests that this is quite possible. Or perhaps the opponents of the Cathars merely attributed to them the arguments earlier attributed to Berengar, since all heretics could be seen as having a single horrid life.[82] If the Cathars denied the Eucharist, then they might well be seen as the same as Berengar. However the connections were made, they clearly occurred and continued to be reenforced as scholar borrowed from scholar throughout the twelfth and into the thirteenth century.

Some heretics are born heresiarchs. One thinks perhaps of Manes. Others achieve such notoriety. Arius might be an example. Berengar, however, seems to have his title by default. Historical events long after his death contrived to thrust his infamy upon him.

---

1. Originally published in *Auctoritas und Ratio: Studien zu Berengar von Tours,* eds. Peter Ganz, R.B.C. Huygens, and Friedrich Niewöhner, Wolfenbütteler Mittelalter-Studien 2 (Wiesbaden: Otto Harrassowitz, 1990) 47–67.

2. For a summary of this literature, see Gary Macy, *Theologies of the Eucharist in the Early Scholastic Period* (Oxford: Clarendon Press, 1984) 189, n. 154. See also Jules Corblet, *Histoire Dogmatique, Liturgique et Archéologique du Sacrement de L'Eucharistie,* 2 vols. (Paris: Société générale de librairie catholique,

1885–6) 1:383; 2:352, 357, 392, and 512. Also Thomas Fredrick Simmons, *The Lay Folks Massbook* (London: N. Trubner & Co., 1889) 281.

3. This study does not go on to examine how later historians and theologians actually made use of the associations between Berengar and later heretics, but rather establishes that such affiliations existed. This second and very interesting question would entail another paper at least of equal length, and so must await development at another time.

4. A. J. MacDonald, *Berengar and the Reform of Sacramental Doctrine* (London: Longmans, Green, 1930) 212–15; Jeffrey Burton Russell, *Dissent and Reform in the Early Middle Ages* (Berkeley: University of California Press, 1965) 163, 165; Joseph Jungmann, *The Mass of the Roman Rite*, 2 vols., trans. Francis Brunner (New York: Benziger, 1951) 1:118–19.

5. Gerard Grant, "The Elevation of the Host: A Reaction to Twelfth-Century Heresy," *Theological Studies* 1 (1940) 228–50. Grant argues that the elevation came about as a reaction to the Cathars rather than to Berengar.

6. "Quae quidam non attendentes, posuerunt corpus et sanguinem Christi non esse in hoc sacramento nisi sicut in signo. Quod est tamquam haereticum abiiciendum, utpote verbis Christi contrarium. Unde et Berengarius, qui primus inventor hujus erroris fuerat, postea coactus est suum errorem revocare et veritatem fidei confiteri." Thomas Aquinas, *Summa Theologiae*, pars III, questio 75, art. 1, *Opera omnia* 12:156. On this subject, see Godfroid Geenen, "Bérenger de Tours dans les écrits de Saint Thomas d'Aquin," *Divinitas* 11 (1967) 439–57.

7. See Margaret Gibson, *Lanfranc of Bec* (Oxford: Oxford University Press, 1978) 94–95, and F. Saverio Festa, "Per il dibattito teologico sull'Eucaristia nell'XI secolo (Guitmondo d'Aversa contro Berengario di Tours)," *Asprenas*, n.s. 25 (1978) 36.

8. "Hinc approbare conati sunt beato me derogare Augustino contra illum sentiendo, quem in sui erroris patrocinium Berengarius citare consueuerat dicta eius malo sensu diripiendo." ed. R. Haacke, *Commentaria in evangelium sancti Iohannis*, Corpus Christianorum, continuatio mediaevalis 9 (Turnhout: Brepols, 1969) 2. On this dispute, see John Van Engen, *Rupert of Deutz* (Berkeley: University of California Press, 1983) 135–80.

9. "Ecce dum catholicam fidem nulla prorsus distinctione indigentem solitis sibi argumentationibus distinguit, alterum se probat Berengarium." *Contra quatuor labyrinthos Franciae*, l. 3, c. 2, ed. P. Glorieux, "Le Contra quatuor labyrinthos Franciae de Gauthier de Saint Victor. Édition critique," *Archives d'histoire doctrinale et littéraire du moyen âge* 19 (1952) 261.

10. "Quod si panis sanctificatus non corpus Christi, sed figura corporis Christi est, ut asseris, ut fert tecum multorum opinio, inio errantium multus error: . . ." *PL* 188: 127C.

11. See the article on Gerland in the *Histoire littéraire de la France*, Académie des inscriptions et belles-lettres and others, eds., 42 volumes and indexes (Paris: Impr. Nationale, 1865–1981) 12, fols. 275–79.

12. "Sed quoniam de domini corpore objectiunculas fieri epistolae auctor dicit, quod signum, et non veritas exstet, pauca etsi exilia, super eo contemplemur." *PL* 156: 530C–D. On the likely background to this letter, see John Van Engen, *Rupert of Deutz*, 173.

13. ". . . modernae haereseos inventores impiique dogmatis conflatores, . . ." *PL* 149: 1393A. ". . . praefatum haeresiarcham Berengarium, . . ." *PL* 149: 1422A. On Durand, see Macy, *Theologies*, 45.

14. ". . . hoc garriunt discipuli atque sequaces tui subversores quidem aliorum et ipsi auro et argento caeteraque pecunia tua a te subversi, errantes, et alios in errorem mittentes, *non intelligentes,* sicut dicit Apostolus, *neque quae loquuntur, neque de quibus affirmant* (I Tim 1:7)." *De corpore et sanguine domini, PL* 150: 436A–B. On this work, see Gibson, *Lanfranc,* 70, 81–91.

15. See Gibson, *Lanfranc,* 65–69.

16. On the influence of Berengar's students, see MacDonald, *Berengar,* 120, 153–54, and Jean de Montclos, *Lanfranc et Bérenger: La controverse eucharistique du XIe siècle,* Études et documents 37 (Louvain: Spicilegium sacrum Lovaniense, 1971) 35, 195–96, 201.

17. On Guitmund's life and works, see Macy, *Theologies,* 48, and F. Saverio Festa, "Per il dibattito teologico sull'Eucaristia nell'XI secolo," 123–36.

18. *De corporis et sanguinis Christi veritate in eucharistia, PL* 149: 1430C-D.

19. See Macy, *Theologies,* 55.

20. "Idque etiam exemplo conantur astruere, quia videlicet in vitis Patrum cuidam seni visus sit angelus ad communionem sacram indignis accedentibus corpus Domini subtrahere, et loco ejus carbonem dare. Si igitur, inquiunt, tales carnem et sanguinem Domini non sumunt, necesse est, id quod accipiunt, aut non fuisse mutatum, aut in naturam priorem esse reversum." *De corpore et sanguine Christi, PL* 149: 1491C.

21. "Soli filii Dei accipiunt corpus Christi, qui Christo sunt incorporandi et Deum visuri; hi autem qui in Christo non manent, quamvis videantur ad os porrigere, corpus Christi non sumunt, sed judicium manducant et bibunt. Corpus autem Christi per manus angelorum in caelum defertur; carbo vero a daemone eis in os projicitur, ut Cyprianus testatur." l. 1, c. 195, Yves Lefèvre, ed., *L'Élucidarium et les lucidaires. Contribution, par l'histoire d'un text, à l'histoire des croyances religieuses en France au moyen âge,* Bibliothèque des École françaises d'Athènes et Rome 180 (Paris: E. de Boccard, 1954) 399. On Honorius' career in England, see Lefèvre, 214–30, as well as V.I.J. Flint, "The Career of Honorius Augustodunensis: Some Fresh Evidence," *Revue Bénédictine* 82 (1972) 638–86, and idem, "The Place and Purpose of the Works of Honorius Augustodunensis," *Revue Bénédictine* 87 (1977) 97–127.

22. "Et quia alius et ipse maculatus, sacrificio a sacerdote celebrato, partem cum ceteris ausus est latenter accipere, sanctum Domini edere et contrectare non potuit: cinerem ferre se apertis manibus invenit." *De lapsis,* c. 26, Maurice

Bévenot, *De lapsis and De Ecclesiae Catholicae Unitate* (Oxford: Clarendon Press, 1971) 40.

23. See Macy, *Theologies,* 55–57.

24. *Epistola ad quemdam monachum, PL* 180: 342A. On this letter, see John Van Engen, "Rupert of Deutz and William of St. Thierry," *Revue Bénédictine* 93 (1983) 327–36.

25. Abelard, *Theologia christiana* l. 4, *PL* 178: 1286B. Zachary of Besançon, *In unum ex quatuor,* c. 4, *PL* 176: 508B. I have used the translation by Gibson, *Lanfranc,* 93.

26. Gregory of Bergamo, *Tractatus de veritate corporis Christi,* H. Hurter, ed., *Scriptorum veterum de eucharistia opuscula selecta,* Sanctorum patrum opuscula selecta 39 (Leipzig: Libraria Academica Wagneriana, 1879) 1–123; Peter the Venerable, *Contra petrobrusianos hereticos,* J. Fearns, ed., Corpus christianorum, continuatio medievalis 10 (Turnhout: Brepols, 1967).

27. On the teaching of the Cathars on the Eucharist, see Macy, *Theologies,* 57–58, especially the references given in n. 116. See also Jean Duvernoy, *Le Catharisme: La Religion des Cathares,* (Toulouse: Privat, 1976) 28, 39, 149, 214–15, 325, 352–54, and 385.

28. See Macy, *Theologies,* 73–105.

29. On the dispute at Liège, see John Van Engen, *Rupert of Deutz,* 135–80. William condemned the teaching, attributed to Abelard, that the accidents of the bread and wine subsist in the substance of the air after the substantial change has taken place. This teaching does not appear in any of Abelard's works, although it does in those of his students. On this criticism see William, *Dialogus,* c. 9, *PL* 180: 280C. See also Macy, *Theologies,* 114–18.

30. "Constat enim apud eruditionem tuam non minus tropica locutione dici: panis, qui ponitur in altari, post consecrationem est corpus Christi et uinum sanguis, quam dicitur: Christus est leo, Christus est agnus, Christus est summus angularis lapis, totique illi tropice locutionis generi unum patere (non amplius) exitum, ut ubicumque predicatur non predicabile, quia tropica locutio est de non susceptibili, alter propositionis terminus tropice, alter proprie accipiatur. Verbi gratia: *petra Christus erat* inquit apostolus constatque subiectum terminum, qui est 'petra,' ilia quae in deserto manavit aquas, susceptibilem eius predicati quod est 'Christus,' . . ." *Rescriptum* 1:1360–71, R.B.C. Huygens, ed., *Rescriptum contra Lanfrannum, (RCL)* Corpus christianorum, continuatio mediaevalis 84 (Turnhout: Brepols, 1988) 73–74.

31. "Fatentur enim moris esse Apostolo, ut sacramentum quodlibet ejus rei, cujus est sacramentum, notet vocabulo, quia solet in apostolicis sacrisque literis res, quae significat eius rei nomen sortiri, quam significat. . . . Et paulo post: *Petra erat Christus.* Non dixit petra significabat Christum, sed tamquam vere hoc esset, quod utique non erat proprietate sed significatione. Ostendimus, inquiunt, rem significantem significatae rei nomine nuncupari; more

igitur suo Apostolus utens res significantes idem panem et vinum, corpus et sanguinem maluit appellare, quae sunt res non substantialiter verae, sed sacramentaliter significatae." *Tractatus,* Hurter, 93–94.

32. "Manichaeus. Illa verba accipiuntur significative, unde *Hoc est corpus meum,* id est significat corpus meum, sicut illud *Petra autem erat Christus,* id est figurat Christum." *Disputatio inter catholicum et paterinum haereticum,* Edmond Marténe and Ursin Durand, eds., *Thesaurus nouus anecdotorum* 5 (Paris: F. Delaulne, 1717) 1731C. On the dating of this work see Antoine Dondaine, "Le Manuel de l'Inquisiteur (1230–1330)," *Archivum fratrum praedicatorum* 17 (1947) 174–80.

33. "Si enim, sicut erras, non sunt in altari nisi portiuncula sensualiter carnis Christi et sanguinis, quae, id est carnem Christi et sanguinem, tropica locutione panem et uinum constet appellari, illa omnino omni non sunt obnoxia corruptioni. Porro quae de altari tam probus quam reprobus accipit manibus franguntur, dentibus atteruntur, ut alia taceam, quae corruptionis esse dissimulare usquequaque non poteris." *Rescriptum* 1:2217–23; Huygens, *RCL,* 97. See also ". . . ita oportuit a domino institui, ut quod de bibendo precipit sanguine suo non ad proprietatem quantum ad os et uentrem accipias, sed ad similitudinem, ut sacramentum, quod est similitudo, in quo quid iure horreas non sit, ore accipias, ventre excipias, sed tamen verae naturae corporis uirtutem—unde ipse dominus: *qui manducat me, etiam ipse uiuit propter me* quantum ad refectionem cordis, . . ." *Rescriptum* 2:3063–70; Huygens, *RCL,* 184–85, and "Pronominis enim vis ad hoc valet, quia, si per subiecti absumeretur corruptionem, ut non per subiectum superesset altaris oblatio sed adesset recens facta per generationem subiecti porciuncula carnis, porciuncula sanguinis, non solum hominibus, sed etiam pecudibus, auibus, putredini atque ignibus corpus fieret Christi et sanguis oblatio altaris. Nec solum hoc, sed et uerbum ipsum 'fiat' a precedentibus verbis perpendendum est sacerdotalis deprecationis." *Rescriptum* 3:518–25; Huygens, *RCL,* 204.

34. "Si enim prudenter advertisses, quod dominus, qui te ecclesie sue prefecit, non per sophystas seu aristotelicos, sed per simplices et idiotas ecclesiam suam per omnes gentes fundaverit et diffuderit, non tot et tantos motus et gemitus viscerum Christi super te concitasses, ne cum Berengero tu (ah pudet) stercorianista dici et agnominari, sicut Francigenarum scripta que ad nos pervenerunt edocent, meruisses." K. Francke, ed., "Zur Charakteristik des Cardinals Humbert von Silva Candida," *Neues Archiv der Gesellschaft für ältere deutsche Geschichtskunde* 7 (1882) 614. See Montclos, *Lanfranc et Bérengar,* 108.

35. For Montclos' argument concerning the accusation against Berengar, see *Lanfranc et Bérengar,* 104–05, 140–41, 144.

36. "Sed, o perfide Stercorianista, qui putas fideli participatione corporis et sanguinis Domini quadragesimalia atque ecclesiastica dissolvi jejunia, omnino credens coelestem escam velut terrenam per aqualiculi fetidam et

sordidam egestionem in secessum dimitti, plane sentis cum Ario." *Responsio contra Nicetas,* Cornelius Will, ed., *Acta et Scripta quae de controversiis ecclesiae Graecae et Latinae saeculo undecimo composita extant,* . . . (Paris: Lipsae & Marpurgi, 1861) 144. On the dating of this work, see Anton Michel, *Humbert und Kerullarios* (Paderborn: F. Schöningh, 1924) 1:84–85.

37. "Friuolum est ergo, sicuti in eodem apocripho libro legitur, in hoc mysterio cogitare de stercore, ne commisceatur in digestione alterius cybi." Paschasius, *De corpore et sanguine domini,* c. 20, B. Paulus, ed., Corpus christianorum, continuatio mediaevalis 16 (Turnhout: Brepols, 1969) 107. See also "Neque obseruandum, sicut apocriphorum monumenta decernunt, donec ea degerantur in corpore, ne communis cybus accipiatur." Ibid., Paulus, 106.

38. "Qui autem residua corporis domini quae in sacrario relicta sunt consumunt, non statim ad communes accipiendos cibos conveniant, ne putent sanctae portioni commisceri cibum qui per qualiculos degestus in secessum funditur." *Epistola Clementis secunda,* P. Hinschius, ed., *Decretales Pseudo-Isidorianae* (Leipzig: B Tauchnitz, 1863) 47. Paschasius wrote some twenty years before the earliest dating of the Pseudo-Isidorian collection. The first two letters of Clement, however, circulated separately before they were included in the Pseudo-Isidorian collection, and it may be to an earlier version of these letters that Paschasius refers. See Horst Fuhrmann, *Einfluß und Verbreitung der pseudoisidorischen Fälschungen,* 2 vols., Schriften der Monumenta Germaniae historica 24 (Stuttgart: Hiersemann, 1972) 1:182–83.

39. ". . . ne ipsis quidem, quibus hoc placet, unde et Stercoritae jure nuncupantur, . . ." *PL* 149: 1382A and "Hic stercorianistae audiant quid tantus doctor dicat: . . ." *PL* 149: 1402C.

40. ". . . obnoxia contendunt ventri et secessui iuxta naturae necessitatem, quae scilicet naturae dominus in federe humanae reconciliationis omnipotentia sua sacramentum fecit et christianae animae escam spiritualem, unde in aeternum vivat, dedit." *Epistola ad Walcherum,* c. 30, R.B.C. Huygens, ed., Corpus christianorum, continuatio mediaevalis 62 (Turnhout: Brepols, 1985) 33. On the dating of this work, see Huygens, ibid., 6.

41. "Corpus Domini inconveniens est in secessum mitti; *Omne autem quod intrat in os,* ut Salvator ait, *in ventrem vadit et in secessum emittitur* (Matt 15:17). Denique de sacramentis istis si multi panes, ut inquiunt, et multa vina sacrentur, potest quis longo tempore vivere, nihil aliud comedens aut bibens; unde igitur habebit secessum illo tempore, nisi ista in secessum vadant? Haec sunt interim quae mihi de rationibus Berengarii occurrunt quibus postquam responderis, auctoritates apponam." *PL* 149: 1450D.

42. *PL* 149, 1452B–53B-C. E.g., "Sed hoc, inquit Berengarius, jam manifeste probatum est (ita enim nonnulli pro eo nobis responderunt) neque ex reliquis praeteritorum ciborum, quippe propter diuturnitatem longi temporis jam consumptis, neque ex defectu propriae carnis, quippe consueta corporis pinguedine permanente, Eucharistia pastos habuisse secessum." *PL* 149: 1452B-C.

43. "Nec solum de veritate corporis Christi, sed et de sacramento ipsius, varii errores, variaeque proveniunt haereses. . . . Alii, quod est deterius, dicunt per comestionem in foedae digestionis converti corruptionem." *De sacramentis corporis et sanguinis dominici, PL* 180: 739D–740C. On Alger, see Macy, *Theologies*, 49–50.

44. On this issue, see John Van Engen, *Rupert of Deutz*, 168–73.

45. Alger referred to the Pseudo-Isidorian Decretals in the same fashion as Durand, although he might also be copying directly from Paschasius. Cf. note 36 above and "Sed nec observandum est quod in quibusdam apocryphorum monumentis decernitur, ne scilicet communis cibus accipiatur, donec sumpta sacramenta per se digerantur, ne vel commistione alterius cibi corrumpantur." Ibid., *PL* 180: 810B-C.

46. Ibid., *PL* 180: 796–97.

47. "Non sunt igitur observanda Graecorum haereticorum, qui merito Stercoranistae vocantur, deliramenta, qui dicunt participatione corporis et sanguinis Christi, solvi ecclesiastica jejunia usque ad crapulam et ebrietatem ventrisque distentionem, putantes coelestem escam velut terrenam indifferenter accipi, et in sordidum ventris secessum emitti." Ibid., *PL* 180: 810B.

48. "Sed iterum cum internum aspectum ad eum dirigimus, qui dixit: *Aperi os tuum, et ego adimplebo illud* (Ps 80:11), fidei integritate manente, provocamur respondere, de quo dignum non tacere, de mysterio videlicet corporis et sanguinis Domini; dicentibus quibusdam idem esse quod sumitur de altari, quod et illud quod est ex virgine natum; aliis autem negantibus, et dicentibus aliud esse; quibusdam etiam diabolica inspiratione blasphemantibus, secessui obnoxium fore. Super quibus periculosum esset aliquid respondere, sed magis aures obturare, nisi periculosius foret, eos talia proposuisse; quia hoc est pro lacte ab uberibus butyrum aut sanguinem elicere." Heriger of Lobbes, *De corpore et sanguine Domini, PL* 139: 179A-B and "Sed illorum jam ineptiis respondendum, qui humano aut saeculi sensu in Dei rebus putant loquendum. Dominus etenim noster non de spirituali cibo, sed de carnali locutus est, cum diceret: *Omne quod intrat in os, in ventrem vadit, et in secessum emittitur* (Matt 15:17). . . . Calumniati sunt haeretici ex hoc sermone, Dominum physicae ignarum fuisse; physica enim sic se habet: . . ." Ibid., *PL* 139, 187C-D. On the background to this tract, see Macy, *Theologies*, 31–33.

49. "Diximus superius non minus ore corporis quam ore cordis corpus Domini esse sumendum: sed ex hac ipsa visibili et corporali comestione, quae sacramentotenus fit, nascitur haeresis foedissima stercoranistarum. Dicunt enim tantum sacramentum sicut corporali combustion, sic et secessui esse obnoxium. Violent autem hoc astruere cum multis argumentis, tum ipsius Christi testimonio, ita in Evangelio dicentis: *Omne quod intrat in os, in ventrem vadit, et in secessum emittitur* (Matt 15:17), cum constet hoc eum dixisse non de spirituali cibo, sed de communi et carnali. His igitur obscenis haereticis periculosum esset super hoc aliquid respondere, magisque dignum aures nostras

obturare, nisi periculosius esset eos in scandalum Ecclesiae talia proponere, et tantam eorum falsitatem nos nullis fidei catholicae rationibus reverberare." *PL* 180, 807B-C. Cf. n. 47.

50. "Sed opponunt haeretici: Si multi panes et multa vina sacrentur, diu hominem inde posse vivere, ut non de praeterito, sed de hoc praesenti et diuturno victu illum astruant interim secessum habere. Dicunt etiam aliquos per multa tempora hoc expertos, eo desiderio, ut etiam in hac vita cibo alerentur angelico, quos ne defectu propriae carnis, ut in infirmitatibus solet, secessum habuisse videantur, ita eos carne vegetatos his cibis et saginatos, sicut et communibus astruunt, ut cum negatur defectus carnis, probetur secessus sacrae fuisse communionis." *PL* 180: 811A-B. Alger would be copied by an anonymous *Summa* associated with the School of Anselm of Laon, and found in Fulda, Landesbibliothek, Codex Aa 36 4⁰, quoted by Artur Michael Landgraf, "Die in der Frühscholastik klassische Frage *Quid sumit mus*," *Dogmengeschichte der Frühscholastik* 3 (2) (Regensburg: Friedrick Pustet, 1955) 215–19.

51. "Quod autem Christus ait: *Omne, quod in os intrat*, etc., intelligendum est de cibo materiali, non spirituali; sicut enim materialis cibus vadit in secessum ita spiritualis in mentis excessum." *PL* 210: 363.

52. "Sed iterum obiiciunt, probare nitentes, quod panis ille corpus domini non sit. Dicunt enim quicquid intrat per os, in ventrem vadit, et in secessum emittitur. Item sic argumentantur. Ponatur aliquis saccades ieiunet per octo dies nihil comedens, aut bibens, quousque stomachus euacuetur ab omni cibo, postea accipiat tortam panis integram et ollam vini plenam, celebret inde et sanctificet. Sic enim potest sanctificare illud totum, ac si esset minimum; videbitur quod per secessum pars exiet." Jacob Gretser, ed., *Trias scriptorum aduersus Waldensium sectam,* (Ingoldstadt, 1614), rpt. M. La Bigne, *Maxima bibliotheca veterum patrum, . .* 24 (Lyons: Anissonios, 1677) 1548C-D.

53. "Manichaeus. Dicit Dominus (Matt 15:17) *Omne quod intrat in os, in ventrem vadit, et in secessum emittitur.* Ergo si corpus Christi comeditur, ut vos Christiani dicitis, in secessum emittitur, quod est inconveniens." *Disputatio,* Marténe and Durand, *Thesaurus,* 1731E-1732A.

54. Ilarino Da Milano, *L'eresia di Ugo Speroni nella confutazione del maestro Vacario. Testo inedito del secolo XII con studio storico e dottrinale, Studi e testi* 115 (Vatican City: Biblioteca Apostolica Vaticana, 1945) 523.

55. "Sed adhuc forte dicis: si corpus Christi ubique non est, sed locale, ubi est corpus Christi, uel quid factum est de corpore Christi, postquam sumpsi illud et manducaui?" *Contra amaurianos,* Clemens Baeumker, ed., *Contra amaurianos. Ein anonymer, wahrscheinlich dem Garnerius von Rochefort zugehöriger Traktat gegen die Amalrikaner aus dem Anfang des XIII. Jahrhunderts.* Beiträge zur Geschichte der Philosophie des Mittelalters 224 (Münster, 1926) 45. Garnerius wrote ca. 1208–10, cf. Baeumker, ibid., xxv.

56. John F. Hinnebusch, *The Historia Occidentalis of Jacques de Vitry. A Critical Edition,* Spicilegium Friburgense. Texts Concerning the History of Christian Life 17 (Fribourg: The University Press, 1972) 5, 17, 30, 290.

57. "Respondemus igitur hereticis, quod postquam facta est transsubstantiatio, forme panis et uini remanet contra consuetum nature cursum sine subjecto. . . . Inuenitur tamen scriptum, quod cum quidam sacerdos de ueritate huius sacramenti dubitaret, formam panis et uini post consecrationem in magna sumpsit quantitate. Et cum aliquot diebus alium cibum non sumeret, ex debilitate et exinanitione fere defecit." *Historia Occidentalis,* 230–31.

58. "Rogerius: Si panis et vinum in Christi carnem et sanguinem verterentur, jam toties, inquiunt, talia devorata sunt, ut si Christi corpus tam magnum ut ingentissimus mons fuisset, jam totum devoratum consumptumque fuisset." *PL* 149: 1450B-C.

59. "Simul cum carnem inducas fieri in altari per generationem subiecti eamque carnem sacramentum esse carnis, quae sedet ad dexteram patris, uecordissimi erat carnem, quae nunc primum esse incipiat per generationem subiecti, dicere Christi carnem, quae ante tot annos, quotacumque est, nichil ultra incremento, nichil augmento sicut nichil morti, [nichil] prorsus debet corruptioni." *Rescriptum* 2:188–94, Huygens, *RCL,* 105–06.

60. "Omitto, quod ipso sit refutandum auditu rationi humane, quod indignissimum deo esse facillimum sit cuipiam pervidere, pervincere: quicumque sibi confingit totum Christi corpus sensualiter adesse, quando celebratur mensa dominica, in altari, indissimulabiliter tali figmento suo milies milies Christi corpus caelo quotidie deicit, quia negari non potest milies milies quotidie mensam dominicam ab aecclesia celebrari; nihilominus milies milies in velum revolt quotidie corpus Christi, ludibrio tali milies milies quotidie, quamdiu volvuntur tempora, obnoxium facit corpus Christi, quod constat innegabiliter, quamdiu volvuntur tempora, sessurum esse ad dexteram patris." *Rescriptum* 2:1788–98, Huygens, *RCL,* 150.

61. "Hoc enim est quod quondam Berengarium dixisse audivi. Nam forte Andegauis constitutus et de hoc corporis Christi sacramento cum quibusdam agens, si, inquit, *corpus Christi tante fuisset magnitudinis, quante turris hec que in conspectu nostro immensa mole attolitur, a tot totius orbis populis comestum, ante multa iam annorum spacia defecisset."* *Contra Petrobrusianos,* Fearns, 101–02.

62. *Heresy, Crusade and Inquisition in Southern France 1100–1250* (Berkeley: University of California Press, 1974) 33.

63. "Set forte dicent heretici: Si ipsa est ostia corpus Christi, quomodo fore potest, ut sint tot corpora Christi? Quia in multis locis missa celebratur, et plurime ostie sunt ita consecrate. Si esset quasi mons magnus, totum comederetur." Kurt Victor Selge, ed., *Die ersten Waldenser. Der Liber antiheresis des Durandus von Osca,* 2 vols., Arbeiten zur Kirchengeschichte 37 (Berlin: De Gruyter, 1967) 2:52. On the dating of this work, see Christine Thouzellier,

Catharisme et valdéisme en Languedoc à la fin du XIIe et au début du XIIIe siècle (Louvain: Éditions Nauwelaerts, 1969) 60.

64. "Obijcit etiam haereticus dicens: Si corpus Christi esset tantae quantitatis, quantae est mons unus, jam dudum consumptum esset, ex quo coepit in omnibus mundi partibus manducari." *Adversus catharos et valdenses,* Tommas Augostino Ricchini, ed., *Venerabilis patris Monetae cremonensis ordinis praedicatorum . . . aduersus Catharos et Valdenses libri quinque . . . atque illustravit* (Rome: Palladis et Marcus Palearini, 1743; rpt. Ridgewood, N.J.: Gregg Press, 1964) 300. On the dating of this work see A. Borst, *Die Katharer,* Schriften der Monumenta Germaniae historica 12 (Stuttgart: Hiersemann, 1953) 17–19.

65. "Manichaeus: Si corpus Christi esset tantae quantitatis, quantae est mons unus, jamdudum consumtum esset, ex quo coepit ob omnibus mundi partibus manducari." *Disputatio,* Marténe and Durand, *Thesaurus,* 1729B.

66. Borst, *Die Katharer,* 6–7.

67. "Vir quidam nostri temporis qui infamatus erat, quod de Cathara vestra gustasset, cum interrogaretur in extremis suis, an vellet dari sibi corpus Domini, dixisse memoratur: Si esset illud corpus Domini tantae quantitatis, ut est Petra Eremberti, jamdudum esset consumptum, ex quo primum coepit manducari. Verbum irrisionis erat hoc, et ex infidelitate processit, in qua, ut dicunt, et vos estis absorpti: unde et vos eodem verbo convenio." c. 14, *PL* 195: 92C.

68. "Sacramenta ecclesie usque adeo adnullabant ut sacri baptismatis undam ab aqua fluviali non distare, sacrosancti corporis Christi hostiam a pane laico non differre, publice dogmatizarent; simplicium auribus hanc instillantes blasphemiam quod Christi corpus, etsi magnitudinem Alpium in se contineret, jamdudum consumptum a comedentibus et annichilatum fuisset," *Petri Vallium Sarnaii monachi Hystoria Albigensis,* Pascal Guébin and Ernest Lyon, eds., 3 vols. (Paris: Campion, 1926–39) 1:11–13. Borst, *Die Katharer* 11 dates this work 1213–18.

69. Cf. n. 32 above.

70. "Ecce Novi et Veteris Testamenti nos haec auctoritate probamus: quibus Berengarius tertium addit, quod non minus quam tertium de coelo cecidisse Catonem reprobamus. Eia ergo, post duo Testamenta, tertium hoc; et ideo tertium, quia ab eis alienatur, verbis ipsius auctoris, ita loquitur: Si mures consecratum corpus Christi comederint; non ideo Christus in eis, et ipsi in Christo manebunt, nec vitam aeternam habuit." *PL* 154, 413C-D. On Wolfhelm's letter, see MacDonald, *Berengar,* 174–75, 334–35.

71. "Rogerius: A muribus quoque, vel huiuscemodi quibuslibet animalibus corrodi, vel consumi haec sacramenta posse objiciunt." *PL* 149: 1448C.

72. "Porro vero si quis se vidisse dicat (nam isti contra quos agimus non curant quid proferant, dum tamen aliquid ne recte credant semper objiciant) haec a brutis animalibus devorari, et intra eorumdem corpora inveniri, licet tale testimonium non facile recipiendum, dignumve responsione videatur,

tamen ne quid neglexisse vel evitasse putemur, responderi potest, quoniam si placet Christo, vel propter eas quas modo diximus, vel propter alias quaslibet, quas ipse noverit causas, ut haec sacramenta absque sui corruptione a bestiis sive avibus comedi possint: quid hoc ad veritatem, quam credimus, Dominici corporis obstat?" *PL* 149: 1449A-B.

73. *Iohannis Mantuani in cantica canticorum et de Sancta Maria tractatus ad comitissam Matildam*, Bernhard Bischoff and Burkhard Taeger, eds., Spicilegium Friburgense 19 (Fribourg: Universitätsverlag, 1973) 49. The editors date this work ca. 1081–83, ibid., 2.

74. "Neque horrible debet esse, si a quibusdam irrationalibus creaturis tangatur, cum nichil coram Deo sit immundum excepto peccato et multa etiam inanimata ut vestes et terra eum tetigerunt; immundior enim coram Deo est peccator omni creatura." Ibid., 48.

75. "Sed iterum opponunt haeretici ad tanti sacramenti indignitatem, quod panis et vinum in sacramento mucidum vel putridum fiat, panis a muribus corradatur et in ventre eorum inveniatur, ignibus etiam comburatur." *PL* 180:811D. Alger would be copied by an anonymous *Summa* associated with the School of Laon and now contained in Fulda, Landesbibliothek, Codex Aa 36 4^0 and quoted by Landgraf, "Die in der Frühscholastik Frage," 213.

76. For information on this question, see Landgraf, ibid., 207–22, but also Gary Macy, "Of Mice and Manna: *Quid mus sumit* as a Pastoral Question," *Recherches théologie ancienne et médiévale* 58 (1991) 157–66.

77. L. 1, c. 57, *PL* 210: 359D–360A.

78. "Set hereticus forte dicet aliquis: Non est credendum; nam ostiam illam bene comedit mus aut canis vel porcus, si inveniunt, aut adulter vel homicida bene comedit ostiam illam." *Liber antiheresis*, Selge, *Die ersten Waldenser* 2:52.

79. "Illud etiam potest comburi, putrescere et a muribus corrodi, et postquam comestum fuerit per uomitum potest emitti, et similia que impii homines solent opponere contra fideles, non attendentes uirtutem dei et quod natura cedit miraculis." *Historia occidentalis*, c. 38, Hinnebusch, 229–30.

80. "Hec et consimilia superuacuum et curiosum reputaremus discutere, nisi importunitati hereticorum oporteret nos respondere." Ibid., Hinnebusch, 240. Cf. also Hinnebusch, 226, from the same *capitula:* "Predicta et multa alia obiciunt contra nos heretici qui, dum maiestatem perscrutantur, opprimuntur a gloria, dum quod residuum est in tam profundo sacramento, igni, id est spiritui sancto, reseruare contradicunt."

81. MacDonald, *Berengar*, 221.

82. Alan of Lille, in the introduction to his *Contra Hereticos*, described heresy as having many forms, but a single source: ". . . nostris vero temporibus, novi haeretici, imo veteres et inveteres, veterantes dogmata, ex diversis haeresibus, unam generalem haeresim compingunt, et quasi ex diversis idolis unum idolum, ex diversis monstris unum monstrum; et quasi ex diversis venenatis herbis unum toxicum commune conficiunt." *PL* 210: 307B–308A.

Chapter 5

The "Dogma of Transubstantiation" in the Middle Ages[1]

THE PROBLEM

Under the heading "transubstantiation" in the *Oxford Dictionary of the Christian Church,* one finds that "the word was in wide-spread use in the later part of the 12th cent., and at the Lateran Council of 1215, belief in Transubstantiation was defined as *de fide;* but the elaboration of the doctrine was not achieved till after the acceptance of the Aristotelian metaphysics later in the 13th cent., when it found classic formulation in the teaching of St. Thomas Aquinas."[2] Jaroslav Pelikan, in his magisterial history of Christian thought, concurs, "At the Fourth Lateran Council in 1215, the doctrine of the real presence of the body and blood of Christ in the Eucharist achieved its definitive formulation in the dogma of transubstantiation."[3]

It has become almost a commonplace in the history of Christianity to understand a single phrase in the opening creed of the Fourth Lateran Council, "transsubstantiatis pane in corpus et uino in sanguinem potestate diuina," as a formal definition of the dogma of transubstantiation.[4] Such an interpretation dates back at least to 1656, when John Cosin, later bishop of Durham, thundered out against this novelty.

"That same pope (Innocent III), after having declared to be heretics those who from then on would deny 'the body of Christ and the blood to be truly contained in the sacrament of the altar, under the species of bread and wine, the bread having been transubstantiated into the body and the wine into the blood'; handed over all of them, of whatever rank or office they might be, to be punished by the secular powers, once their crime had been brought to their attention; that is, he handed them over to be burned."[5]

81

Historical events would seem to support the contention of Bishop Cosin. After all, not only were John Wyclif and Martin Luther condemned for their teaching on the Eucharist, but there were also the earlier and less well known cases of the censuring of the eucharistic theology of Peter Olivi and John Quidort of Paris.

Yet, within a decade of the publication of Cosin's work in 1675 another scholar, the Calvinist pastor Pierre Allix, suggested in his own *Historia transubstantiationis* that many theologians writing after the decree of Lateran IV not only taught doctrines other than transubstantiation as orthodox but also denied that transubstantiation was required by faith: "Yet I am not able to leave out that however this Innocentian definition prescribed the substantial change of the bread and wine into the body and blood of Christ to be *de fide;* it was by no means able to take hold completely."[6] Allix offered an impressive collection of witnesses ranging from the twelfth century up to and even after the time of Trent, who clearly did not teach that the substances of the bread and wine were transformed into the substances of the Body and Blood of Christ and who still considered themselves orthodox, and who were so considered. For Allix this proved not only the novelty of transubstantiation, but also the inconsistency and hypocrisy of Rome.

Writing long after Allix and quite independently of him, two important modern studies on the use of the word transubstantiation have argued that at least theologians of the thirteenth century did not understand the creed of the Lateran Council as limiting discussion of the various possible explanations of the change believed to take place in the Eucharist. The first of these, Hans Jorissen's *Die Entfaltung der Transsubstantiationslehre bis zum Beginn der Hochscholastik,*[7] offers an exhaustive study firstly of the discussion by theologians of the orthodoxy of transubstantiation and secondly of the use of the term transubstantiation during the late twelfth and early thirteenth centuries. Jorissen clearly demonstrates in the second of these studies that there was no common understanding of the category of substance, much less agreement on either the use of the term transubstantiation or on what the word might have meant when used. In fact, theologians at the time of the Fourth Lateran Council fell roughly into three camps in regard to the eucharistic change. Some believed that bread and wine remained present along with the Body and Blood of the Lord; others felt that the substance of the bread and wine were annihilated, the substance of the Body and Blood alone remaining. Finally a third group argued that the substance of bread and wine was changed into the substance of the Body and Blood at the words of consecration. Modern terminology would categorize the first theory as "consubstantiation," the second as "annihilation" or "succession" theory, and the third as "transubstantiation."[8]

These terms can be misleading, however, as "transubstantiation," especially after the Council of Trent, came to be associated with the particular explanation given of the eucharistic change by Thomas Aquinas. More importantly, as I hope will become clear, transubstantiation had a far different meaning for medieval writers than it has for post-Reformation writers. "Consubstantiation" can be misleading as well, since this expression has often been used to describe Luther's theology of presence. In order to avoid as far as possible the imposition of post-Reformation concerns onto medieval discussions, I have adopted the following terminology for the purposes of this paper. The first of these options, that is, consubstantiation, I will refer to as "coexistence." I will retain the term "substitution" for the second option and will refer to the third as "transmutation" rather than transubstantiation.

Peter of Capua, the Parisian master writing ca. 1201–02, could accept as orthodox all three of these explanations of the change in the sacrament, even though he himself preferred transmutation as an explanation:

"Concerning the conversion there is a threefold opinion. Some say that there is no change here, but the substance of bread and the substance of wine remaining, at the recitation of the words the flesh and blood of Christ begin to be under the same species, though at first there was nothing here except the substance of bread and wine. Thus wherever something about a change is read, it ought to be understood thus: that where first was only bread and wine, the flesh and blood of Christ also begin to be.

Others say that the substance of bread and wine are completely annihilated and the same species remaining, the flesh and blood of Christ alone begin to be here and in a similar way they explain that change.

We say, and the commentators assert, that the substance of bread itself is converted into the true flesh of Christ which was born of the Virgin, and the substance of wine itself into the true blood, and with the prior species remaining, the flesh and blood of Christ begin to be here. Nor is it an article of faith to believe that conversion takes place this way or that but only to believe that the body of Christ is on the altar at the recitation of those words."[9]

The passage by Peter is interesting, not only because he clearly stated that all three theories are orthodox, but also because his schema of three possible theories of change in the sacrament continued to be copied well into the thirteenth century. This passage also helps in answering the first of Jorissen's questions, that is, whether theologians considered transubstantiation to be a doctrine required by faith. Certainly Peter of Capua did not. According to Jorissen, theologians writing long after Lateran IV continued to discuss the different modes of change listed by Peter as if the council had not definitively spoken.

To give but one example, William of Auvergne, writing perhaps as late as 1240, reviewed the different positions and stated:

"It suffices for the piety of faith, which we intend to establish here, to believe and hold that after the priestly blessing has been correctly performed, the bread of life is placed on the altar before us under the form of material and visible bread, and the drink of life is placed before us under the form of visible wine."[10]

By the end of the thirteenth century, coexistence would find few advocates, although some theologians still saw merit in this explanation, the most famous of these being John of Paris, even if they themselves rejected it. The second theory, that of substitution, found many advocates including Peter the Chanter, Gerard of Douai, William of Auvergne, Roland of Cremona, the *glossa ordinaria* on the *Decretum*, and Duns Scotus to name only the most important.[11] The third alternative found the most widespread support, Albert the Great and Thomas Aquinas being the strongest advocates. Thomas and Albert were also the first to insist that coexistence was not only wrong, but actually heretical.[12] The basis for this condemnation was not, however, the ruling of Lateran IV, but rather the words of institution, "Hoc est corpus meum," which they believed could not be construed to refer to any other substance than that of the Body and Blood of Christ.[13]

An equally important point made by Jorissen concerns the term transubstantiation itself. In the thirteenth, fourteenth, and fifteenth centuries the term referred not only to the third of Peter of Capua's alternatives but also to the second. Important theologians, most notably Duns Scotus, William of Ockham, and Gabriel Biel, espoused the substitution theory and considered it to be one type of transubstantiation and used this term for it.[14] By the time of Trent, the merits of these two ways of understanding transubstantiation would still be bitterly disputed by Dominican and Franciscan theologians, and so, according to Jorissen, Trent wisely decided to leave the question open.[15] As already mentioned, modern terminology for these issues can be very misleading, since "transubstantiation" for modern writers refers almost exclusively to transmutation, the third of Peter of Capua's alternatives, while for many, but not all, medieval writers, it refers to any theory that could explain how the substance of the Body and Blood came to be present, which would include the second and third of Peter's alternatives. A few theologians, the most important of whom was John of Paris, would argue that even coexistence could be a form of transubstantiation in its broader sense. Again in order to avoid this confusion, "transubstantiation" will be given in quotation marks when it is being used in the medieval sense, while transubstantiation without quotation marks will be used for its usual modern sense which equates the transmutation theory of Thomas Aquinas with transubstantiation.

Pierre Allix's examples of writers who rejected transubstantiation after Lateran IV and even after Trent were, not surprisingly, all advocates of the substitution theory. Since many medieval authors copied Peter of Capua's discussion of three alternative explanations for the change, Allix was also able to offer several examples of theologians who at least entertained the possibility of coexistence as a valid explanation long after Lateran IV.[16] Jorissen gives an even later example of how different understandings of "transubstantiation" could affect the interpretation of Roman teaching. The Council of Pistoia, held in 1786, was condemned by Pius VI in 1794 for teaching that "transubstantiation" was merely an academic opinion, and that it would suffice to teach that the substance of bread and wine cease to exist and that the accidents remain. The Jansenists at Pistoia held to a very loose interpretation of Trent, while Pius VI upheld a narrower interpretation. Yet even the pope's understanding would have allowed for the substitution theory.[17] Jorissen concludes, therefore, that Lateran IV certainly did not define transubstantiation, not even in the broad medieval sense of "transubstantiation," and that even Trent did so only in this broader sense, leaving open the question of how a substantial change takes place.[18]

A second study of this issue by James McCue, "The Doctrine of Transubstantiation From Berengar Through the Council of Trent,"[19]

depends heavily on Jorissen's study, but follows up on Jorissen's almost off-handed remark that Scotus, Ockham and Biel all interpreted
Lateran IV as having ruled out coexistence as an orthodox understanding of "transubstantiation"[20] McCue agrees that all three of
Peter's options were accepted as orthodox immediately after the
Fourth Lateran Council, but argues that as the century progressed,
coexistence came under more and more criticism.

According to McCue, a drastic change took place with the writings
of John Duns Scotus, the Franciscan master, whose *Opus Oxoniense,* a
commentary on the *Sentences,* was probably completed ca. 1306–07.
Scotus argued strongly against transmutation and concluded that
both coexistence and the substitution theory make more sense than
transmutation. He ended his discussion, however, by asserting the
truth of "transubstantiation," basing his decision on the authority of
the Fourth Lateran Council.

"The Church declared this to be understood to be of the truth of the
faith in that creed edited under Innocent III in the Lateran Council,
'We firmly believe, etc.' . . . And, in short, whatever is said here to be
believed, ought to be held to be of the substance of the faith, after this
solemn declaration having been made by the Church."[21]

God is free, according to Scotus, to choose any means of effecting the
presence in the Eucharist. In this case, God had chosen a less "reasonable" approach than God might have. Further, we know that this is
God's choice because the Church has declared it to be so.[22]

McCue's article offers four other witnesses to support his contention that transubstantiation came to be seen by medieval theologians
as having been defined by Lateran IV. The first of these is William of
Ockham. McCue holds that, by the time of Ockham's later writings,
"His position is now more exactly like that of Scotus."[23] McCue then
cites Durand of St-Pourçian, Thomas of Strasbourg, and the condemnation of Wyclif at the Council of Constance to prove his contention
that "this position [that of Scotus and Ockham], or a position very
much like it, seems to have become rather commonplace from about
Ockham's time, and apparently remained so down to Luther's time."[24]

McCue concludes with an analysis of Luther and of Trent's response to Luther. Luther, according to McCue, did not object to anyone else believing in transubstantiation, however stupid an opinion
he himself found it to be. Rather, Luther objected that such an unim-

portant and badly argued theory should not be considered a matter of faith.[25] Trent's response was to reassert the claim of Scotus: transubstantiation was true by the *fiat* of early *auctoritates,* the chief of which was Lateran IV.[26] McCue thus concludes: "Fourteenth- and fifteenth-century theologians considered themselves bound by a decree which they misinterpreted."[27]

McCue offers a significant addition to Jorissen's conclusions by pointing out the important role which Lateran IV played in the theology of Scotus, Ockham, and ultimately, Trent. What he does not do is to distinguish between transubstantiation and transmutation. As a consequence, whenever his sources refer to a change in substance occurring in the sacrament, he assumes that they mean transmutation. His thesis that Lateran IV was seen as an authoritative limitation of transubstantiation to mean simply transmutation only holds if one assumes that this identification of transubstantiation was also made by his sources. A closer reading shows that the authors he cites do in fact refer to Lateran IV as the basis of their rejection of coexistence, but not always as basis for accepting transmutation.

When Scotus, for instance, explained his understanding of "transubstantiation," what he described was a form of substitution theory. The bread and wine disappear and the Body and Blood of Christ appear in separate actions; the substance of the Body and Blood "succeeding" the substance of the bread and wine.[28] There are two points worth noting here. First, as McCue rightly points out, Scotus is the first theologian to appeal to the Fourth Lateran Council as upholding "transubstantiation" in his discussion of the three possible modes of change. Secondly, Scotus' own understanding of "transubstantiation" would certainly not have identified "transubstantiation" with transmutation as would Thomas Aquinas, Albert the Great or many modern writers.

William of Ockham opposed coexistence in his commentary on the *Sentences,* basing this rejection not only on Lateran IV, but also on a passage in the *Decretales,* in the section entitled *De celebratione missae.* The passage in question reads:

"Because, however, the determination of the Church is in opposition, as *extra de summa trinitate et fide catholica* [a reference to the creed of Lateran IV contained in the *Decretales*] and *de celebratione missae* [again a reference to the *Decretales*] demonstrate, and as all the teachers also commonly hold the opposite, therefore I hold that the substance of bread does not remain, but only its species, and that the body of Christ coexists with them."[29]

In this case, Ockham rejected only coexistence, but did not, as did Scotus, also go on to canonize "transubstantiation." In a later quodlibetal question quoted by McCue, however, Ockham did follow Scotus in accepting "transubstantiation" based on the authority of Lateran IV alone. The text reads: "The second [transubstantiation] is the common opinion of all the theologians, which I hold according to the determination of the Church, and not on account of any reason."[30] Like Scotus, though, when Ockham did define what he understood by "transubstantiation" (and the belief required by Lateran IV), he described a position that was clearly a form of substitution theory.[31] The Dominican, Durand of St-Pourçian, offered a similar analysis. Three versions of Durand's commentary on the *Sentences* exist, and McCue uses the third recension completed ca. 1313–27.[32] The text reads: "But because this mode [coexistence] ought not to be held *de facto,* as the Church, which is presumed not to error in such matters, has determined the opposite, therefore the other part [that the substance of bread and wine do not remain] ought to be held."[33] Once again, Durand appealed to Lateran IV in rejecting coexistence, but did not go on to evoke the council in favor of transmutation.

The third witness given by McCue in support of his thesis did argue for a narrower reading of Lateran IV. The Augustinian hermit, Thomas of Strasbourg, who lectured on the *Sentences* at Paris between 1336 and 1341 wrote:

"Always subject to a better judgment, it does not seem to me from this that before the determination of holy mother Church, which I have repeated above, this opinion [coexistence] would have been considered heretical. I do not know of anyone who after that determination asserted this opinion except John of Paris of the Order of Preachers, who posited that the breadness remained, lest the accidents might be in the symbol without a subject. Because of this, he is said to have been excommunicated by the bishop of Paris."[34]

The "determination of holy mother Church" to which Thomas had earlier referred, was indeed Lateran IV,[35] to which Thomas also appealed in his rejection of any form of annihilation which denied a *conversio* in the sacrament.[36] These three theologians, Ockham, Durand, and Thomas did, then, appeal to Lateran IV in their determination of the mode of change in the Eucharist, but did not agree as to the extent of the authority of the decree, Thomas preferring a narrower definition to that of Ockham or Durand.

The final case to which McCue alludes is that of the condemnation of the theology of John Wyclif at the Council of Constance. The error condemned reads: "The material substance of the bread and similarly the material substance of the wine remain in the sacrament of the altar."[37] Once again, this condemnation does not define transubstantiation; it merely asserts that one must believe that the "material substance" of the bread and wine no longer remain after the words of consecration. Even less restrictive than the condemnations by the theologians discussed above, this vague wording would allow for some subtle forms of coexistence, as well as for any form of substitution theory, or any of several different understandings of transmutation.

Further support for the contention that the basis of Wyclif's condemnation was his teaching of coexistence comes from a list of questions that were to be asked of suspected Lollards. The list is contained in the Register of Thomas Polton, bishop of Worcester, and seems to be part of the proceedings of the convocation of 1428. The only question dealing with the Real Presence reads: "First of all, whether after the consecration the true Body of Christ might be on the altar and not the material substance of the bread nor of the wine."[38] The question asked, therefore, concerned only a belief in the continued existence of the bread and wine and not in any other aspect of the eucharistic change.

In concluding this analysis of the work of Jorissen and McCue, one can agree with these two scholars that thirteenth-century theologians did not understand the Fourth Lateran Council as defining transubstantiation, nor did they feel compelled to condemn other possible theories that explained the Real Presence. On the other hand, McCue's further thesis that from the time of Scotus theologians did understand the council to have ruled out all but transmutation as orthodox cannot stand without some modification. The evidence in fact shows that theologians differed over the narrowness of the "definition" of Lateran IV, some understanding the council only to have ruled out coexistence, others holding that the council ruled out some forms of substitution theory as well.

An author not discussed by Jorissen or McCue, Pierre d'Ailly, witnessed to the wide range of opinions about the status of "transubstantiation" in the fourteenth century. D'Ailly defined transubstantiation as the immediate succession of two things having no common matter or subject; one which ceased to be, the other which begins to be.[39] D'Ailly then went on:

"It is known that Catholics would agree in this, that the body of Christ truly and principally is in the sacrament under the species of bread and wine or where the species appear. However the master [Peter Lombard] tells us in distinction eleven [of book four] and the *glossa* on the *de celebratione missarum*, cap. *cum marthae* [a reference to the *Decretales*], there were different opinions to be considered in the way in which this might be explained."[40]

D'Ailly judged all the opinions, even that of coexistence, to be acceptable "if they accord with the determination of the Church," which he seemed to consider possible, since he concluded his discussion:

"The fourth opinion and the more common is that the substance of the bread does not remain but simply ceases to be. . . . And although this does not follow thus evidently from scripture nor even, it seems to me, from the determination of the Church, because it is more supportive of them and of the more common opinions of the saints and teachers, therefore I hold it."[41]

D'Ailly's position did not differ significantly from that of William of Auvergne written a hundred years earlier. More significantly, it is this very passage of d'Ailly to which Luther would refer when he argued that transubstantiation ought not be considered a doctrine of the Church.[42]

Jorissen and McCue are correct, therefore, in their insistence that Lateran IV was not assumed by all medieval theologians to have defined transubstantiation. McCue is also correct when he argues that, starting with Scotus, some medieval theologians appealed to Lateran IV as an authority in determining the mode of change. He is incorrect, however, in assuming either that there was unanimity in how theologians would understand either the term "transubstantiation," or how the creed of Lateran IV might delimit the explanation of that term.

A great deal of confusion has resulted from the identification of the broader medieval term "transubstantiation" with the much narrower explanation of the eucharistic change which I have called "transmutation." Roman Catholics and Protestants both came to identify transubstantiation with transmutation, although for different historical reasons. The claim by scholars such as Bishop Cosin that Lateran IV defined transubstantiation *de fide* actually amounts to a claim that

Lateran IV defined transmutation *de fide*. The research of Jorissen and McCue demonstrates that medieval theologians did not understand the matter in the same way at all. Even claims that "transubstantia-tion" enjoyed a privileged doctrinal status did not necessarily entail such a status for transmutation. Some theologians did make this equation; others did not.

THE CANONISTS IN THEORY

So far, the discussion has mostly centered on theological discus-sions of Lateran IV and its authority in the matter of transubstantia-tion. Theologians were only some of the players in the drama, however. Theologians might propose, but lawyers disposed, some-times of theologians. If the theologians did not reliably assert the dogma of transubstantiation as transmutation, or understand Lateran IV as promulgating one, perhaps the canonists did, and it was the canonists teaching in the schools who trained the myriad of officials who would enforce the teachings of the Church. It seems reasonable to suppose that if anyone understood Lateran IV to have defined transubstantiation in the narrow sense of transmutation, it would be the lawyers.

The earliest commentaries on the decrees of Lateran IV, however, fully support the contention of Jorissen and McCue that contempo-raries did not understand the council as limiting discussion of euchar-istic change. Antonio García y García has recently edited four commentaries on the decrees of Lateran, all written before 1220. Only one of the commentaries, that of Vincent of Spain, offered any com-ment at all on the section of the creed which used the word "transsub-stantiatis." The passage reads: *"under the species:* and so whiteness, roundness and other accidents are here without a subject and thus miraculously, or they are in the air. Vincent. *bread and wine:* with water, *extra iii. de celebrati[one]. missar[um]. Cum Marthe."* The first commentary on the existence of the Body and Blood under the species actually rules out transmutation, since Vincent described the acci-dents as existing without any substance, or else as joined to the sub-stance of the surrounding air.[43] The second commentary on the bread and wine contained the same reference provided by William of Ockham and Pierre d'Ailly in their discussions of coexistence. The reference is to a letter of Innocent III to the archbishop of Lyons written in 1202 which was included in the *Decretales Gregorii IX,* Lib. III, tit. 41, *De celebratione missarum,* as c. 6. Clearly some thirteenth-century writers considered this text as important in discussions of the Eucharist, and it is to this text that we shall shortly turn.

A fifth early witness to the reception of the decrees of Lateran IV was Thomas of Chobham in his *Summa confessorum*. According to F. Broomfield, the editor of the *Summa,* Thomas had completed his work before the council, but added whatever material he could gather from the council before finally publishing his text.[44] This makes him a very unreliable witness to the council, but Thomas did include a discussion *de transsubstantiatione* which paralleled that of Vincent of Spain:

"It is, however, known and firmly believed that after the confection of the body and blood of the Lord, nothing remains of the substance of the bread, nor of the substance of the wine, but only accidents, namely, taste and color; and this happens through a miracle, whether [the accidents] are without any subject or in the surrounding air. Nor is a person here able to see, or touch, or taste any substance or matter of the bread and wine, but only accidents, and through a miracle a person is able to be fed and nourished by the accidents alone."[45]

Leaving aside for a moment Thomas's rather strange and (by the early thirteen century) antiquated theology, it is clear that he did hold as a matter of faith that the substance of the bread and wine cease to exist, and this could be read as a rejection of coexistence. Given Thomas's limited understanding of metaphysics, he probably did not have anything so definite in mind, but his text could be taken as such.

If the immediate commentators on the decrees of Lateran IV indicated little interest in the reference to transubstantiation by the council, the question still remains whether later canonists commenting on sections of the *Decretum* and the *Decretales* might have understood transubstantiation to be an approved doctrine of the Church. The discussions of the Eucharist by the canonists of the thirteenth century occur in three places. First, there are commentaries on the section of the *Decretum* called the *De consecratione*. This was an addition to the *Decretum* made soon after Gratian finished his work in the middle of the twelfth century. By 1166, commentaries on the *De consecratione* begin to appear. Distinctio II of the *De consecratione* contains an impressive collection of ninety-seven *sententiae* dealing with eucharistic belief and practice. The standard commentary on this material was compiled by Johannes Teutonicus, a doctor of canon law at Bologna, and was completed about 1216. This commentary was revised by another Bolognese professor, Bartholomew of Brescia, who completed his work in 1245. This *glossa ordinaria* became the standard text for all students of canon law in the Middle Ages.[46]

Another important set of glosses are those on the two sections of the *Decretales* dealing with the Eucharist. The first of these are the commentaries on the actual text of the creed of Lateran IV which is included as the very first entry in the *Liber extra* prepared by Raymond of Peñafort for Gregory IX and issued in 1234.[47] I have been able to consult three glosses on this passage. The earliest is that of the canonist, Henry of Susa (Hostiensis), who published his *Summa aurea* in 1253 while archbishop of Embrun. The second commentary comes from Thomas Aquinas, who commented on the first and second article of the *Liber extra* in a letter to the archdeacon of Todi (most likely Giffredus d'Anagni) written sometime in the 1260s.[48] A third discussion occurs in Henry of Susa's commentary on the *Liber extra* which he worked on until his death in 1270.[49]

Secondly, I have consulted two commentaries on the letter of Innocent III. The first is an extensive discussion by Henry of Susa in his commentary on the *Liber extra*. A second and much shorter commentary occurs in the *glossa ordinaria* on the *Decretales* by Bernard of Parma, the final revision of which was completed in 1263.[50] A final commentary is at least worth mentioning. The canonist Sinibalde of Fiesche, later Innocent IV, wrote an *Apparatus* on the *Liber extra* as well as on his own laws as pope. Although Sinibalde discussed both the creed of Lateran IV and the letter of Innocent III, he mentioned nothing about the eucharistic change.[51]

These texts give a fairly accurate picture of what was being taught to the budding young canonists at Bologna during the thirteenth century, and given the influence of Johannes Teutonicus' and Bernard of Parma's *glossa ordinaria* well beyond.

Innocent III wrote to the archbishop of Lyons in 1202 in response to a number of questions addressed to him by the archbishop. Two of these questions concern the Eucharist. The first deals with how to respond to certain people who say that the Body and Blood of Christ are not really present in the sacrament, but only present as under an image or sign. Innocent responded heatedly, arguing that if the presence in the sacrament was not real, then neither would be the death and resurrection of Christ. Innocent continued to give the archbishop a little lesson in theology, and moved on to the second question concerning the Eucharist. The archbishop wished to know if the water added to the wine is converted along with it into the Blood of Christ.

Innocent admitted that scholars differ, but after a long discussion of the different views, held as more probable the opinion that the water is transformed along with the wine.[52] Innocent did not directly address the question of the orthodoxy of any one explanation for the change, but the letter, once included in the *Liber extra,* would often be referred to as a supporting text for the Real Presence, starting with the commentary of Vincent of Spain quoted above.

The *glossa ordinaria* on the *Decretum* referred to this letter in the commentary on the first chapter of the *De consecratione,* dist. 2. The glossator followed Innocent in his theology of the Eucharist and in his discussion of the changing of the water into the Blood of Christ. This led to a discussion of the different theories about the eucharistic change, and the glossator offered three theories of change, as had Peter of Capua. The three theories put forward do not quite parallel those of Peter, however. The first merely asserts a change without further specification. The second opinion argues that the bread and wine cease to exist, and then the Body and Blood begin to exist under the accidents; a form of substitution theory. Although he is not named, the glossator here seems to be following the gloss of Vincent of Spain. The third opinion is clearly coexistence. All the opinions are accepted as confessing the real presence, although the glossator holds the second opinion to be truer, based on the creed of Lateran IV.[53] There is no indication in the text that any of these theories would be unorthodox.[54]

The glossator debated the merits of coexistence as opposed to substitution theory in the commentary on c. 34. There is no indication that either theory is heretical, and coexistence is supported by references to *sententiae* by Ambrose and Augustine.[55] In the same gloss, the author listed several terms that could be used to describe the change which takes place in the sacrament. "Transubstantiation" is only one of several acceptable terms.[56] The glossator here was following the gloss of Stephen of Tournai, one of the first of the commentators on the sentences of Gratian.[57] Further discussion by the glossator clarifies his understanding of "transubstantiation." He described "true transubstantiation" as occurring when the substance of bread and wine cease to exist, and the new essence of the Body and Blood begin to exist. He did not hesitate to speak of the disappearance of the substance of the bread and wine as *corruptio.*[58] The glossator's underlying theological assumption was that the species of bread and wine were a true sign, whose sign quality begins when the consecration takes place and ends when the bread or wine are no longer recognizable as signs. Thus there is no presence when the species are in the throat, or in the stomach, or digested, or disfigured, or eaten by a mouse.[59] As soon as the teeth of the faithful touch the species, the Body of Christ returns to heaven.[60] The glossator even entertained the idea that the presence ceases to exist when the most wicked people attempt to receive the sacrament.[61]

The theology of "transubstantiation" put forward here was far different than that which would be espoused and defended by Albert the Great or Thomas Aquinas, and is similar to that of Alexander of Hales.[62] The idea that the Body of the Lord might just disappear when descending into the stomach or when eaten by a mouse particularly infuriated Albert and Thomas. This is the kind of teaching Albert had in mind when he ripped into the canon lawyers for their sacramental theology, calling them ignorant in both Scriptures and the Fathers, incapable of teaching without sinning.[63] Clearly what was taught at Bologna in the Middle Ages as the standard gloss on the *Decretum* was not what would be considered standard theology by post-Reformation Roman theologians, nor is there any hint in the gloss that the term "transubstantiation" had any particular canonical standing.

Commenting on the creed of Lateran IV ca. 1253 in his *Summa aurea*, Henry of Susa repeated the tripartite distinction between different theories of change contained in the *glossa ordinaria*. The order is different, however, as coexistence was placed second, and transmutation third. Henry placed more importance on transmutation than the *glossa ordinaria* had, holding that "the general council seems to sanction this third (opinion), as well as Innocent III." He did not take this sanction as ruling out the other possibilities, as all of them profess the true Body to be on the altar. Only the belief that the Body and Blood are not truly there was condemned. The sources that Henry gave for his opinion were both the creed of Lateran IV and the letter of Innocent III.[64] Again, although this gloss is somewhat more definite about the approbation of transmutation, there is no indication that the other opinions mentioned would be heretical.

The gloss of Thomas Aquinas, written in the 1260s, shows quite a change from any of the earlier glosses. Thomas, as one might imagine, identified transubstantiation with a very technical understanding of transmutation, and held that this is the meaning of the creed of Lateran IV. He went further than this, however, and explicitly held that the creed condemned coexistence: "It (the creed) says, however, *under the species* in order to exclude the error of certain persons who have said that in the sacrament of the altar the substance of bread and the substance of the body are contained together."[65] Thomas then went on to prove this from Scripture, again insisting that this is the meaning of the letter of Innocent. Although Thomas did not use the word "heretical" of this opinion, he certainly intended it. The parallel usage of the word "error" for the denial of the Real Presence makes this clear.[66] Thomas, then, not only introduced the teaching that coexistence was heretical into the theological tradition, he also introduced it into the canonical tradition.

Thomas's opinion, however, remained Thomas's opinion, and when Henry of Susa commented a second time on the creed of Lateran IV, ca. 1270, he either did not know of it or ignored it. Henry simply repeated his earlier gloss, again holding that any of the three opinions about the change was acceptable, and only a denial of the change was heretical.[67] In the same work, Henry also glossed the letter of Innocent III, and here he gave a more detailed analysis of his views. He repeated what he had said earlier, this time explicitly mentioning Johannes Teutonicus as his source. He then proceeded to spell out more clearly what orthodox belief might be.

"In the first opinion, all Catholics concur, of course, that substance, which first was bread and wine, afterwards becomes the body and blood; this 'becomes' however, according to what is said, denotes conversion. All words, then, that denote conversion, or transubstantiation, can be properly used here; so if I say 'the bread is transubstantiated into the body of Christ,' this is true; similarly if I say 'converted' or 'changed.'"[68]

Henry ended this discussion by claiming that the second opinion is the "catholic opinion."[69] A quick glance at the second opinion shows that this opinion, ascribed to Vincent of Spain, was the substitution theory put forward by the *glossa ordinaria*. The bread ceases to be, and the Body of Christ succeeds it. Henry even argued that the substance of the bread might be reduced to nothing, a good description of the substitution theory of change. Henry responded to objections to this theory and concluded that this opinion seemed to have been approved by the creed of Lateran IV.[70] Henry repeated his opinion that transubstantiation referred to substitution theory in his gloss on the word "transubstantiatur."[71]

Henry of Susa offered no indication that any particular opinion should be understood as heretical. He himself preferred the substitution theory, probably influenced by the *glossa ordinaria,* and held that, if anything, the creed of Lateran IV supported this opinion. The commentary comes to a very different conclusion than that of Thomas Aquinas.

The *glossa ordinaria* of Bernard of Parma on the letter of Innocent III, written about the same time as Thomas's gloss, added little to the discussion as it merely repeated the gloss of Johannes Teutonicus on the *Decretum.* As did the earlier glossator, Johannes preferred the substitution theory, and felt that Lateran IV upheld it.[72]

What then can be concluded from this investigation of canonical sources? Simply that different scholars held different opinions. In fact, the situation is not much different from that of the theologians discussed above. By the beginning of the fourteenth century, John Duns Scotus thought that the creed of Lateran IV limited belief to "transubstantiation," but transubstantiation understood as a form of substitution theory. Thomas Aquinas and Albert the Great were certain in their opinion that coexistence was heretical, and it appears that they influenced at least William of Ockham, Durand of St-Pourçian, and Thomas of Strasbourg through both theological and canonical writings. The canonists seemed to go their own way, insisting that any description of the change that asserted a Real Presence was orthodox, although they appeared to favor the substitution theory. Certainly the students of Bologna were not being taught that transmutation was a *de fide* belief of the Church.

If McCue is right in his assertion that by the end of the fourteenth century transmutation had come to be seen as required for belief based on the creed of Lateran IV, it seems surprising that an early sixteenth-century edition of the *glossa ordinaria,* especially one revised by a fifteenth-century canonist, would provide no indication of this. Two of the greatest canonists of the Middle Ages, Henry of Susa and Innocent IV, did not seem to think that belief in transmutation was required. Henry said so more than once, and Innocent's silence is at least a weak argument supporting the conclusion that the canonists did not understand Lateran IV as requiring a *de fide* belief in transmutation.

ENFORCEMENT IN PRACTICE

If, however, the canonists considered a range of beliefs as orthodox, how did Peter Olivi, John Quidort of Paris and John Wyclif end up by being condemned for their teaching on the Eucharist? The stubborn fact remains that people *were* condemned for their teachings, despite the wide range of views voiced by the masters of Paris and Bologna. Since I have already noted that Wyclif was technically condemned by the Council of Constance for teaching coexistence, and that it was this teaching that came to be associated as well with Lollardry, I will concentrate rather on the cases of Peter Olivi and John of Paris.

David Burr offers an excellent study of the censuring of Peter Olivi's theology in *The Persecution of Peter Olivi*.[73] Peter studied in Paris during the 1260s and by the 1270s was teaching in southern France. There he roused the ire of some of his fellow monks and scholars. Why exactly Peter earned this opprobrium is uncertain, but at least two reasons are possible. First, Peter espoused a fairly strict interpretation of *usus pauper,* and secondly, he despised the introduction of "the pagan Aristotle" and "the Saracen Averroes" into theological discussions. Peter connected these two beliefs into an apocalyptic vision where Aristotle becomes the Antichrist who had introduced false ideas of wealth into the Church. Olivi explained,

"Aristotle's view of riches and human happiness is, I believe, . . . the root of the error of the Antichrist. . . . And just as the Arian heresy proceeded from the erroneous doctrine of Plato the master, so, according to some masters, from the erroneous doctrine of this one proceeded the heresy of the Antichrist, which is a disciple of the Arian heresy just as Aristotle is a disciple of Plato."[74]

Whatever the cause, the complaints reached the ears of the minister general, Bonagratia, who appointed a commission of four masters and three bachelors to examine Peter's works. The commission produced a *rotulus* made up of excerpts from Peter's writings, which are marked with different degrees of disapproval ranging from heretical to ignorant, as well as a list of twenty-two orthodox articles, known as the *Letter of the Seven Seals,* to which Peter was forced to assent at Avignon in 1283 before a special council. Peter's own books were seized, and all copies of his works were to be turned over to the minister general.

An eclectic group of opinions, ranging from *usus pauper* to the divine essence, were challenged by the commission, and Peter's teaching on the Eucharist played a somewhat minor role in the proceedings. In fact, the actual teaching in question dealt not with the Eucharist, but with the proposition that "to say that the predicaments are not really distinct is contrary to the philosopher and especially dangerous in the cases of relation and quantity."[75] Behind this philosophical issue, however, lies an attack by Peter on Albert's and Thomas's theory of transmutation, which held that the quantity of the bread and wine remained after the change and provided the substratum to which the other accidents inhered. To quote Burr, "Olivi's view of quantity, if accepted, would have necessitated a basic reconsideration of eucharistic presence not only by the Dominicans but by many of his fellow Franciscans."[76] In a treatise on quantity written some years before the censure, Peter offered an intriguing glimpse into his motives for challenging the standard views on quantity:

"I am not concerned about whether the opinion is accepted, except insofar as I am unwilling to see either myself or anyone else drawn into accepting either side of the controversy without careful thought, for I do not want to see those things which do not directly affect the articles of our faith treated or held as if they were themselves articles of faith. Such things should rather be treated as ancillary to it. That is the reason why I sometimes recite diverse opinions and theories regarding such questions. In such matters no single opinion should be advanced as the faith, for unless I am mistaken about such matters (which I do not believe) dangers of the highest order lurk in such an assertion and in reliance upon the support of human opinions, be they of Aristotle, Averroes, or anyone else except the holy doctors authoritatively received and approved by the Roman Church."[77]

The condemnation of Peter Olivi's teaching on the Eucharist, then, was just a small part of a much larger challenge by Peter to the reception of Aristotle at Paris, and even more, to the authority of the masters at Paris, who had just recently received a severe reprimand on that account by the bishop of Paris, Étienne Tempier. The orders during this time were all carefully monitoring their scholars in an attempt to defend their own people, as well as to avoid censure.[78] Local politics brought Peter to the attention of the higher authorities, who saw him as a dangerous nuisance.

The story does have a more or less happy ending. Peter somehow was able to gather enough of his writings, and those of his opponents, to write a defense of his views in 1285. At the general chapter meeting at Montpellier in 1287, he defended some of his views, which were then accepted as orthodox. His rehabilitation was completed by his being appointed *lector* of the Franciscan *studium* in Florence by the new minister general, Matthew of Aquasparta.[79]

The opposition to Olivi did not quite stop there, however. David Burr in his study of the controversy over the role of *quantitas* in the explanations of eucharistic presence espoused by Olivi and Ockham, points out that at least three theologians attacked the claims of Olivi in their writings. Richard of Mediavilla, who had been a member of the original commission which judged Olivi, Raymond Rigalidi, and Augustinus Triumphus all argued that Olivi's opinion was contrary to the beliefs of the Church. Richard of Mediavilla was perhaps the most explicit in his claims: "the holy Church holds most firmly (and we should firmly hold with it) that in the sacrament of the altar quantity remains through divine power without the substance of the bread and wine."[80] Neither Richard nor Augustinus appealed to Lateran IV in their arguments, but their claims for Church teaching do suggest that theologians other than Albert the Great, Thomas Aquinas, and Thomas of Strasbourg understood Church teaching in a rather narrow sense.

John Quidort of Paris was twice censured for his teaching on the Eucharist, once as master of the *Sentences,* and once as a regent master. Information about John Quidort's early life is uncertain, but the most reliable version suggests that he was born in Paris and was already a master in the arts before joining the Dominican Order. He lectured on the *Sentences* between 1284 and 1286, which would mean that he was a student in theology during the condemnation of 1277 and possibly a recent member of the very suspect arts faculty.[81] Sixteen propositions taken from his commentary on the *Sentences* were reported to the master general as erroneous. John's defense of his teaching survives and was printed by P. Glorieux in 1928.[82] Two of these propositions touched on the Eucharist. The third in the list of sixteen opinions condemned dealt with the ongoing controversy with the Greek Church over the use of leavened bread in the liturgy, and, according to John, was simply a mistaken report of his teaching, which he claimed to be that of Thomas Aquinas.[83] The fifteenth article is the more relevant and once again involves the controversy over quantity. John was accused of teaching that "whiteness" could be visible, even without quantity underlying it. John responded that he had indeed taught on this matter in his lectures on the Eucharist, but held only that it was possible for God to make accidents without subjects, "whiteness" without quantity and a soul outside a body.[84] John's defense was a success and his teaching was not censured, although his inception as master was delayed until 1304. As in the case of Olivi, the real issue behind the doubts concerning John's teaching on the Eucharist was a lively thirteenth-century dispute about quantity.[85]

In the very year he became master, John wrote a *Determinatio de modo existendi corpus Christi in sacramento* in which he argued that through the consecration, the substance of the bread and wine were drawn into the existence *(esse)* of the Lord in such a way that they now become accidents of the one self-existent being of the Lord.[86] This might at first glance seem a very strange proposition indeed, but a very similar explanation of the incarnation had been discussed at least from the time of William of Auxerre, and John explicitly based his theology on the model of the incarnation.[87] He even went so far as to suggest that every Holy Thursday and in fact every Mass is a "Feast of the Impanation," just as there is a feast of the incarnation.[88] John felt comfortable describing such a change in the Eucharist as "transubstantiation"[89] Basing himself on both the *glossa* on the *Decretum* and on the commentaries of Henry of Susa discussed above, John insisted that no council or pope had determined a particular explanation of the change as *de fide*.[90] The discussion received immediate attention. The bishops of Paris, Bourges, Orléans, and Amiens censured John for his teaching on the Eucharist, and a board of examiners at Paris suspended him from his teaching position.[91] He appealed to Rome, but died while awaiting the decision of the pope.

There is no question that it was John Quidort's theology of the Eucharist that got him into this trouble, although he might well have been able to clear himself at Avignon. John Hilary Martin has suggested that John Quidort did not actually hold the theory he put forward, but only meant it as a true *determinatio*, that is, a theologically defensible possibility. This may well be the case, since John's commentary on the *Sentences* specifically denied coexistence,[92] and he was known as a keen, although independently minded, defender of Thomas Aquinas, writing in Thomas's defense some time before 1284.[93] Furthermore, John specifically stated in the beginning of the *Determinatio* that he believed that a substantial conversion took place in the sacrament, although he did not feel that such an explanation was a matter of faith.[94]

If John's teaching were only one among many theories, and only a suggestion at any rate, why was he hauled up before the authorities? It is hard to know for certain, but some shrewd guesses can be offered. John Quidort, as Étienne Gilson phrased it, "never was completely trusted."[95] First, he may have been suspect as a master of the school of arts located by Tempier as the hotbed of heretics. Secondly, he wrote a very influential study of the power of popes and kings. According to Roensch, "Quidort is best known for his work on the origin, rights, and limits of ecclesiastical and civil power. It is evident even from his sermons that he took a particularly firm stand against the abuses of justice, not only in matters of multiple benefices, but also concerning the crimes of the wealthy and powerful."[96] He was also one of the signatories of an appeal directed to the council called by Philip the Fair against Boniface VIII.[97] This is not the kind of activity calculated to win friends in high places. John Quidort could easily have had many powerful enemies for whom his theology of the Eucharist was a Godsend.

What then can be made of these two cases of people condemned for their teaching on the Eucharist? First, and most obviously, they died of natural causes. Not Peter Olivi, not John Quidort, not even John Wyclif, met the fate of other heretics. Secondly, none of these teachers was condemned for denying transmutation. Even Wyclif was actually condemned, it seems, for teaching coexistence, as was John Quidort (although he called it transubstantiation). In fact, these men held quite disparate opinions from one another. Nor do these three cases include all those censured for their teaching on the Eucharist. William of Ockham was censured by John Lutterall for teaching the substitution theory.[98] The Dominican, Durand of St-Pourçian, was continuously censured by his order for deviating from the teaching of Thomas Aquinas and kept having to rewrite his commentary on the *Sentences*. One of the teachings for which he was condemned was the opinion that the Body of Christ is present in the Eucharist without any quantity.[99]

These were all academics, censured in one way or another for positing theories far too complicated for the ordinary cleric or layperson. Wyclif was probably right when he jibed that "The people and a thousand bishops understand neither accident nor subject."[100] But what about the ordinary Christian? Was Bishop Cosin right when he claimed that belief in transubstantiation was thrust upon Christians, "through excommunications, armies, rebellions, tortures, and burning alive," as he so graphically put it?[101] There were Lollards, no doubt, who met just these fates, although their beliefs on the Eucharist were but one small part of a whole package of errors for which they were condemned. Further research needs to be done, but at least insofar as I have been able to determine, few people, at least in the Middle Ages, seem to have been brought before the Inquisition specifically for mis-understanding the mode of change in the Eucharist. They might deny that the Eucharist had any value, as did the Cathars. They might deny that unworthy priests or that the priest alone could consecrate, as did the Waldensians. Bishop Cosin appears to have been wrong, however, when he ascribed to the machinery of the Inquisition the enforcement of transubstantiation (even in its larger sense).

This does not mean, however, that one could not be investigated for suspicious teaching on the Eucharist, especially if the Inquisitor was particularly malicious or had a larger agenda into which eucharistic teaching might fit. One particularly instructive case of this kind was recorded in the *Directorium inquisitorum* of Nicolas Eymeric, the in-quisitor of Aragon from 1357 to 1360 and then again from 1387 until 1393.

Nicolas appealed to Gregory XI against a Franciscan who taught that the Body of Christ ceases to be present when the host falls into any inappropriate place, or is eaten by an animal, or even when it is chewed and digested by recipients.[102] Gregory responded by banning this teaching in the areas under Nicolas' control, without specifying any wider condemnation. The preacher Johannes de Latone was also sent a letter and asked to stop preaching these things in the churches of Aragon.[103] It is somewhat surprising that Johannes received even this mild reproof, since he was simply following the teaching of Inno-cent III, Alexander of Hales, Bonaventure, Nicholas of Lyra, and even of the *glossa ordinaria* on the *Decretum*.[104] Less surprisingly, this letter is not referred to in either the medieval canonical or theological discus-sions I have read.[105]

Why did Nicolas pounce on a Franciscan merely for following the teaching of his order's greatest masters? More work needs to be done, but two factors help explain how this could happen. First of all, Nicolas *liked* to pounce. He is described by one source as "the most tenacious, the most aggressive and the harshest inquisitor in the en-tire history of the Catalan Inquisition."[106] Removed by his own order from his post as Inquisitor in 1360, he was banned from the realm of Aragon by Pedro IV in 1375. Upon the death of Pedro, he returned as Inquisitor in 1387, only to be banished again in 1393.[107] He seems not to have been an easy man with whom to get along.

Secondly, Nicolas may have had particular reasons for attacking Johannes. Eymeric single-mindedly pursued the followers of Ramon Lull both while in Catalonia and while in exile in Avignon. The spiritual Franciscans received the same hostile reception from the Inquisitor.[108] Nicolas could well have found a convenient target for his bile in the Franciscan preacher, especially if Johannes were associated in any way with Lull or the Spirituals.

As in the cases of Peter Olivi and John Quidort discussed above, the accusation of eucharistic heresy depended more on particular local circumstances than on the orthodoxy of the teaching. Johannes de Latone was teaching the wrong thing in the wrong place, despite the fact that what he was teaching would have been considered orthodox almost anywhere else in Europe. Again, it is worth pointing out that Johannes de Latone appears to have escaped unharmed from his brush with the Inquisition.

SOME CONCLUSIONS

The conclusions of Jorissen and McCue, then, stand firm and can even be expanded. Lateran IV did not intend to define transubstantiation, and medieval theologians and canonists never reached a consensus concerning the canonical weight of the decree. Thomas Aquinas and Albert the Great in the thirteenth century, and Thomas of Strasbourg in the fourteenth century, argued that Lateran IV imposed a narrow understanding of transubstantiation as transmutation *de fide*. Duns Scotus, William of Ockham, and Gabriel Biel argued that "transubstantiation" was indeed declared as the *de fide* understanding of the Church, but interpreted "transubstantiation" to include the substitution theory. Peter Olivi, John Quidort of Paris, Pierre d'Ailly and the thirteenth-century canonists argued for a much broader understanding of Lateran IV, restricting its weight to at most a condemnation of coexistence. Durand of St-Pourçian and the Council of Constance specifically interpreted Lateran IV to exclude only coexistence.

Further, "transubstantiation" itself did not have a fixed meaning. It could refer to the narrow definition which included only theories which argued for a transmutation of the substance of bread and wine into the Body and Blood, or it could include any theory that posited a change in the substance of the bread, including the substitution theory. The more common medieval usage would appear to be the second of these positions, and Jorissen has argued that it was this broader definition of transubstantiation that the Council of Trent wished to impose. The insistence of the Franciscans at the council that the substitution theory should not be disallowed, and the examples of its continued teaching after the council, both of which are described by Jorissen and by Pierre Allix, argue strongly in favor of this interpretation.[109]

To say, however, that there was no clearly and canonically defined "dogma of transubstantiation" during the Middle Ages does not mean that theologians, or even ordinary preachers, were not subject to the scrutiny of their respective authorities when they taught about the Eucharist. If there was an academic or preacher whom others felt needed disciplining, then an examination of his theology of the Eucharist was a good place to look for heresy. Heretical teaching about the Eucharist often appears among the charges brought against theologians because it was a complicated, touchy, and much-debated subject which could readily provide useful additions to the mix of accusations brought against a theologian. As the case of Johannes de Latone makes clear, however, such charges should not be taken as proof that what was taught was actually heresy or that a settled doctrine existed against which this teaching could easily be judged as heresy.

To conclude, then, despite a surprisingly tenacious belief that a "dogma of transubstantiation" was promulgated by the Fourth Lateran Council and enforced by the medieval Church, the evidence suggests that this was never the case, especially if by this one equates transubstantiation with transmutation.[110] At most one can argue that coexistence was dismissed as an orthodox option by the fifteenth century. The instances of charges against the eucharistic teaching which do occur in the Middle Ages usually seem to be part of a larger political or theological agenda, and not instances of the transgression of an established body of Church teaching.

---

1. Originally published in the *Journal of Ecclesiastical History* 45 (1994) 11–41.

2. *The Oxford Dictionary of the Christian Church*, F. L. Cross and E. A. Livingstone, eds., 2nd ed. (Oxford: Oxford University Press, 1974) 1390.

3. *The Growth of Medieval Theology (600–1300)*, The Christian Tradition: A History of the Development of Doctrine 3 (Chicago: University of Chicago Press, 1978) 268. For an excellent discussion of the first use of transubstantiation, see J. Goering, "The Invention of Transubstantiation," *Traditio* 46 (1991) 147–70.

4. The text of the council has been critically edited by Antonio García y García, *Constitutiones Concilii quarti Lateranensis una cum commentariis glossato-*

rum, Series A: Corpus glossatorum 2 (Vatican City: Biblioteca Apostolica Vaticana, 1981). This section of the creed appears on p. 42. García y García feels that the wording may well be that of Innocent III himself (pp. 6–8). The relevant text of the creed reads: "Vna vero est fidelium universalis ecclesia, extra quam nullus omnino salvatur, in qua idem ipse sacerdos est sacrificium Iesus Christus, cuius corpus et sanguis in sacramento altaris sub speciebus panis et uini ueraciter continentur, transsubstantiatis pane in corpus et uino in sanguinem potestate diuina, ut ad perficiendum mysterium unitatis accipiamus ipsi de suo quod accepit ipse de nostro."

5. The entire passage reads: "Idem vero pontifex, postquam haereticos esse pronunciavit quicumque deinceps: "Christi corpus et sanguinem in sacramento altaris, sub speciebus panis et vini, transubstantiatis pane in corpus et vino in sanguinem, veraciter contineri" negaverint; eosdem omnes, cujuscunque tandem dignitatis aut officii sunt, secularibus potestatibus animadversione debita puniendos, id est cremandos tradit, in suspectos inquiri jubet, receptores et fautores eorum infames, intestabiles, atque haereditatum et officiorum omnium incapaces esse judicat, et reliquos christianos adversus eos extimulat." *Historia transubstantiationis papalis* (London: Thomas Roycroft at Henry Brome, 1675) 150. John Cosin wrote this work in 1656, but it was not published until after his death in 1672. On his life and works, see the *Oxford Dictionary of the Christian Church,* 350.

6. The entire passage reads: "Verum omittere nequeo quod cum haec Innocentiana definitio substantialem conversionem panis et vini in corpus et sanguinem Christi praescribat esse de fide, neutiquam tamen integra potuit obtinere, imo ex disputandi, ut videtur, aestu, quo ferebantur qui Joannis Parisiensis impetebant sententiam de panis subsistentia, illius annihilatio defensa est a plurimis, cui successura fuit Christi corporis e coelis deductio in locum substantiae panis et vini." *Determinatio Fr. Joannis Parisiensis praedicatoris, De modo existendi corpus Christi in sacramento altaris* (London: J. Cailloues, 1686) 77. The *Historia* is contained in a long preface to Allix's edition of the *Determinatio de modo existendi corpus Christi* of John of Paris. Allix's treatise is a rambling affair, in which he recorded the teaching of several medieval scholars who disagreed openly with Thomas Aquinas's teaching on transubstantiation, or who argued that the question of the mode of change in the Eucharist was still an open one. The most important of these for Allix was, of course, John of Paris. On Allix, see John Hilary Martin, "The Eucharistic Treatise of John Quidort of Paris," *Viator* 6 (1975) 197–99, and the *DTC* 1:894–95.

7. *Die Entfaltung der Transsubstantiationslehre bis zum Beginn der Hochscholastik,* Münsterische Beiträge zur Theologie 28 (1) (Münster: Aschendorff, 1965).

8. This is the terminology used, for example, by James F. McCue, "The Doctrine of Transubstantiation from Berengar through the Council of Trent," *Harvard Theological Review* 61 (1968) 385–430.

9. "De conversione triplex est opinio. Quidam dicunt quod non est ibi aliqua mutatio, sed remanente substantia panis et substantia vini ad prolationem illorum verborum incipit sub eisdem speciebus esse caro et sanguis Christi, cum prius non esset ibi nisi substantia panis et vini, et ubicumque legitur aliquid de conversione, sic intelligitur; ubi prius erat tantum panis et vinum, incipit esse etiam caro Christi et sanguis.

Alii dicunt quod substantia panis et vini penitus adnihilatur et manentibus speciebus eidem incipit ibi esse sola caro et sanguis Christi, et simili modo exponunt conversionem illam.

Nos dicimus et expositores hoc asserunt, quod ipsa substantia panis convertitur in carnem Christi veram quam traxit de Virgine, et substantia vini in verum sanguinem, et manentibus prioribus speciebus incipit ibi esse caro et sanguis Christi. Nec est articulus fidei credere quod sic vel sic fiat illa conversio, sed tantummodo credere quod corpus Christi ad prolationem illorum verborum sit in altari." Jorissen, *Entfaltung*, 24. On the dating of this work, see Gary Macy, *Theologies of the Eucharist in the Early Scholastic Period* (Oxford: Clarendon Press, 1984) 129, n. 225. For a similar discussion, cf. Gerard of Novara, *Summa*, Vatican City, Biblioteca Apostolica Vaticana, Vaticana latina MS 10754, fol. 37ra-b.

10. "Sufficit enim ad pietatem fidei, quam hic intendimus stabilire, credere, et tenere, quod sub forma panis materialis atque visiblis, in altari post benedictionem sacerdotalem rite factam apponitur panis vitae, et sub forma vini visibilis, potus vitae." *Magisterium divinale, De sacramentis* in *Opera omnia* (Paris: Franciscus Hotot, 1674; rpt. Frankfurt: Minerva, 1963) 434.

11. Jorissen, *Entfaltung*, 55.

12. See the references given in nn. 61 and 65 below for a more detailed discussion.

13. Jorissen, *Entfaltung*, 56.

14. Ibid., 57–58.

15. Ibid., 56 and 57, esp. nn.170 and 171. The discussion recorded in the Acts of the council does not differentiate between the different theological understandings of transubstantiation, cf. the Acts of Sessions 6 and 12 in *Acta genuina ss. oecumenici concilii Tridentini*, August Theiner, ed. (Zagreb: Societatis bibliophilae, 1874) 1:406–63, 488–529. The council settled for the rather restrained wording, "Si quis dixerit, in sacrosancto eucharistiae sacramento remanere substantiam panis et vini, una cum corpore et sanguine D. N. Jesu Christi, negaveritque mirabilem illam et singularem totius substantiae panis in corpus, et totius substantiae vini in sanguinem, manentibus dumtaxat speciebus panis et vini, conversionem, quam catholica ecclesia aptissime transubstantiationem appellat: anathema sit." Ibid., 525.

16. *Determinatio*, 36–38, 41–51.

17. Jorissen, *Entfaltung*, 9. The text of Pius's condemnation is given in Heinrich Denzinger and others, *Enchiridion symbolorum definitionum et declarationem*, 36th ed. (Freiburg: Herder,1976) n. 2629.

18. Jorissen, *Entfaltung*, 10, 59–64.

19. See n. 8 above.

20. Jorissen, *Entfaltung*, 62, n. 183.

21. "Ecclesia declaravit istum intellectum esse de veritate fidei in illo symbolo edito sub Innocentio III in Concilio Lateranensi *Firmiter credimus* etc. . . . Et breviter, quidquid ibi dicitur esse credendum, tenendum est esse de substantia fidei, et hoc post istam declarationem solemnem factam ab Ecclesia" IV Sent., d. 11, q. 3, *Questiones in liber quartum sententiarum* (Opus Oxoniense) *Opera omnia* 8 (Lyons: Laurentius Durand, 1639, rpt. Hildesheim: Georg Ohlms, 1968) 618–19. See McCue, "The Doctrine of Transubstantiation," 405–06, but also David Burr, *Eucharistic Presence and Conversion in Late Thirteenth-Century Franciscan Thought*, (Philadelphia: The American Philosophical Society, 1984) 92.

22. Burr, *Eucharistic Presence and Conversion*, 91–93, has a very intriguing discussion on this point of which I will quote only a part: "Thus two different factors would seem to coalesce in the formation of Scotus' more 'positivistic' approach. On the one hand, emphasis upon divine freedom leads to emphasis upon the contingency of the divinely instituted order, which in turn leads to greater emphasis upon revelation as opposed to natural theology. On the other hand, a critical evaluation of the 'proofs' provided by previous theologians leads to a greater awareness of the insufficiency of these 'proofs' which in turn leads to a similar emphasis upon revelation as opposed to natural theology."

23. McCue, "The Doctrine of Transubstantiation," 409.

24. Ibid.

25. "[Luther's] question was whether the Church should, indeed whether it can, require as a sine qua non of communion the confession of a doctrine that is neither necessary nor important." Ibid., 429, cf. 412–17.

26. Ibid., 417–28. McCue is arguing against the contention of the modern theologian, Edward Schillebeeckx, who argues that Trent saw transubstantiation as a necessary corollary to an assertion of the Real Presence.

27. Ibid., 430

28. Ibid., 403–07. The discussion by Burr, *Eucharistic Presence and Conversion*, 76–98, is much preferable. See also idem, "Scotus and Transubstantiation," *Medieval Studies* 36 (1972) 336–50.

29. "Quia tamen determinatio Ecclesiae est in contrarium, sicut patet *Extra, De Summa Trinitate et fide catholica* et *De celebratione missarum*, et communiter omnes doctores tenent oppositum, ideo teneo quod non remanet ibi substantia panis sed illa species, et quod illi coexsistit corpus Christi," lib. 4, q. 8, *Questiones in librum quartum sententiarum, Opera philosophica et theologica* 8 (St. Bonaventure, N.Y.: Editiones Instituti Francescani Universitatis S. Bonaventurae, 1984) 139–40.

30. "Secunda est communis opinio omnium theologorum, quam teneo propter determinationem Ecclesiae et non propter aliquam rationem. Unde

dicit Innocentius tertius, *Extravagantes: De Summa Trinitate et fide catholica, Firmiter,* sicut allegatum est in praecedenti quaestione, quod corpus Christi continetur sub illis speciebus, transsubstantiatis pane in corpus et vino in sanguinem potestate divina," Quodlibet 4, q. 30 in *Quodlibeta septem, Opera philosophica et theologica* 9 (St. Bonaventure, N.Y.: Editiones Instituti Francescani Universitatis S. Bonaventurae, 1980) 449–50. The editor dates this quodlibetal to 1323, see p. 38*. For a more detailed discussion of Ockham's theology, see David Burr, "Quantity and Eucharistic Presence: The Debate from Olivi through Ockham," *Collectanea Franciscana* 44 (1974) 5–44.

31. *Tractatus de corpore Christi,* cap. 6, e.g., "Dico tamen quod substantia panis non manet, sed desinit esse et sub illis speciebus incipit esse corpus Christi," *Opera philosophica et theologica* 10 (St. Bonaventure, N.Y.: Editiones Instituti Francescani Universitatis S. Bonaventurae, 1986) 99–101. The editor dates this work 1323/4, p. 27*. The matter is further complicated by the fact that Scotus and Ockham rejected the third of Peter of Capua's alternatives, and accepted the second. It is only later on in both their discussions that it becomes clear that they understand Peter's second alternative in the medieval sense of "transubstantiation" and so felt free to adopt a form of the substitution theory. Again, the best explanation of this appears in the articles of Burr cited above.

32. On the dating of this work, see James Weisheipl, *Friar Thomas D'Aquino: His Life, Thought and Work* (Washington, D.C.: The Catholic University of America Press, 1974) 343, and the *DMA* 4:313–14. For a discussion of Durand's theology, see Kenneth Plotnick, *Hervaeus Natalis, O. P. and the Controversies over the Real Presence and Transubstantiation* (Munich: F. Schoningh, 1970) esp. 15–19.

33. "Sed quia hic modus non debet teneri de facto cum ecclesia determinaverit oppositum, quae non praesumitur errare in talibus, ideo tenendo de facto aliam partem respondendum est ad argumenta quae sunt in contrarium." *In IV libros sententiarum,* l. IV, dist. 9, q. 1, n. 15. Durand of Saint-Pourçian, *D. Durandi a Sancto Porciano, . . . in Petri Lombardi sententias theologicas commentariorum libri IIII* (Venice: Guerraea, 1571, rpt. Ridgewood, N.J.: Gregg Press, 1964) fol. 318vb; McCue, "The Doctrine of Transubstantiation," 411. Cf. Allix's use of Durand, *Determinatio,* 36–37, 41–42.

34. "Unde semper, salvo meliori iuditio, non videtur mihi quod ante determinationem sanctae matris ecclesiae, quam superius recitavi, ista opinio fuerit haeretica reputanda. Nec scio aliquem qui post illam determinationem istam opinionem asseruerit, nisi Ioannes Parisiensis ordinis praedicatorum qui posuit paneitatem remanere ne accidentia in isto sacramento essent sine subiecto: propter quod, ut dicitur, excommunicatus fuit per episcopum Parisiensem." *Thomae ab Argentina, . . . Commentaria in IIII. libros sententiarum, . . .* (Venice: Officina Stellae, Iordanus Ziletti, 1564, rpt. Ridgewood, N.J.: Gregg Press, 1965) fol. 93va. See McCue, "The Doctrine of Transubstantia-

tion," 411–12. For the dating of Thomas's work, see D. Trapp, "Thomas v. Straßburg," *LThK* 10, cols. 147–48.

35. *Commentaria in IIII. libros sententiarum,* fol. 93ra.

36. "Quia vel ista opinio supponit conversionem panis in corpus Christi, vel sic ponit annihilationem, quod negat hiusmodi conversionem. . . . Si secundo modo, tunc auctoritates sanctorum, et determinatio sanctae matris ecclesiae non minus sunt contra istam opinonem, quam contra primam. Ex quo sequitur, quod sicut opinio praecedens non est asserenda ab aliquo catholico, sic nec ista." Ibid. fol. 94ra-b. Since Ockham, and later Biel, insisted that the form of substitution theory they espoused was a theory of *conversio,* these theologians would not fall under Thomas's condemnation.

37. "Substantia panis materialis et similiter substantia vini materialis remanent in sacramento altaris." Denzinger, *Enchiridion,* n. 1151. See also n. 1152: "Accidentia panis non manent sine subiecto in eodem sacramento." Cf. McCue, "The Doctrine of Transubstantiation," 412.

38. "In primes an post consecrationem sit in altari verum corpus Christi et non substantia panis materialis neque vini." The list of questions is published and discussed by Anne Hudson, *Lollards and Their Books* (London: Hambleton Press, 1985) 125–39. A second list of questions contains the following: "An corpus sic confectum sit in altare terrestri corpus Christi naturale et non panis naturalis neque vinum." Ibid., 135. Dr. Hudson contends that this list was actually used, and that similar questions were asked of Lollards in other places in England. I want to thank Dr. Thomas Goodman of the University of Miami for this reference. Cf. also the "Interrogationes Wyclifitis et Husitis proponendae" of Martin V, nos. 16 and 17. "16. Item, utrum credat, quod post consecrationem sacerdotis in sacramento altaris sub velamento panis et vini non sit panis materialis et vinum materiale, sed idem per omnia Christus, qui fuit in cruce passus et sedet ad dexteram Patris. 17. Item, utrum credat et asserat, quod facta consecratione per sacerdotem, sub sola specie panis tantum, et praeter speciem vini, sit vera caro Christi et sanguis et anima et deitas et totus Christus, ac idem corpus absolute et sub unaqualibet illarum specierum singulariter." Denzinger, *Enchiridion,* nos. 1256–57.

39. *Quaestiones super libros sententiarum cum quibusdam in fine adjunctis* (Strassburg 1490, rpt. Frankfurt: Minerva, 1968) n. p.; lib. 4, q. 6. "Ideo aliter describo transsubstantiationem et dico quod est successio immediata duarum rerum non habentium communem materiam, vel subiectum quarum posterior est substantia quam incipit de per se, vel principaliter esse ubi alia res totaliter desinit esse." Francis Oakley, *The Political Thought of Pierre d'Ailly: the Voluntarist Tradition* (New Haven: Yale University Press, 1964) 10, dates this work 1377–78. Gabriel Biel held a similar opinion to that of d'Ailly, see Jorissen, *Entfaltung,* 57–58.

40. "Sciendum est quod licet catholici concordaverint in hoc quod corpus Christi vere et principaliter est in sacramento sub speciebus panis et vini sive

ubi apparent species, tamen sicut recitat magister distinctio xi et glossa *de cele-bratione missarum, cum marte,* circa modum ponendi fuerunt diverse opinones," *Quaestiones,* lib. 4, q. 6.

41. The entire passage reads: "Quarta opinio et communior est quod substantia panis non remanet sed simpliciter desinit esse. Cuius possibilitas patet quia non est deo impossibile quod illa substantia subito desinat esse quamvis non esset possibile creata virtute. Et licet ita esse non sequatur evidenter ex scriptura nec etiam videre meo [*sic*] ex determinatione ecclesie quia tamen magis favet ei et communi opinioni sanctorum et doctorum ideo teneo eam. Et secundum hanc viam dico quod panis transsubstantiatur in corpus Christi ad sensum expositum in descriptione transsubstantiationis." Ibid.

42. "Some time ago, when I was studying scholastic theology, I was greatly impressed by Dr. Pierre d'Ailly, cardinal of Cambrai. He discussed the fourth book of the *Sententiae* very acutely, and said it was far more likely, and required the presupposition of fewer miracles, if one regarded the bread and wine on the altar as real bread and wine, and not their mere accidents—had not the church determined otherwise. . . . I adopted this view, because I saw that the opinions of the Thomists, even though approved by pope and council, remained opinions still, and would not became articles of faith even if decreed by an angel from heaven." *The Babylonian Captivity of the Church* in John Dillenberger, ed., *Martin Luther: Selections From His Writings* (Garden City, N.Y.: Doubleday, 1961) 265. Cf. McCue, "The Doctrine of Transubstantiation," 414–15.

43. *"sub speciebus:* Et ita albedo, rotunditas et alia accidentia sunt ibi sine subiecto et hoc miraculose, uel sunt in aere. vin[centius]. *panis et uini:* cum aqua, *extra iii. de celebrati[one]. missar[um]. Cum Marthe":* García y García, *Constitutiones Concilii,* 288. The teaching that the species existed supported by the substance of the surrounding air was the teaching of the School of Abelard, see Macy, *Theologies,* 114–18. I have filled in the abbreviations by providing the missing text in parentheses. I will use this format for all the canonical texts cited in this paper.

44. *Thomae de Chobham summa confessorum,* F. Broomfield, ed. (Louvain, Paris: Editions Nauwelaerts, 1968) XL–LXII.

45. "Est autem sciendum et firmiter credendum quod post confectionem corporis et sanguinis domini nulla remanet substantia panis, nulla substantia vini, sed sola accidentia, scilicet sapor et color, et illa per miraculum, vel sunt sine omni subiecto, vel sunt in aere circumposito, nec homo ibi videt vel tangit vel gustat aliquam substantiam sive materiam panis et vini, sed tantum accidentia, et per miraculum ex illis solis accidentibus posset pasci et nutriri homo." *Summa confessorum,* 121.

46. On the formation of this text, see Stanley Chodorow, "Decretum," *DMA* 4:128–30; idem, "Law, Canon: after Gratian," *DMA* 7:413–17; Kenneth Pennington, "Huguccio," *DMA* 6:327–28; A. M. Stickler, "Bartholomaüs v. Brescia," *LThK* 2, col. 11; idem, "Benecasa," *LThK* 2, col. 200, and J. Gründel,

"Johannes Zemecke (Semeca) Teutonicus," *LThK* 5, cols. 1091–92. The edition of the *glossa* which I was able to consult was printed in Venice in 1584 and also contains material by the canonist Benedictus de Benedictis who wrote ca. 1420. Identification of the authors of the various glosses is possible, however, since glosses on the text are ascribed to different canonists by use of abbreviations: "Io" is used for Johannis Teutonicus, and "Bar" for Bartholomew of Brescia. Two other abbreviations appear as well. "H" or "Hug" for Huguccio, a canonist writing ca. 1188–98 who is much quoted by Johannes, and "Ben," an ambiguous abbreviation which might stand for Benecasa, a late twelfth-century canonist often quoted by Bartholomew or Benedictus, the fifteenth century canonist. Unmarked passages are assumed to be from the original gloss of Johannes.

47. See Chodorow, "Law, Canon: after Gratian."

48. On the dating of this work, see Thomas Aquinas, *Expositio super primam et secundam decretalem ad Archidiaconum Tudertinum,* H.-F. Dondaine, ed., *Opera omnia* 40 (Rome: S.C. de Propaganda Fide, 1969) E38.

49. On Henry of Susa and his works, see Elisabeth Vodola, "Hostiensis," *DMA* 6:298–99, and Clarence Gallagher, *Canon Law and the Christian Community: The Role of Law in the Church According to the Summa Aurea of Cardinal Hostiensis* (Rome: Universitas Gregoriana, 1978) 21–45.

50. See Chodorow, "Law, Canon: after Gratian," as well as Paul Ouliac, "Bernard de Parme," *DDC* 2: cols. 781–82.

51. On Innocent IV and his works, see Vodola, "Innocent IV," *DMA* 6:465–67. The edition of this work I used was *Innocenti Quarti pont. maximi super libros quinque decretalium* (Frankfurt: Sigismudus Feierbent, 1570, rpt. Frankfurt: Minerva, 1968).

52. *Decretales D. Gregoriani IX,* Lib. III, tit. 41, *De celebratione missarum,* c. 6, *Cum Marthae,* Emil Friedberg, ed., *Corpus Iuris Canonici* (Graz: Akademische Druck- u. Verlagsanstalt, 1959) 2, cols. 638–39. Part of Innocent's letter was copied directly from his *De sacro altaris mysterio* written before he became pope. Cf. *PL* 217: 878D.

53. "*In sacramentorum* [c. 1] . . . De eo tamen quod dicitur quod panis convertitur in corpus Christi variae sunt opiniones. Una asserit quod illa substantia quae fuit panis primo postea est caro et sanguis Christi; argumentum infra eadem. *panis est in altari* [*de consecratione,* II, c. 55] et c. *quia corpus* [c. 35]. Secunda opinio tenet quod substantia panis et vini ibi desinit esse et remanent accidentia tantum, scilicet sapor, color, pondus, et similia, et sub illis accidentibus incipit ibi esse corpus Christi. Tertia tenet quod remanet ibi substantia panis et vini et in eodem loco et sub eadem specie est corpus Christi. argumentum infra eadem *ego* [c. 42] Quelibet tamen opinio fatetur ibi esse corpus Christi. Secunda opinio verior est, ut extra *de summa. trinitate, firmiter* [c. 1] ¶ *una*" *Decretum Gratiani emendatam et notationibus illustratum una cum glossis* (Venice: n.p., 1584) col. 2504.

54. Jorissen, *Entfaltung,* 29–30, cites this passage to show that the glossators accepted a variety of opinions, and that they preferred the substitution theory.

55. "*Sunt.* [c. 34 *Species et similitudo*] id est. retinent et ita vox interitu rei non amittit significationem, liceat res pereat. Et hic est argumentum contra eos qui dicunt substantiam panis et vini ibi esse post consecrationem quia non convertuntur in corpus Christi ut dicunt. Sed contra eos est infra eadem. *nos autem* [c. 41] et c. *panis* [c. 55]. Sed exponunt quia antea fuerunt sola, sed modo non sunt sola, quia ibi iam latet corpus Christi. Alii dicunt quod desinit sibi esse panis et vinum sed differunt nam quidam dicunt ipsa mutari et converti in corpus Christi, alii in nihilum redigi vel in primordialem materiam resolvi. Istis utrisque obiicitur de forma, sapore, colore et aliis accidentibus in quo subiecto sunt. Et eorum quidam dicunt quod in aere, alii esse sine subjecto miraculose nam cedit natura miraculo. Extra. *de celebr[atione] mis[se] cum Marthe* ¶ i" *Decretum Gratiani.,* col. 2523.

56. "*Convertuntur.* Bene dicit convertuntur vel transubstantiantur ut alii transeunt vel transeant, sed non fiunt nec incipiunt. Nihil enim fit vel incipit esse corpus Christi. Potest tamen concedi quod de pane conficiatur vel fiat corpus Christi sicut de aqua fit crystallus, non tamen est crystallus, sed securius non conceditur hoc et ubicumque invenitur panis vel de pane fit vel conficitur corpus Christi, sic intelligatur, id est transit in corpus Christi, ut infra eadem *panis* [c. 39]. . . . Non intelligas ergo quod aliquod augmentum sumat ex tali conversione, nec eo modo quo cibus convertitur in carnem, sed est ibi corruptio, id est desinit ibi esse substantia panis et vini, nulla tamen generatio. Unde potest dici quod sit ibi vera transubstantiatio quantum ad hoc ut nova essentia ibi generetur." Ibid., col. 2525.

57. "Determinabat autem eam sic: Id quod fuit panis etc. convertitur, transformatur, transsubstantiatur in corpus Christ; cum enim omnia verba communionis admittantur, ut transsubstantiatur convertitur et huiusmodi, transsubstantiatum ut est vel erit vel fuit non admittitur, ne tanquam ex materia fieri credatur ut avis ex ovo, ita enim panis convertitur in corpus, ut non sit verum hoc: erit illud, vel ex hoc tamquam ex materia fiet illud." Johann Friedrich von Schulte, *Stephan von Doornick, Die Summa über das Decretum Gratiani* (Giessen: E. Roth, 1891, rpt., Aalen: Scienta Verlag, 1965) 274. Stephan wrote ca. 1166; see Schulte, *Die Summa,* 9–19.

58. See text in n. 56 above. Cf. also "*Significatur.* [c. 40 *Ante benedictionem*] Et licet verba successive proferantur, non tamen successive consecratio fit, sed in uno instanti corrumpitur panis, scilicet in ultimo instanti prolationis verborum. Et licet panis fit corpus compositum, momentanea est tamen eius corruptio, secundum eadem *quia corpus* [c. 35] verbis. *ergo*" *Decretum Gratiani,* col. 2529.

59. "*In terram* [c. 27 *Si per negligentiam*] Id est in tabulam terrae adhaerentem ut patet per capitulum sequens. Sed nunquid sacramento cadente cecidit ibi corpus et sanguis? Dic quod sic et tamdiu credas ibi esse corpus et sanguinem quamdiu apparuerint ibi accidentia. Cum vero propter rasuram

non apparuerint, dic ibi non esse." Ibid., col. 2520. "*sacramentum*. [c. 55 *Panis est in altare*] Dum panis est nullum est ibi sacramentum quia nihil significat. Sed cum incipit transire in corpus Christi statim species panis incipit significare corpus Christi et esse sacramentum. Cum autem nihil significaret, tunc non erat sacramentum, non tamen panis vel sacramentum vel corpus Christi consecratur precibus, sed in sacramentum quod est corpus Christi panis sit transubstantiatio." Ibid., col. 2542. "*Adoraverit* [c. 92 *Accesserunt Iudei*] Argumentum hic quod mus non potest accipere corpus Christi. Argumentum contra infra eadem *qui bene* [c. 94] sed statim desinit esse." Ibid., col. 2571.

60. "*Miscere*. [c. 23 *Tribus gradibus*] Sed nec species ille aliis cibis permiscentur, non enim in stomachum descendunt quare per secessum non emittuntur. Licet enim ex ipsis aliquis reficiatur, non tamen incorporantur nec in stomachum descendunt nec per secessum emittuntur. Interdum enim odore recreatur homo qui tamen nec in stomachum nec in secessum dirigitur. Dici potest quod species bene descendunt in stomachum nam aliter quando evomerentur, infra eadem *si quis per ebrietatem* [c. 28] unde forte per sudorem emittitur de corpore. Certum est quod species quam cito dentibus teruntur, tam cito in celum rapitur corpus Christi." Ibid., col. 2517. See also text in n. 59 above.

61. "*Comederit*. [c. 94 *Qui bene*] Nec dicendum quod mus sumat corpus domini, statim enim desinit esse sacramentum ex quo ab eo tangitur. Si tamen dicatur quod sumat non est magnum inconveniens cum sceleratissimi homines illud sumant. Sed B[enecasa? Benedictus?] non concedit quod ab eo sumi possit, immo statim desinit esse sacramentum. Sed iterum non posset consecrari, quia non est ibi iam panis, immo tantum species. Sed numquid desinit esse sacramentum si transit super illud corpus mus vel aranea? Non credo quod desinat esse sacramentum." Ibid., col. 2572. This opinion concerning reception by the wicked was held by Honorius Augustodunensis, based on a story of Cyprian of Carthage. For references, see Gary Macy, "Berengar's Legacy as Heresiarch," reprinted as the fourth essay in this volume.

62. On the differences between the theology of Albert and Thomas, and that of Alexander and his followers, see Burr, *Eucharistic Presence and Conversion*, but also Gary Macy, "Reception of the Eucharist According to the Theologians: A Case of Diversity in the 13th and 14th Centuries," reprinted as the third essay in this volume.

63. ". . . tamen in scientia sacramentorum non multum attendenda est sententia decretistarum quia pro certo multa falsa de cordibus vel talibus scribunt et dicunt, eo quod sunt homines ignari in sacram scriptura, nescientes originalia sanctorum, nec possunt non peccare docentes in fide Catholica quae ignorant," *De corpore domini*, dist. 3, tr. 3, c. 1, n. 2, B. *Alberti Magni*, . . . *Opera omnia* 38, A. and E. Bognet, eds. (Paris: Vives, 1899) 307. See Jorissen, *Entfaltung*, 47, note 145.

64. "De corpore autem Christi tres sunt opiniones. Una dicit quod illa substantia quae prius fuit panis et vinum, postea sit corpus et sanguis; *de conse[cratione]* dist. 2, *panis est in altari* [c. 55] et c. *quia corpus* [c. 35]. Secunda asserit quod remanet ibi substantia panis et vini, et in eodem loco et sub eadem specie est corpus et sanguis Christi; argumentum. *de consec[ratione]* dist. 2, *ego* [c. 42]. Tertia dici, quod substantia panis et vini desinit ibi esse; transsubstantiatur enim in corpus et sanguinem, et tantum accidentia ipsorum ibi remanent, scilicet sapor et color et pondus, et sub illis speciebus, id est accidentibus, est corpus Christi; infra titulus 1, *cum Marthae* [c. 6] ¶ *quaesivisti*. Et hanc tertiam videtur comprobare concilium generale, secundum *de summa trinitate* ca. 1 ¶ *una est* et Innoc[entius] III infra titulus 1, *cum Marthae* [c. 6] ¶ *verum inter opiniones*. Quaelibet autem istarum fatetur verum corpus esse in altari. Sed est alia quarta pessima opinio, quae astruere nititur, non esse in altari corporis et sanguinis veritatem sed imaginem tantum et speciem et figuram et haec reprobatur; infra titulus i *cum Marthae* [c. 6] ¶ *ex eo.*" *Summa Aurea Henrici de Segusio Cardinalis Hostiensis Summa Aurea* (Venice: Iacobus Vitalis, 1573, rpt. Turin: Bottega d'Erasmo, 1963) liber 3, *De consecratione ecclesiae vel altaris*, col. 1183.

65. The entire passage reads: "Dicit autem *sub speciebus panis et vini* ad excludendum errorem quorundam qui dixerunt quod in sacramento altaris simul continetur substantia panis et substantia corporis Christi, quod est contra verbum Domini dicentis, «Hoc est corpus meum», esset enim secundum hoc magis dicendum «Hic est corpus meum», ut ergo ostendat quod in hoc sacramento non remanet substantia panis et vini sed solum species, id est accidentia sine subiecto, dicit *sub speciebus panis et vini*" *Expositio super primam et secundam decretalem ad Archidiaconum Tudertinum*, E38, col. 2.

66. Cf. "Dicit autem *veraciter* ad excludendum errorem quorundam qui dixerunt quod in hoc sacramento non est corpus Christi secundum rei veritatem, sed solum secundum figuram sive sicut in signo." Ibid.

67. "*Veraciter* . . . Circa hoc tamen tres sunt opiniones. Nam quidam dicunt quod illa substantia que prius fuit panis et vinum, desinit esse; *de cons[ecratione]* di. 2, *panis est in altari* [c. 55] et c. *quia corpus* [c. 35] Secundum quod ille substantie transsubstantiantur et remanet color et sapor sub illis accidentibus et corpus et sanguis Christi et istam tene. Tertii dicunt quod remanet substantia panis et vini et sub eadem specie est corpus Christi; *de conse[cratione]*. di. 2, *ego* [c. 42]. Et quilibet istorum asserunt corpus verum esse in altari. Quarti asserunt in sacrament altaris non esse corporis et sanguinis veritatem. Hoc reprobatur *de cel[ebratione] mis[se], cum Marthe* [c. 6], ¶ *quesivisti*. Opinio vero secundarum ibi approbatur et hic ut sequitur." *In Primum Decretalium librum Commentaria Henrici de Segusio Cardinalis Hostiensis . . . In Primum Decretalium Librum Commentaria* (Venice: Ivntas, 1581, rpt., Turin: Bottega d'Erasmo, 1965) fol. 6va.

68. "In prima vero opinione omnes catholici conueniunt, scilicet quod illa substantia, quae prius fuit panis et vinum, postea fit corpus et sanguis. Ita tamen ut hoc quid dicit fit, notet conuersionem. Omnia enim verba quae notant conversionem vel transubstantiationem, proprie hic ponuntur, ut si dico panis transubstantiatur in corpus Christi, haec est vera. Item si dico convertitur vel mutatur." *In Tertium Decretalium librum Commentaria, Henrici de Segusio Cardinalis Hostiensis . . . In Tertium Decretalium Librum Commentaria,* . . .Venice 1581, rpt. Turin, 1965, fol. 163ra.

69. "Secunda etiam opinio catholica est." Ibid.

70. "Secundum Vin[centium] ita quod panis esse desinit et corpus Christi succedat. Si quaeritur quid de substantia panis et vini fiat? Dicunt quod in praeiacentem materiam resolvitur vel in nihilum rediguntur, quod potest ille facere qui de nihilo cuncta creavit. Hanc vero quidam reprobant, dicentes quod si quis induatur vestibus alterius non ideo dicitur converti vel transire in illum cuius vestes induit. Tamen et haec videtur approbari secundum *de summa Tri[nitate]* c. 1, in fine." Ibid.

71. "*Transubstantiatur* Et haec vera est et ita desinit ibi esse species panis et vini," ibid., fol. 163va.

72. "*Sanguinis veritatem* De corpore Christi tres sunt opiniones. Una dicit quod illa substantia quae prius fuit panis et vinum, postea fit corpus et sanguis Christi; *de conse[cratione]* dist. 2 *panis in altari* [c. 55] et c. *quia corpus* [c. 35]. Secunda tenet quod substantia panis et vini desinit esse et tantum accidentia ipsorum remanent, scilicet sapor et pondus et sub illis accidentibus est corpus Christi. Et hoc approbatur secundum *de summa trinitate et fide cath[olicae],* c. 1. Tertia dicit quod remanet substantia panis et vini et sub eadem specie est corpus Christi. Io[hannis]" *Decretales D. Gregorii Papae IX. suae integritati una cum glossis restitutae* (Rome: Populus Romani, 1582) col. 1370.

73. *The Persecution of Peter Olivi* (Philadelphia: The American Philosophical Society, 1976).

74. Quoted in Burr, *The Persecution,* 31.

75. Ibid., 55.

76. Ibid., 57.

77. Quoted ibid., 59.

78. Ibid., 8–9.

79. Ibid., 67.

80. The entire passage reads: "Vides ergo quod illa evasio magnam absurditatem contra phylosophiam ponit, et veritati quam tenet sancta ecclesia de sacramento altaris derogat cum firmissime tenet sancta ecclesia et firmiter debemus tenere cum ea, quod in sacramento altaris remanet per divinam potentiam quantitas, sine substantia panis et vini, haec etiam quantitas panis sine substantia panis et quantitas vini sine substantia vini," Quolibet 2, art. 2, q. 2, *Quolibeta Doctoris eximii Ricardi de Mediavilla . . . Quaestiones octvaginta* (Brescia: Vincenzo di Sabbio, 1591, rpt. Frankfurt: Minerva, 1963) 50, col. 2.

For a more thorough discussion, see David Burr, "Quantity and Eucharistic Presence: The Debate from Olivi through Ockham," *Collectanea Franciscana* 44 (1974) 22–23. I have used Burr's translation of this passage.

81. I am basing myself on the summary of previous scholarship given by Fredrick Roensch, *Early Thomist School* (Dubuque: Priory Press, 1964) 98–104, but see also Plotnick, *Hervaeus Natalis,* 57, and Martin, "The Eucharistic Treatise."

82. P. Glorieux, "Un mémoire justificatif de Bernard de Trilia," *Revue des sciences philosophiques et théologiques* 17 (1928) 408. Glorieux has wrongly ascribed this text to Bernard of Trilia. The change in attribution in favor of John Quidort was made by Glorieux himself, and is widely accepted, see J. P. Muller, "À propos du mémoire justificatif de Jean Quidort," *Recherches de théologie ancienne et médiévale* 19 (1952) 343–51.

83. The copy of John's *Commentaria super sententias* which has survived in Paris, Bibliothèque Mazarine, MS 889. The discussion of this question in fol. 83va supports his contention that he copied the teaching of Thomas Aquinas.

84. The entire passage reads: "*Quod albedo sine quantitate esset visibilis actu, quia esset extensa quadam extensione effecta ab extensione quantitatis, sicut apparet de vase et aqua, sigillo, etc. Item huiusmodi albedo esset visibilis, etiam dato quod non esset extensa, et hoc non actione sed aptitudine.*—Hoc duos articulos quandoque investigando tetigi, scilicet primo libro, et etiam in quarto libro ubi quesivi: utrum in sacramento altaris sint accidentia sine subiecto; et modum inquisitionis mee vidi in reportatione fratris N. et aliorum fratrum 4. Sed tandem totam illam inquisitionem retractavi expresse dicens quod circa illam hoc solum teneretur quod Deus potest facere accidentia sine subiecto et albedinem sine quantitate, et animam extra corpus. Cetera vero in duobus articulis continentur, dixi in scolis quod nolebam tenere sed volebam pro non dictis haberi; quod patet in reportatione de Sancto Vic[tore] super 4." Glorieux, "Un mémoire justificatif," 412–13. Here John is being somewhat disingenuous; e.g., "Propter quartum, scilicet, color in isto sacramento si separaretur a quantitate esset visibile." *Commentaria,* Bibliothèque Mazarine, MS 889, fol. 84vb.

85. For a thorough discussion of this issue, see Plotnick, *Hervaeus Natalis,* 19–25.

86. E.g., "ut substantia panis maneat sub accidentibus suis, non in proprio supposito, sed tracta ad esse et suppositum Christi, ut sic sit unum suppositum in duabus naturis: et sic est verum substantiam panis manere sub suis accidentibus in sacramento altaris." Martin, "The Eucharistic Treatise," 215, ll. 23–26.

87. See ibid., 203–05. William of Auxerre had argued that the human Jesus had an accidental relationship to the Word in a similar fashion. See Walter Principe, *William of Auxerre's Theology of the Hypostatic Union* (Toronto: Pontifical Institute of Mediaeval Studies, 1963).

88. "Dico quod imo sit festum de Impanatione, sicut in die Coenae." Martin, "The Eucharistic Treatise," 222, ll. 308–09.

89. "Panis etiam est transsubstantiatus, vel conversus in corpus Christi" ibid. 220, ll. 232–33. See also 221, ll. 274–79.

90. Ibid. 218, ll. 140–78; 220, ll. 226–35; 221, ll. 263–79. The *Determinatio* ends with a summary which includes the following: "Dicit tamen quod nullus est determinatus per Ecclesiam, et idcirco nullus cadit sub fide, et si aliter dixisset, minus bene dixisset, et qui aliter dicunt, minus bene dicunt. Et qui determinate assereret alterum praecise cadere sub fide, incurreret Sententiam Canonis et Anathematis." Ibid., 225.

91. Roensch, *Early Thomist School,* 144, n. 198, and Étienne Gilson, *History of Christian Philosophy in the Middle Ages* (N.Y.: Random House, 1955) 731–32.

92. "Ad hec dicendum quod magister in littera recitat opinionem illorum qui ponunt quod substantia remanet cum corpus Christi. Sed opinio illorum non stat. Immo error erit dicere," *Commentaria,* Bibliothèque Mazarine, MS 889, fol. 84ra. See also Plotnick, *Hervaeus Natalis,* 57.

93. Plotnick, *Hervaeus Natalis,* ibid.

94. "Et licet teneam et approbem illam solemnem opinionem, quod corpus Christi est in sacramento altaris per conversionem substantiae panis in ipsum, et quod ibi maneant accidentia sine subjecto; non tamen audeo dicere quod hoc cadat sub fide mea; sed potest aliter salvari vera et realis existentia corporis Christi in sacramento altaris." Martin, "The Eucharistic Treatise," 214, ll. 5–8.

95. Gilson, *History of Christian Philosophy,* 413.

96. Martin, "The Eucharistic Treatise," 196–97; Roensch, *Early Thomist School,* 100.

97. Ibid.

98. David Burr, "Ockham, Scotus, and the Censure at Avignon," *Church History* 37 (1968) 144–59.

99. Roensch, *Early Thomist School,* 100.

100. Quoted by Margaret Aston, "Wyclif and the Vernacular," Studies in Church History, Subsidia 5, *From Ockham to Wyclif* (Oxford: B. Blackwell, 1987) 313. On the question of what the clergy and laity were expected to know about the Eucharist, see Miri Rubin, *Corpus Christi: The Eucharist in Late Medieval Culture* (Cambridge: Cambridge University Press, 1991) 83–129.

101. "Atque in hunc modum Innocentius tertius per excommunicationes, exercitus, rebelliones, carnificinas, et vivicomburia novum fidei suae dogma stabilire voluit," *Historia transubstantiationis,* 151.

102. The entire matter is described in Eymeric's *Directorium inquisitorum.* The condemned articles read: "Primus quod si hostia consecrata cadat seu proiiciatur in cloacam, lutum seu aliquem turpem locum quod speciebus remanentibus sub eis esse desinit corpus Christi et redit substantia panis. Secundus quod si hostia consecrata a mure corrodatur seu a bruto sumatur,

quod remanentibus dictis speciebus sub eis desinit esse corpus Christi et redit substantia panis. Tertius quod si hostia consecrata a iusto vel a peccatore sumatur quod dum species dentibus teritur, Christus ad coelum rapitur, et in ventrem hominis non traiicitur." *Directorium inquisitorum F. Nicolai Eymerici* (Venice: Marcus Antonius Zalerius, 1595) 44a. [For a recent discussion of this incident, see Gary Macy, "Nicolas Eymeric and the Condemnation of Orthodoxy," *The Devil, Heresy, and Witchcraft in the Middle Ages: Essays in Honor of Jeffrey B. Russell*, A. Ferreiro, ed. (Leiden: E. J. Brill, 1998) 369–81.]

103. Nicolas recorded the papal missive, the bulk of which reads: "Miseratione divina Petrus sancti Eustachii et Guillermus sancti Angeli diaconi cardinales reverendis patribus Tarraconensis et Cesaraugustanensis provinciarum., archiepiscopis eorumque suffraganeis necnon inquisitoribus haereticae pravitatis a sede apostolica in ipsis provinciis deputatis, salutem et sinceram in Domino caritatem. Relatione religiosi fratris Nicholai Eymerici magistri in theologia ac in dictis provinciis haereticae pravitatis inquisitoris ad audientiam domini nostri pape nuper pervenit quod tam in vestris quam in suffraganeorum vestrorum ecclesiis palam et publice per certos religiosos predicati fuerunt tres articuli subsequentes in effectu. . . . Idem dominus noster papa nobis ibidem praesentibus vivae vocis oraculo expresse commisit quatenus auctoritate sua apostolica vobis mandaremus ut omnis morae sublato dispendio in dictis vestris provinciis sub poena excommunicationis inhibeatis ne quis deinceps dictos articulos publice praesumat praedicare. Nos igitur Petrus et Guillermus cardinales praedicti huiusmodi mandatum apostolicum cupientes exequi ut tenemur, vobis et vestrum cuilibet in virtute sanctae obedientiae praecipimus et mandamus ne ab inde in antea dictos articulos seu eorum alterum sub eisdem vel aliis verbis idem sonantibus in substantia seu in effectu in vestris ecclesiis vel alibi palam seu publice praedicari a quoquam permittatis et hoc sub pena excommunicationis qua contrarium facienties innodetis ipso facto. Notificantes vobis nihilominus simili mandato per ipsum dominum nostrum papam nobis facto quod idem dominus noster papa fratri Iohanni de Latone ordinis fratrum minorum qui aliquos de dictis articulis in vestris ecclesiis frequenter recitando praedicaverat inhiberi fecit sub poena excommunicationis ne dictos articulos de caetero publice praedicare presumat." Ibid.

104. See Macy, "Reception of the Eucharist," 15–36, as well as nn. 59, 60, and 61 above.

105. Two private repositories of orthodoxy do include these teachings as condemned. Carolus du Plessis d'Argentré, *Collectio iudiciorum de novis erroribus qui ab initio XII saeculi post incarnationem verbi, usque ad annum 1632 in ecclesia proscripti sunt et notati,* 3 vols. (Paris: Coffin, 1724–36) 1, pars 1, p. 390, cols. 1 through 391, col. 2 included this teaching under the year 1371, the date of the papal letter to Nicolas Eymeric. Du Plessis d'Argentré was copied by Denziger, *Enchiridion,* nn. 1101–03.

106. "fra Nicolau Eimeric, que havia d'esdevenir l'inquisidor mès tenaç, mès agressiu i mès dur de tota la història de la Inquisiciò catalana." Eufenià Fort y Cogul, *Catalunya i la Inquisiciò,* (Barcelona: Editorial Aedos, 1973) 87.

107. On Eymeric's life, see André Duval, *DSAM* 9: cols. 277–79; R. Chabanne, *DDC* 6: cols. 1007–09, and Fort y Cogul, *Catalunya i la Inquisiciò,* 87–112.

108. Fort y Cogul, *Catalunya i la Inquisiciò,* 87–102. See also Marcelino Menéndez Pelayo, *Historia de los Heterodoxos Españoles,* 2: *Obras Completas* 26 (Santander: Aldus, 1947) 302–11, 339–44.

109. Jorissen, *Entfaltung,* 56–57, and Allix, *Determinatio,* 77–80. The exact meaning of the teaching of the Council of Trent on the Eucharist is a much debated issue among Roman Catholic theologians. For an exhaustive discussion of this issue, see Josef Wohlmuth, *Realpräsenz und Transsubstantiation im Konzil von Trient* (Frankfurt: Peter Lang, 1975).

110. The extremely interesting question of how such a belief started and why it continues to persist is unfortunately beyond the scope of this paper. The author hopes to present his research on this matter in a future article.

Chapter 6

Demythologizing "the Church" in the Middle Ages[1]

One frequently comes across references in scholarly works to "the Church in the Middle Ages," usually in conjunction with the verbs "taught" or "believed." These statements appear to be made with some confidence that there existed a fairly easily identifiable authority which can be consulted to ascertain what "the Church" taught and believed. Although fairly common and seemingly harmless, the practice in fact carries with it some highly questionable assumptions. This article will explore some of the problems inherent in presuming the existence of such a monolithic "Church in the Middle Ages."

The first and most pestering of these problems would, of course, entail what exactly the expression "the Middle Ages" might mean. The designation is a highly politically charged appellation invented in the nineteenth century, and usually carrying a derogatory implication.[2] This is more true in the United States than in Europe as the new study, *Il medioevo secondo Walt Disney*, by Matteo Sanfilippo, points out.[3] As important as an exploration of the expression might be, I can do no more than mention it.

A related and equally prickly issue involves *who* exactly "the Church in the Middle Ages" might be. The phrase is often accompanied by a footnote which refers the reader to either a theologian (usually Thomas Aquinas), or to some legislation (ranging from the decree of a universal council—e.g., Lateran IV—to an episcopal letter). One might infer then that the views of theologians, or of a particular theologian (i.e., Thomas Aquinas), embody "the teaching of the Church." The difficulty with this approach lies in the obvious disagreement between generations of theologians and even among theologians who were contemporaries. There seems to be no apparent reason why we should pick Thomas Aquinas as the embodiment of "the teaching of the Church" over any of this contemporaries, such as Bonaventure, or over any of the many famous theologians of other generations, such as Alexander of Hales or Duns Scotus. Yet these four theologians, for example, held very different opinions on central issues such as the Real Presence of Christ in the Eucharist.[4] Of course, the obvious reason why a modern scholar might choose Thomas Aquinas over the aforementioned theologians is because Thomas received the endorsement of the Council of Trent as an authority for the council's particular form of Roman Catholicism. This argument in favor of Aquinas creates a whole new and interesting set of problems, however, since this would imply a strange form of anachronism in which Reformation claims determine the identity and orthodoxy of the medieval Church.

A second possibility might be that any or some ecclesiastical legislation represents "the Church." Again this solution simply raises more problems. What weight should each form of legislation be given: the validity intended by its authors, or the validity understood by its recipients, or that interpretation favored by the scholars of Bologna (when, if ever, they reached a consensus on that interpretation)? Again, to appeal to later interpretations of such laws as "definitive" (such as the interpretation given to the Fourth Lateran Council by the Council of Trent) would involve the same sort of anachronism raised in regard to the theologians, especially in those cases where contemporaries either did not accept such decrees as definitive or disagreed among themselves about such a designation. Contemporaries, for instance, did not understand the Fourth Lateran Council to have "defined" transubstantiation by the inclusion of that term in the opening creed. From the fourteenth century on, however, a growing number of theologians did so understand this council, and certainly the majority of post-Tridentine writers assumed such a definition was indeed intended. Which interpretation is therefore determinative of "the teaching of the Church": that of the contemporaries of Lateran IV, or that of some fourteenth-century theologians, or that of post-Tridentine polemicists?[5]

The more closely one investigates the issue the harder it becomes to identify reliable *loci* for "the teaching of the Church" in the Middle Ages. The problem, I would suggest, stems from the underlying assumption that "the Church" in the Middle Ages had a cohesive self-understanding on behalf of which certain voices could speak. When one investigates the understanding Christians themselves had of their own "Church," one is struck with a diversity of opinions on the subject which coexisted in the Middle Ages.

HOW THE MEDIEVAL THEOLOGIANS SAW "THE CHURCH"

The phrase, "the Church" when it appears in the late Middle Ages, however, was often ambiguous and largely depended on context. When not referring to a local ecclesiastical authority, the term meant different things to different people. The extensive studies of the understanding of "the Church" during this period point out the difficulties. The broadest and most popular definition of "the Church" in the twelfth and thirteenth centuries was based on that of Augustine. "The Church" consists of all just people from Abel until the end of time; in short "the Church" refers to all saved people. Augustine (and his medieval followers) specifically included in this Church "just" people who were not Christians, and specifically excluded unjust people who were within the institutional boundaries of Western Christianity. This mystical, spiritual Church was the real Church; the Church which would be finally known only in heaven. It was, nevertheless, an operative reality in the Middle Ages. It was always an open question whether individual heretics, Muslims, Jews, or even Greeks might be, in fact, more truly a member of "the Church" than their orthodox Christian contemporaries.[6] Dante could, then, describe the pagans Trajan and Ripheus, now in heaven as *"non gentili, ma christiani."*[7] Pope Nicholas III, meanwhile, burns in hell and awaits his fellow pontiff, Boniface VIII.[8]

Of course, given this description of "the Church," the warning that "there is no salvation outside the Church" becomes merely tautological and hardly a threat. The point is an important one. The context in which claims for "the Church" are made become as important as the claims themselves. Certainly medievalists are not free to read an institutional understanding of the Church into any passage which makes claims about the necessity of membership in the Church for salvation. To quote Avery Dulles in his summary of the ecclesiology of Thomas Aquinas,

"St. Thomas does not speak of subjection to the pope and the bishops, or of acceptance of the dogmas and disciplinary regulations of the Church, as positive constituents of membership [in the Church]. These conditions come into his discussion only negatively or indirectly, when he is treating of heresy, schism, and excommunication. For Saint Thomas a rejection of Church doctrine or law might involve the sin of heresy or schism, and for that reason sever or weaken the bonds of communion. Inculpable dissidence would not result in loss of membership or communion."[9]

Yves Congar, upon whose research Dulles's study of Thomas is based, makes the further point that what one says about St. Thomas "is equally true of St. Bonaventure, Alexander of Hales, Albert the Great and the other scholastics of that epoch. Excluding some certain delicate distinctions which do not affect the general structural outlines, all these scholastics offer the same ecclesiology as St. Thomas. In short before the 'first treatises on the Church,' no other method was known."[10]

Extreme caution should be urged, then, in the use of medieval authors in justifying claims about the medieval ecclesiastical structure. When medieval writers speak of "the Church," most likely they do not have in mind any earthly institution at all.[11]

Finally, and perhaps most importantly, Christians throughout most of their history would not identify "the Church" with the hierarchy and in fact would vehemently reject such an identification. According to Avery Dulles in his classic study of the different ways in which Christians have viewed the Church, the identification of "the Church" with the institution was and is a "deformation of the true nature of the Church." Further, this particular understanding of the Church arose out of particular historical situations. Again to quote Dulles,

"Catholic theology in the Patristic period and in the Middle Ages, down through the great Scholastic doctors of the thirteenth century, was relatively free of institutionalism. The strongly institutionalist development occurred in the late Middle Ages and the Counter-Reformation, when theologians and canonists, responding to attacks on the papacy and hierarchy, accented precisely those features that the adversaries were denying. . . . The institutional outlook reached its culmination in the second half of the nineteenth century, and was expressed with singular clarity in the first schema of the Dogmatic Constitution on the Church prepared for Vatican Council I."[12]

The identification of "the Church" with the hierarchy and its official pronouncements was fully developed only after the Middle Ages.

Not that medieval writers were uninterested in the "Church militant," that is, the Church on earth. Indeed, most of the great debates of the Middle Ages involved conflicts over authority within this Church.

In the late Middle Ages, in particular, claims for control of ecclesiastical governance became more strident.[13] Certainly one of the groups claiming ultimate authority for the Church militant during this period did argue for papal supremacy. The Dominican Cardinal Juan de Torquemada, who wrote his *Summa de ecclesia* in 1453, is generally credited with setting the pattern for a full-blown defense of papal authority; but even he was aware of earlier definitions, listing sixteen different meanings for *ecclesia* ranging from a reference to the hierarchy alone to a reference to all the faithful.[14]

But if Cardinal de Torquemada offered the papacy as the ultimate authority for Christians on earth, other writers had other ideas. Dante, and the polemicists of Philip the Fair championed the notion that the ecclesiastic and secular governments were autonomous authorities within Christianity.[15] William of Ockham postulated a freedom of the individual conscience over against either ecclesiastical or secular authority.[16] John Wyclif (who died within the institutional Church) held that only the just have legitimate authority within the Church, a position also held by John Hus (who was burned as a heretic).[17] The conciliarists offered yet another alternative—that a general council of the Church took precedence over either pope or king.[18] Marsilius of Padua weighed in with still another famous alternative, placing the civil authority over the ecclesiastical authorities even in matters of faith and morals.[19]

In short, what Brian Tierney described as the situation at the beginning of the fourteenth century became even more confused as time went on and led inexorably to the split of Western Christianity during the Reformation.

"At the beginning of the fourteenth century the whole field of Catholic ecclesiology was in a state of considerable disarray. Theologians were not certain whether Scripture was the sole fount of revealed truth or whether Tradition also was a source of divine revelation. The old doctrine of indefectibility was giving way to a different theory of ecclesiastical inerrancy, but this had not yet been given any clear, definitive expression; it could be twisted in different ways, either to attack the public institutions of the visible church or to exalt them more than ever before. The proper structure of ecclesiastical institutions—the right form of government for the church—was again a matter of vigorous debate, with no agreement in sight. Conciliarists were attacking the principle of papal sovereignty. Dominicans, seeking to defend the papacy, were deploying Scriptural arguments that were bound to offend influential sections of the episcopate, and that were very vulnerable to attack from traditionally-minded theologians. Franciscans were developing a theory of papal power that, although it was couched in deferential terms, could hardly in the long run be acceptable to the popes themselves."[20]

Alongside the formal claims for authority by pope, council, and king came other less organized, but no less potent claimants to the voice of "the Church." Theologians made up what was described in the thirteenth century as a "third force," a counterweight to that of priesthood and empire.[21] Jo Anne McNamara, in her excellent article on the role of women in the struggle against heresy, demonstrates that women clearly felt that they had authority within the Church given to them often directly by the Holy Spirit.[22] Catherine of Siena claimed even more, asserting that she was an apostle, anointed with the Holy Spirit as surely as were the original apostles at Pentecost. It would be hard to deny that she did not at times exercise that authority even over the pope.[23] Penelope Johnson expresses clearly the authority women could claim (and achieve), in her recent study of religious women in medieval France:

"If we posit that medieval women in general accepted their role in patriarchal society, religious women still often challenged the authority of their male superiors. The high birth of some nuns, like Agnes of Barbezieux, helped to create a climate in which assertive behavior seemed natural. But the presence of some noblewomen does not explain the common experience of the rank and file of nunneries which routinely jockeyed with prelates over issues of control. . . . By becoming participants in the church's liturgy and life, by belonging to the church more completely than was possible for any secular person—female or male—nuns collectively were empowered by their communal privileges and status to think and act with self-confidence."[24]

To reply that neither theologians nor women held any "official" authority within "the Church" appears to be the same sort of anachronistic mistake made when historians claim a privileged voice for

Aquinas (himself a mere theologian) in the Middle Ages. The question of who spoke for "the Church" and what "the Church" might be were the very issues under dispute at the time, and thus to pick one of the groups as "the (official) Church" prejudges the legitimate claims of the others.

In any case, not all the Christian groups which emerged from late medieval Christianity denied or denigrated the authority assumed by some theologians and some women in medieval Christianity. The groups that did not deny this authority would seem to have just as legitimate a claim to the inheritance left by the outspoken theologians and women of late medieval Christianity as those who presently seek to discredit or silence their voices.

What conclusions can be drawn, then, from this rather straightforward recitation of the struggles over authority in the late Middle Ages? First, it seems wildly unfair to identify "the Church in the Middle Ages" or "the teaching of the Church in the Middle Ages" with only one medieval group, that of the papists. This is to silence the others, to deny them their claims to be valuable and authentic voices of "their Church" (to use the poignant phrase of Professor McNamara). To prejudice the claims of one group while the struggle is still on seems to me to be both historically inaccurate and politically suspect.

And this second issue brings me to my other point. It is extremely interesting to identify those who get excluded from "the Church" when "the Church" is limited to the definition of the papal claimants. Most noticeably, of course, women—who certainly considered themselves part of the Church, and believed themselves to have authority within that Church—would be excluded by such a definition. I have not yet come across a sentence which reads "The Church in the Middle Ages taught . . ." which cites Catherine of Siena as a reference, and yet she is considered a "doctor" (i.e., a definitive teacher of "the Church") even by the most conservative of the descendants of the late medieval Church, the Roman Catholic papacy.

It is not just women, however, who would no longer belong to "the Church." Neither would practitioners of popular devotion, nor would any layperson, nor even would kings and princes count as "the Church," at least in the sense that what they believed or taught or practiced should be considered as "the Church." Indeed, they are portrayed most often by modern historians as subjects or even adversaries of "the Church." How odd that would seem to the medieval opponents of the papal theorists!

Disputes which are often portrayed as struggles between "the Church" and some other group would have been understood by contemporaries more as struggles between different authorities *within* the Church. Jeffrey Burton Russell makes this point eloquently when describing the contending claims of hierarch and heretic in his many studies on medieval heresy. The struggle between pope and king, between bishop and pope, between popular devotion and theologian, between heretic and orthodox might be better expressed as struggles within the Church over authority rather than struggles between "the Church" and some outside group.[25]

A PROCESS OF MARGINALIZATION

Equally interesting in this mix is *who* is doing the excluding and *why*. If the studies by Dulles and Congar (cited at the opening of this paper) are correct, those twentieth-century medievalists who define "the Church" as the hierarchy are doing so based on criteria developed by the defenders of the Tridentine Church and perfected by the nineteenth-century ultramontanists. In short, they are describing late medieval Christianity as if it were the Roman Catholic Church, just as the cardinals of Vatican I would have envisioned it. Gavin Langmuir, to give but one example of a modern historian who makes this erroneous conflation, asserts that "When medieval historians speak of the Church instead of the Roman Catholic Church, they may only be engaging in a convenient ellipsis, but their language echoes the assumption expressed as dogma by Pope Boniface VIII in 1302: 'We are bound to believe and to hold, our faith urging us, that there is one holy Catholic and Apostolic Church.'"[26]

Now, of course, there is a sense in which referring to late medieval Christianity as "Roman" and "Catholic" is quite correct. Western Christianity was focused upon Rome as a source of unity, and the papacy did claim a growing authority in later centuries of the Middle Ages. The term "Catholic" also applies, if used in its original Greek sense of "universal" as opposed to a local or national church. But twentieth-century American readers do not usually use these terms in these ways. "Roman Catholic" refers in ordinary parlance to that group of Christians who remained in communion with the papacy in the sixteenth century and who continue to do so to the present day. And it is this more modern sense of "Roman Catholic" to which those medievalists who use the expression seem to be referring. It was the fathers at the Council of Trent, for example, who declared Thomas

Aquinas to be an authority for their Church, and it was the nineteenth-century papacy that encouraged the study of Thomas's theology. However, Thomas had no such standing in the Middle Ages and, therefore, to appeal to his teaching as that of "the medieval Church" only makes sense in light of the later history of Roman Catholicism.

Professor Langmuir, again to give but one example, would appear to define "Roman Catholic" in terms of even more recent history, that of the more extreme forms of ultramontane nineteenth- and early twentieth-century Roman Catholicism:

"Whatever the ultimate source of Catholic beliefs, an adherent of the Roman Catholic religion is one who obeys the commands of the Roman Catholic Church in which ultimate authority, treated in practice as infallible, and legally so defined since 1870, belongs to the pope. If any important question as to what or who is Catholic arises, the judgment must be ratified explicitly or tacitly by the pope. . . . Reference to the authority of God aside, the ultimate criterion, in theory if not in practice, of what Catholicism is and who is a Catholic at any given moment is the decision of the pope, and a Catholic is one who accepts that authority."[27]

Many Roman Catholics (including some popes) would, and have, rejected such an understanding of their beliefs.[28] Such a definition would represent but one *extreme* theory of ecclesiastical governance in late medieval Christianity. To speak of the medieval Church as Roman Catholic, in this modern sense, seems oddly anachronistic.

Since all of the traditions of the Reformation emerged from the late medieval confusion that was Western Christianity, and not just that group which emerged from the reforms of the Council of Trent, it would seem more historically accurate to reserve the designation "Roman Catholic" for this latter form of Christianity (while also realizing that even within this tradition there are varying opinions as to the role of the papacy and of the hierarchy).

THE MIDDLE AGES AND ROMAN CATHOLICISM IN THE UNITED STATES

If some medievalists are, often uncritically and even unintentionally, describing the late medieval Church as if it were nineteenth-century ultramontanist Roman Catholicism, the question remains why they do so. Matteo Sanfilippo's study of perceptions of the

Middle Ages in the United States suggests one possible and disturbing element in the solution of this enigma.[29]

Sanfilippo points to two major strands in U.S. thought about the Middle Ages. On one hand, the Middle Ages represent much of what the U.S. believes to have rejected in its revolution from England—ignorance, religious oppression, and the tyranny of feudal lordship. The U.S. views itself, in fact, as the polar opposite of medieval Europe, a utopia created by freedom, frankness and the ingenuous use of technology. This theme Sanfilippo sees exemplified in Mark Twain's *A Connecticut Yankee in King Arthur's Court* and in his *Innocents Abroad*. The word "medieval" is still used in this sense, in common parlance, as equivalent to "brutal, or superstitious, or ignorant."[30]

On the other hand, the Middle Ages were also seen in the United States of the nineteenth century as the forebear of democracy. But the founders of the democratic tradition were not the Mediterranean peoples of the former Roman Empire, but the Teutonic barbarian tribes. This tradition was introduced into the United States, according to Sanfilippo, with the influential *History of the United States* written by George Bancroft between 1831 and 1874. In his history, "in the face of the pretenses of a tyrannical king, the descendants of the Pilgrim Fathers rose up and finally realized the reign of liberty on earth, ideally concluding the process begun by the Germanic barbarians."[31]

According to Sanfilippo, these two general strands in U.S. thought about the Middle Ages, one represented by Twain and another by Bancroft, continue to influence the views on the Middle Ages in the United States, both at the scholarly level and at the level of mass culture. In neither strand, however, does the medieval Church fare well. On one hand, it is the tyrannical guardian of superstition, standing against enlightened science and technology; and on the other, it is the main opponent of democracy.

Americans thus began to think of the medieval Church as a ruthless, monolithic institution, united in thought and action by a united hierarchy. Quite apart from the analysis by Sanfilippo, the reasons for such a perception are easily identifiable. The post-Reformation propaganda of both Romans and Protestants made precisely this claim. For Romans, the one true Church had always and everywhere agreed on the fundamental dogmas proclaimed at Trent (although some periods might have had a better doctrinal understanding than others), thus preserving a unified voice down through the centuries. For Protestants, that medieval invention—the Roman Curia—used its totalitarian powers to ruthlessly enforce its heretical will. This mythology suited equally well the anticlerical agendas of the Enlightenment and of the nineteenth century. In this scenario, religion—especially institutional religion—presented a unified opposition to science, education and any form of liberation.[32] According to the "Disney" version of this myth, "It was the Dark Ages and men's minds were dark" (. . . and going to stay that way if the Church had anything to say about it).[33]

The United States in the nineteenth century was Protestant and revolutionary, and Roman Catholic immigrants became the enemy. The Reformation and Enlightenment vision of the ruthless and merciless "papist Church" particularly suffused and empowered the nativist propaganda directed against the influx of mostly Roman Catholic immigrants.[34] This picture is clearly painted in the widely read English anti-Catholic writer, Walter Walsh:

"Looking abroad throughout the whole world, we find that Popery degrades the nations, instead of raising them to a higher level. The ritualists cannot point to a single Roman Catholic country which is even on a level with, much less superior to, Protestant countries. On the contrary, Popery has dragged down Spain from her proud eminence, to be the most degraded and poverty-stricken nation in Europe, excepting Turkey. It has kept the South American republics and nations in a state of degradation, immorality, and ignorance deplorable to behold. Would any Englishman wish this Protestant country to become what the Papal States were under the temporal rule of Pope Pius IX? Would English working men wish to exchange wages with their brethren in any Roman Catholic country in the world? Every part of Ireland is under the same government. Why, then, is it that the Roman Catholic portions of that unhappy land are those in which more poverty, dirt, disloyalty, and ignorance are to be found, than in the Protestant portions? The answer to this question must be that the religion of Popery is at the bottom of this marked difference."[35]

The nativists in the U.S. were quick to follow Walsh's lead. One such tract from 1912 entitled *America's Menace* features a cover with a bloody hand inscribed "Papism" reaching out for the innocent Statue of Liberty (with no good intent, one suspects). With "scientific" and impressive economic statistics, similar to those of the proponents of California's recent Proposition 187, the tract's authors "prove" that Roman Catholics are the poor, uneducated, lazy, and superstitious dupes of their Church. Roman Catholics are, in short, medieval.[36]

Sanfilippo points out, for instance, that it became extremely important in the nineteenth century to prove that the medieval Vikings, not Columbus, discovered America, since Columbus was "Italian, Catholic and in the service of Spain" while the Vikings were the ancestors of the Nordic democratic and Protestant world.[37]

It is from this thought-world that medievalists draw when they unwittingly and uncritically paint "the medieval Church" as a "Roman Catholic" monolith. Thanks to the work of some modern historians, summarized in Edward Peters' *Inquisition*,[38] this central symbol of the ruthless "Church in the Middle Ages" has begun to be demythologized. This process has much farther to go, I would suggest, because the picture of a ruthless, totalitarian Church in the Middle Ages is historically inaccurate, as I hope I have indicated here. Furthermore, as we in the Southwest are all too well aware, since the majority of today's immigrants into the United States are still Roman Catholic, still largely poor and uneducated, they are still subject to vicious anti-Catholic propaganda. To quote the conclusion of Stephen Vicchio's article, "The Origins and Development of Anti-Catholicism in America":

"The contemporary discussions in the 1980s of what some officials in the national government call the 'Mexican immigration problem' gives one cause to wonder if we are not sitting on the edge of yet another version of American nativism. And where there is nativism, as we have seen, there is often anti-Catholicism."[39]

Medievalists should not, even unintentionally, provide aid and comfort to this form of bigotry.

WHAT IS NOT BEING SAID

To make the case as I do in this article can easily be misunderstood and, therefore, I want to be very clear as to what I am *not* saying here. First of all, by arguing that late medieval Christianity was more complex than some medieval historians admit, I am not suggesting that there was no "Church" in the late Middle Ages. There certainly was a quite distinct clerical culture with its own set of laws and rituals, which even some contemporaries referred to as "the Church." Clearly this expression is an important category for studying that institutional phenomenon in the late Middle Ages (and in other time periods). But just as clearly, some other groups within the Church held greater power, and these too were often referred to by their contemporaries as "the Church." What I am advocating is a recognition that references to "the Church" are a form of shorthand, and that more careful nuancing and respect for the different groups within late medieval Christianity would give a truer picture of its diversity.

Second and more importantly, I am not saying that the evil perpetrated by certain groups within late medieval Christianity become any less vicious by denying that those groups exhausted the meaning of "the Church." Individuals and institutions acting in the name of Christianity could be very cruel indeed, and a growing bureaucracy within the hierarchy (and within secular government) became less and less tolerant of diversity as the Middle Ages progressed, as Robert Moore recently pointed out in his study, *The Formation of a Persecuting Society*.[40] No fewer people would die, no fewer lives would be destroyed, no fewer people would be displaced, no less suffering would take place if historians were more careful when ascribing blame for such actions to particular groups within late medieval Christianity rather than making sweeping condemnations of "the Church" or Christianity. Furthermore, condemnations of such tyranny should be no less firm as they become more precise. To honor the claims to Christianity made by those opposed to such cruelty, or by those who were the victims of that cruelty, does not mean that historians are not obligated to analyze and condemn the aspects of Christianity which were used to justify the institutions perpetrating the tyranny.

Thirdly, I am not claiming that medievalists (or others) who refer to "the Church" as a monolithic organization in the Middle Ages are the least sympathetic to the anti-immigrant, nativist agenda. This essay does not purport to establish any direct historical link between Reformation and Enlightenment anti-Roman propaganda and the present approach to the medieval Church on the part of contemporary historians, although I am strongly suggesting that this link would be an interesting topic for further research.

What I am proposing is that references to "the Church" in the Middle Ages, especially when "the Church" is designated as Roman Catholic, can be perceived as supporting two very different contemporary political agendas. First, such references can be perceived as supporting those within the Roman Catholic Church who make the most extreme claims for papal power. While of concern mostly to Roman Catholics, this can be very annoying to those within that community who do not accept such extreme assertions. Secondly, the very same references can be perceived to support the anti-Catholic agenda of the anti-immigrant movement. Of course, one of these groups proclaims the benefits of an ostensible fourteen hundred years of papal monarchy, while the other fears and decries that monarchy, but both welcome references to (understood as historical support for) a monolithic and strictly hierarchical "Church" in the Middle Ages.

Finally, any Christian community which wishes to claim the late medieval Church as an important part of its tradition, and certainly Roman Catholicism would make such a claim, must also accept the historical burden of the intolerance and cruelty of those groups which acted in the name of Christianity during the late medieval period. The rejection and repudiation of those actions should come all the more strongly from groups, like the Roman Catholics, who wish to retain an historical link with this period.

However, the same caveats apply to present Roman Catholicism as apply to late medieval Christianity. For example, some groups within Roman Catholicism wish to continue to deny full membership in that Church to women (at least the majority of the hierarchy), while others reject and condemn this practice (at least the majority of theologians). This means that one cannot simply claim that the Roman Catholic Church holds that women should not be ordained. The hierarchy at the moment may refuse to do so but, despite its claims, the hierarchy does not exhaust Roman Catholicism and a significant part of the Roman Catholic Church actively opposes this decision of the hierarchy. Furthermore, those within Roman Catholicism, and those outside of it, should not refer to the views of the majority of the hierarchy simply as the views of "the Church," merely because the hierarchy insists that this is the case. The claims of absolute power sometimes made by the hierarchy are not (and were not) always accepted by all Roman Catholics. Roman Catholics do not have to accept such claims to remain Roman Catholics. As Avery Dulles (among many others) points out, such institutional claims are actually a perversion of a proper understanding of "Church" within Roman Catholicism itself.[41]

SOME TENTATIVE CONCLUSIONS

If the arguments as laid out in this essay are substantially sound, then a number of interesting implications for modern Catholic theology, and especially Hispanic/Latino theology seem to follow. First, and most obviously, this essay suggests that research into the history of the mythology developed in the United States about the "Roman Catholic" Church in the Middle Ages would demonstrate how such a mythology gradually marginalized Hispanic/Latino groups. The connection is simple. If the Church in the Middle Ages was tyrannical, corrupt, and immoral, and the Church in the Middle Ages was (and is) Roman Catholic, then Roman Catholics are immoral, corrupt, and tyrannical. Hispanics, as Roman Catholics, can (therefore) be expected to be devious, immoral, lazy, technologically underdeveloped, and ignorant. The quoted texts cited earlier should suffice to make the point.[42]

Less obviously, a broader and more historically accurate reading of late medieval Christianity would not only allow long silenced voices to speak on behalf of "their Church," but also open up the possibility of a more diverse reading of present-day Roman Catholicism. If Roman Catholics wish to claim late medieval Christianity as their heritage, then surely, they should also claim its diversity. Today's hierarchy may wish to make large and growing claims for their authority, but that represents but one (albeit important) voice within Roman Catholicism. Professor Orlando Espín has argued eloquently against the reduction of Roman Catholicism to its Euro-American and post-Tridentine forms:

"Most theologians have (inaccurately) taken for granted, and their social scientific colleagues have agreed, that Latino popular religion is usually coextensive with popular Catholicism and, worse still, that the latter is certainly a 'popularized' version of *Roman* Catholicism. Furthermore, theologians (as social scientists had before them) have also uncritically taken the post-Reformation and post-Enlightenment operative definitions of 'Church,' of 'Roman Catholicism,' of 'Protestantism,' of 'religion,' and of 'western medieval Christianity,' as sufficiently and substantially correct."[43]

Espín would argue that Latino popular Catholicism is better understood on its own terms as a cultural expression independent of, but in dialogue with, both Tridentine or Euro-American Roman Catholicism.[44] The present diversity within U.S. Catholicism, of which Latino popular Catholicism is perhaps the largest component, is better explained as the result of the antecedent diversity of western medieval Christianity than as a perversion of a reified (and imaginary) monolithic Tridentine establishment.

In conclusion, then, the assumed identification which medievalists tend to make between late medieval Christianity and post-Tridentine Roman Catholicism presents several problems. First, it appears to unfairly represent the diversity of this rather chaotic period in the history of Christianity. By allowing a broader understanding of "the Church" during this period, a number of hitherto excluded voices can be reintroduced as authoritative into the tradition of Christianity. Secondly, certain anachronisms (such as references to Thomas Aquinas as an official spokesperson for "the medieval Church") can be more easily avoided. Finally, and most tentatively, it would seem that at least one factor which influences historians when speaking of a unified "Church" in the later Middle Ages is the mythology about this Church which arose in the Reformation and became very influential in the United States during the nineteenth century.

If, as most historians of late medieval Western Christianity claim, there was no unified perception of what constituted, or even who spoke for, "the Church," then medievalists (and others) should take care when referring to hierarchy, theologians, or canon lawyers during this period as speaking for "the Church." Sloppy or careless history is never acceptable, but when it can be perceived to justify questionable or even vicious political agendas, it should not be tolerated.

---

1. Originally published in the *Journal of Hispanic/Latino Theology*, 3 (1995) 23–41, this essay won the Essay Award of the College Theology Society for 1995. Preliminary discussions of this topic were contained in papers delivered at a summer meeting of the Ecclesiastical History Society, held in Nottingham, England (July 21, 1994), and at the conference "Reinventing the Middle Ages and the Renaissance," held at the Arizona Center for Medieval and Renaissance Studies, Arizona State University (February 18, 1995). The first of these papers was published as the essay, "Was there a 'the Church' in the Middle Ages?," *Unity and Diversity in the Church*, Robert Swanson, ed., Studies in Church History 52 (Oxford: Blackwell, 1996) 107–16.

2. The most detailed and interesting discussion of the origins of the use of the expression "Middle Ages" is found in the yet unpublished study by Robert M. Stein, in his "Medievalisms and the Structure of the Middle Ages: An Inquiry into Some Principles of Historiography," read at The Medieval Academy of America's annual meeting (April 2, 1993) in Tucson, Arizona.

3. *Il medioevo secondo Walt Disney. Come l'America ha reinventato l'Età di Mezzo* (Rome: Castelvecchi, 1993). See especially chapter one, "Un'età brutale e corrotta?," 15–38.

4. For the details of this disagreement, see my "Reception of the Eucharist According to the Theologians: A Case of Diversity in the 13th and 14th Centuries," published as the third essay in this volume.

5. The issue is discussed in my "The Dogma of Transubstantiation in the Middle Ages," published as the fifth essay in this volume.

6. ". . . enfin, que tous les justes, même ceux de l'Ancien Testament, même ceux du paganisme, appartiennent à un seul peuple, à une même cité, a un même corps: l'Eglise." Y. Congar, "Ecclesia ab Abel," *Abhandlungen über Theologie und Kirche. Festschrift für Karl Adam* (Dusseldorf, 1952); rpt. in *Etude d'ecclésiologie médiévale* (London: Variorum reprints, 1983) 2:83.

7. *Paradiso,* canto 20, vv. 67–70, 103–05.

8. *Paradiso,* canto 19, vv. 53–87.

9. "The Church According to Thomas Aquinas," A. Dulles, *A Church to Believe In* (N.Y.: Crossroad Publishing Co., 1982) 157.

10. Y. Congar, "The Idea of the Church in St. Thomas Aquinas," *The Mystery of the Church: Studies by Yves Congar,* A. V. Littledale, trans. (Baltimore: Helicon Press, 1960) 98.

11. "Être sauvé, être du Christ, être de l'Eglise: ces trois termes ne constituent qu'une unique affirmation," Y. Congar, "Ecclesia ab Abel," 92.

12. *Models of the Church,* expanded ed. (Garden City, N.Y.: Doubleday & Co., Inc., 1987) 36.

13. Y. Congar, *L'Eglise de Saint Augustine à l'époque moderne* (Paris: Ed. du Cerf, 1970) 270–71, n. 2, identifies over twenty-five tracts written on state/papal relations between 1280–81 and 1376–77.

14. T. Izlicki, *Protector of the Faith. Cardinal Johannes de Turrecremata and the Defense of the Institutional Church* (Washington: The Catholic University of America Press, 1981). A. Dulles says (in his "The Church According to Thomas Aquinas," 164): "Cardinal Juan de Torquemada (1388–1468), whose *Summa de ecclesia* set the pattern for many centuries, greatly admired Saint Thomas but put the accent far more on the external, visible features. Cardinal Robert Bellarmine (1542–1621), polemicizing against the Protestants, gave still greater emphasis to the juridical."

15. "The two swords signified a dualism *(dualitas)* of the powers. Dualism meant the autonomy of the lay power; the pope had no power over the emperor. Two-swords doctrine taught the co-operation of the powers, not the jurisdictional superiority of the spiritual power. This principle, which we may very properly call dualistic, since that was Henry IV's own word, continued to be asserted and justified by Frederick Barbarossa, Frederick II, the polemicists of Philip the Fair, and Dante, champion of Henry VII. Its echoes rumbled on in the later middle ages, occasionally, as with the pen of William of Ockham, finding a new burst of vitality," J. A. Watt, "Spiritual and Temporal Powers," *The Cambridge History of Medieval Political Thought c. 350–1450,* J. H. Burns, ed. (Cambridge: Cambridge University Press, 1988) 372.

16. "Ockham's insistence that legitimate political power be exercised only over free persons, while supported by Aristotle's distinction between political and despotic rule, was inspired above all by the idea of liberty in the New

Testament. Authority which robbed people of the spiritual liberty given by Christ could not be legitimate; and an authority which demanded that they believe or behave contrary to Scripture or reason was doing precisely that. In other words, the supremacy of the individual conscience flowed from Ockham's interpretation of the New Testament. In him the Church–state controversy inspired an original statement of individual rights. None of this should surprise us, coming from an ardent follower of St. Francis and a diligent reader of the New Testament; and it would be hard to deny that the spirit of philosophical nominalism was blowing here too." A. Black, *Political Thought in Europe 1250–1450* (Cambridge: Cambridge University Press, 1992) 77. For a different interpretation of Ockham's thought, see B. Tierney, *The Origins of Infallibility* (Leiden: Brill, 1973) 235–36: "In the end Ockham's conclusions were simply perverse. He wanted the institutional church to crush error while denying that any church institution could certainly define the truth. He offers us only dogma without order, anarchy without freedom, subjectivism without tolerance."

17. See, for example, A. Black, *Political Thought in Europe*, 79: "Wycliff held that the only human group that had spiritual significance was the true church, consisting exclusively of those predestined to salvation, 'the community of the just.' It alone had a legitimate claim to spiritual authority. But, since no one except God knew who these persons were, this group is unrecognizable, and therefore non-institutional. What is commonly called 'the church'—the clergy, bishops and papacy and the identifiable community of baptized Catholics—is but an institution of human contrivance with no divine sanction." On Hus's basic agreement with Wyclif, cf. Steven Ozment, *The Age of Reform, 1250–1550* (New Haven: Yale University Press, 1980) 165–70.

18. For an overview of conciliar theories, see, for example: A. J. Black, "What was Conciliarism? Conciliar Theory in Historical Perspective," *Authority and Power: Studies on Medieval Law and Government Presented to Walter Ullmann on His Seventieth Birthday,* B. Tierney and P. Linehan, eds. (Cambridge: Cambridge University Press, 1980) 213–25. For the theory of a representative of the conciliarists, cf. T. E. Morrissey, "Franciscus Zabarella (1360–1417): Papacy, Community, and Limitations upon Authority," G. F. Lytle, ed. *Reform and Authority in the Medieval and Reformation Church* (Washington, D.C.: The Catholic University of America Press, 1981) 54: "Perhaps the clearest way to describe Zabarella's system is to say that no matter what body was called to act, whether the pope, the bishops, cardinals or a council, it had to act with the authority given to it according to the divine plan. It had to act with a structured and rational authority *(potestas ordinata)* and so any notion of absolute power *(potestas absoluta)* was denied to every human person or institution and even the very claim or mere appearance of a claim to any such absolute power had to be avoided. In the end Zabarella's scheme was that of a jurist or lawyer who thought in terms of a corporation, that is of groups of people

bound together by inescapable ties and relationships. These very ties embodied duties and obligations that had to be respected, for if this ordered system could be disregarded by any member or combination of members, then the whole system was endangered and this would be subversion of the state of the Church which was never to be allowed."

19. "With the correct identification of the lawful sovereign, Marsilius removed pope and clergy from jurisdiction in civil affairs. There was a second consequence of this identification: the lawful sovereign was also the sole authority in ecclesiastical affairs, beginning with the definition of the Bible. The lawful sovereign, the whole body of the citizens *(universitas civium)* reappears as the whole body of the faithful *(universitas fidelium)* or, more pertinently, as the general council of believers *(generale concilium credentium),"* J. A. Watt, "Spiritual and Temporal Powers," 420.

20. *The Origins of Infallibility,* 170.

21. "Les théologiens ont formé ainsi une sorte de troisième Pouvoir, à côté du sacerdoce et de l'Empire, un peu comme les moines l'avaient fait par moments. L'idée est deveue un lieu commun dans la trilogie Sacerdotium, Imperium, Studium dont le Haut Moyen Age présente quelques antécédents, qu'Alexandre de Roes systématise (1281) et qui est même officiellement admise," Y. Congar, *L'Eglise de Saint Augustine,* 243.

22. "The Rhetoric of Orthodoxy: Clerical Authority and Female Innovation in the Struggle Against Heresy," *Maps of Flesh and Light: The Religious Experience of Medieval Women Mystics,* U. Weithaus, ed. (Syracuse, N.Y.: Syracuse University Press, 1993) 9–27.

23. See K. Scott, "'Io Catarina': Ecclesiastical Politics and Oral Culture in the Letters of Catherine of Sienna," *Dear Sister: Medieval Women and the Epistulary Genre,* K. Cherewatuk and U. Wiethaus, eds. (Philadelphia: University of Pennsylvania Press, 1993) 87–121, esp. 111–12.

24. *Equal in Monastic Profession: Religious Women in Medieval France* (Chicago: University of Chicago Press, 1991) 99–100.

25. Most recently, see J. B. Russell, *Dissent and Order in the Middle Ages: The Search for Legitimate Authority* (N.Y.: Twayne Publishers, 1992). On a similar understanding of Church/state relations in the late Middle Ages, see, for example, A. Black, *Political Thought in Europe,* 43–44: "The church–state dispute was about where the boundary lay, and about who, if anyone, had authority to say where, in a disputed case, it lay."

26. *History, Religion and Antisemitism* (Berkeley: University of California Press, 1990) 65. I chose Professor Langmuir's study because, unlike most medievalists, he carefully defines the terms he uses in speaking of medieval religion. He has also spent most of his career as an outspoken opponent of any form of prejudice and would certainly never intentionally misrepresent any religious or cultural group.

27. *History, Religion and Antisemitism,* 137.

28. The most obvious recent example being the Dogmatic Constitution on the Church *(Lumen gentium)* from the Second Vatican Council.

29. A much more detailed examination of the influence of nineteenth-century thought on contemporary presentations of late medieval Christianity than either Sanfilippo or this essay can present would be necessary to explain fully the present approaches to that subject. The following discussion is intended only as a starting point for further study.

30. *Il medioevo*, 15–38.

31. Ibid., 41. For the entire discussion, cf. 39–58.

32. In the words of the influential study by A. White, *A History of the Warfare of Science with Theology*, 2 vols. (N.Y.: D. Appleton and Company, 1900) 2:65–66: "In summing up the history of this long struggle between science and theology, two main facts are to be noted: First, that in proportion as the world approached the 'ages of faith' it receded from ascertained truth, and in proportion as the world has receded from the 'ages of faith' it has approached ascertained truth; . . ." On the continuing importance and influence of White's work, cf. the Introduction to *God and Nature: Historical Essays on the Encounter Between Christianity and Science*, D. Lindberg and R. L. Numbers, eds. (Berkeley: University of California Press, 1987); as well as D. Lindberg, "Science and the Early Church," ibid., 19–22.

33. The quotation comes from the Halloween episode of the television show, "Walt Disney Presents," and was accompanied by a dark and scary "medieval" street scene. On the attitude of Disney productions toward the Church, see Sanfilippo, *Il medioevo*, 108: "Dio non si manifesta, forse non esiste nemmeno nell'universo disneyano, e i suoi rappresentanti sono speso figure comiche, il frate Tuck di *Robin Hood*, o addirittura deteriori, i missionari cristiani del *Drago del lago di fuoco*." Cf. also 103–04.

34. "In secondo luogo, verso la metà del secolo XIX il *nativismo*, scatenato dall'arrivo massiccio di emigrati europei (in particolare irlandesi), focalizza l'odio degli americani bianchi, anglosassoni e protestanti contro i cattolici. Per i nativisti la Chiesa di Roma è il sostegno dell'ingiustizia e sta tentando di riportare tutto il mondo, ivi compresa l'America, ai secoli bui del Medioevo." Sanfilippo, *Il medioevo*, 27.

35. *The Secret History of the Oxford Movement*, 4th ed. (London: Swan Sonnenschien, 1898) 362. The connection between medieval Christianity and modern Roman Catholicism is assumed by Walsh: "If Rome had ceased to be what she once was, we would not bring her past crimes and murders to her remembrance. But in this point, alas! more than in any other, she is *semper eadem*. Her persecuting laws are still the same as when in the Dark Ages her infernal Inquisition performed, unhindered, its bloodthirsty work. The modern authorities of the Church of Rome still glory in the intolerant work of their Church in those days." Ibid., 367. On the influence and importance of

Walsh's work, see W.S.F. Pickering, *Anglo-Catholicism: A Study in Ambiguity* (London: Routledge, 1989) 177–78.

36. "It is estimated that at least seven-eighths of the twenty million inhabitants in Spanish-America, which consists of the countries of Mexico, Cuba, Central America, and the north and west parts of South America, are unable to read, and in Mexico alone, 90 per cent of the inhabitants cannot read or write, neither do they know their alphabet: thus you can see what Roman Catholicism does for the countries which she controls." C. W. Bibb, *America's Menace, or Popery a Political System* (Minneapolis: C. W. Bibb & Co., 1914) 21–22. On the Middle Ages as controlled by the papacy, cf. ibid., 49–50.

37. "In secondo luogo, la possibilità di provare il primato norreno risponde a una richiesta pressante del mondo protestante, che non ama Cristoforo Colombo, perché questi era italiano, cattolico e al servizio della Spagna. Il desiderio protestante oggi può, forse, far sorridere, ma si pensi a quanto già scritto a proposito del movimento nativista e alle fobie anti-cattoliche negli Stati Uniti." *Il medioevo,* 137.

38. (Berkeley: University of California Press, 1989).

39. Published in *Perspectives on the American Catholic Church, 1789–1989,* S. J. Vicchio and V. Geiger, eds. (Westminster: Christian Classics, 1989) 83–103.

40. *The Formation of a Persecuting Society: Power and Deviance in Western Europe, 950–1250* (Oxford and New York: Blackwell, 1987).

41. *Models of the Church,* 198.

42. Even a scholar as sensitive to prejudice as Gavin Langmuir seems to more than hint at the superiority of Euro-American culture as opposed to traditional societies when he argues: "The unparalleled development of rational empirical knowledge in Europe and North America and its application to natural phenomena and many aspects of human conduct challenged or overthrew many traditional beliefs, and those rational doubts reinforced any nonrational doubts people already had about Christianity." *History, Religion and Antisemitism,* 311.

43. "Popular Religion as an Epistemology (of Suffering)," *Journal of Hispanic/ Latino Theology* 2 (1994) 64–65.

44. See "Popular Religion as an Epistemology (of Suffering)," as well as the earlier studies by O. Espín referenced in that article.

Chapter 7

Commentaries on the Mass
During the Early Scholastic Period[1]

INTRODUCTION

From the late eleventh century throughout the twelfth century, and into the early years of the thirteenth century, some two dozen commentaries on the Christian ritual meal, the Eucharist, appeared in Western Christendom. They were not a new phenomena, indeed such commentaries had always had a place in Christian literature and had flourished under the Carolingians. Nor did this genre die out in later centuries, although few new commentaries were written in the late thirteenth or fourteenth centuries.[2]

Still, this set of treatises has several remarkable characteristics. First, the works were extremely popular in their own time, and, secondly, they remain to a large extent, unappreciated by modern scholarship. They remain nevertheless an important witness to a period which marked a turning point in eucharistic devotion. During the twelfth century, stories of miracle hosts proliferated, new forms of devotion, like the elevation of the host, appeared, and in theology the first uses and explanations of transubstantiation made their debut.[3]

It is the way in which the commentaries encode this important change that discourages modern interest, for they are written in an elaborate allegorical style that leaves most moderns cold (and frankly bored). Unfortunately, the most important studies on the commentaries remain the unpublished doctoral theses of Dennis W. Krouse,[4] David F. Wright,[5] Ronald J. Zawilla,[6] Mary Schaefer,[7] and Douglas L. Mosey.[8]

The most extensive published discussion of these works remains that of Adolf Franz, in his book *Die Messe in deutschen Mittelalter*, published in 1902 and reprinted in 1963. The book is a storehouse of strange liturgical customs adopted during the Middle Ages and the author tips his hand early in the work regarding his opinion of medieval worship: "The praxis of the church (during this period) was most often influenced by a distorted and superstitious conception (of the liturgy), dominating both people and clerics."[9] Franz represents only the major voice in a chorus of scholars who decry the commentaries as a stage in the decay in the understanding of the liturgy in which the original meaning of the eucharistic rite was lost under an avalanche of meaningless and disconnected symbolism. F. M. Martineau condescendingly remarked of these works:

"The interest of these little *summae* is not in their exegesis nor in the imagination which gives free rein to the most fantastic interpretations, a naive symbolism which seduced contemporaries, but which today disconcerts a spirit better prepared to appreciate these pious allegories."[10]

Many people, even liturgical scholars, I fear, still perceive the medieval allegorical literature much as James Thurber viewed that epitome of evil, the Todal, in his book *The 13 Clocks:* "(It) smells of old unopened rooms," and "feels as if it had been dead at least a dozen days."[11]

Although space does not allow for a complete analysis of all the works written during this period, a brief overview of the eucharistic devotion described in some of the less well known of the commentaries may hopefully lift the sense of dread with which modern liturgical scholarship has cloaked this genre.[12] In a separate appendix a tentative guide to the commentaries has been provided to those readers willing to brave unopened rooms.

MASS COMMENTARIES

Whatever might be said about Martineau's own dislike for this form of literature, he is quite right in pointing out the popularity of these works among contemporaries. The works appear not only to have survived, but also to have been read and copied. A sermon on the canon of the Mass given at Clairvaux by an unknown Premonstratensian canon named Richard has survived in some sixty manuscripts dating from the twelfth to the fifteenth centuries,[13] while the extremely popular commentaries of John Beleth and Innocent III exist in well over one hundred manuscripts each.[14]

If these commentaries were read, who read them, and to what end were these then captivating allegories produced? The first question is easier to answer than the second. Several of the commentators mention that their works were undertaken by request. Odo, bishop of Cambrai from around 1095 to 1113, wrote his commentary on the canon of the Mass as a favor to Fulgentius, abbot of the Benedictine monastery of Affligem.[15] Isaac, abbot of the Cistercian house at Stella, wrote a similar commentary dated to the years 1162–67 at the request of John, bishop of Poitiers.[16] Honorius Augustodunensis and Gerhoh of Reichersberg both wrote commentaries to answer the demands of the religious of their individual houses.[17] Ivo, bishop of Chartres from 1090 to 1115, and the Premonstratensian Richard both delivered sermons which expounded the allegorical meaning of the Mass; Ivo presumably addressing his clergy at Chartres and Richard delivering his sermon before the monks of Clairvaux.[18]

The works appear for the most part to be addressed to the clergy, diocesan and religious. The fact that the commentaries were written in Latin, and presumed a knowledge of the prayers of the Mass rules out the possibility that these works, at least in the form in which they have survived, were intended for an uneducated audience. Their purpose was not, then, to explain the external ritual of the Mass, something with which the intended audience was presumed to be familiar, but to explain the inner meaning of the outward rituals, the invisible things understood by the visible signs.

John Beleth

The first commentator on the Mass to be studied here, John Beleth, remains a somewhat obscure figure in the history of the schools of the twelfth century. Scholars know only that he was in Chartres ca. 1135, was a student of Gilbert of La Porrée and taught in Paris in the mid-twelfth century. His commentary on the offices of the Church year, *Summa de ecclesiasticis officiis,* was completed between 1160 and 1164. The work was extremely popular in the Middle Ages, and reached a large audience.[19] According to Beleth, his work was intended to explain the offices of the Church to those who heard, but could not understand the words of the services.[20] He seems to have intended his book for clerics, but not necessarily priests.[21] Perhaps the book was written for his students at Paris.[22] Modern scholars have praised Beleth's book for its simple, straightforward, learned style, offering a distinct change from the heavily allegorical commentaries of his predecessors.[23]

Indeed, most of Beleth's commentary on the Mass offers little more than etymologies on the words of the liturgy and a description of the action of the ceremony interspersed with canonical notes. Surprisingly enough, much of his material is borrowed from the allegorical commentary of Honorius Augustodunensis.[24] Unlike many of the commentators, Beleth offers no overall conception of the eucharistic action.[25]

In his commentary on the Offertory, he mentions three things which ought to be offered: first, ourselves; second, those things necessary for the sacrifice, that is, bread and wine; and third, the gifts of the faithful.[26]

The Canon of the Mass is obviously the most important part of the office for Beleth. The section of the Mass from the Secret to the Lord's Prayer is properly called the Mass (proprie missa dicitur).[27] Further, Beleth argues that even the words of consecration themselves can be properly called the Mass.[28] He refuses to comment on the words of consecration, because these words should be known only by the priests.[29] In explaining the silence of the Canon, he offers the traditional story of the shepherds in the early Church who recited the words of consecration over their lunch of bread and wine and were destroyed by divine wrath as proof of the danger which common knowledge of these words would incur.[30] Only a vested priest, with the proper books, on a proper altar, is allowed to offer Mass, and any deviation from this procedure is prohibited under anathema.[31]

Beleth's commentary on the Communion offers a standard history of the gradually diminishing frequency of reception in the Church due to the growing unworthiness of the recipients. Beleth describes three practices introduced to succor those people who cannot receive the Eucharist frequently: the kiss of peace, the prayer over the people at the end of Mass, and the distribution of the blessed bread at the end of Mass.[32]

Although Beleth offers no theology of the Eucharist as such, his position as regards the act of consecration is clear. The purpose of the Mass lies in the power of the words of consecration to make the Body and Blood of Christ present on the altar. He surrounds these words with mystery and power, and understands the presence they bring about as a dangerous thing, never to be taken lightly, either in the act of consecration, nor in the reception of Communion. Only in the commentary on the Offertory does his attitude of pure adoration waver, when he adjures the believer to join the offering of himself to the offerings which will bring about the divine presence.

Isaac of Étoile

Unlike the commentary on the Mass written by John Beleth, the commentary on the Canon of the Mass written by the Cistercian abbot, Isaac of Étoile, offers a rich theological and allegorical yield.[33] The commentary is contained in a letter of Isaac, written to John, bishop of Poitiers, between 1162 and 1167.[34] The short work had much influence in the twelfth century, and was copied by at least two other commentators of the period.[35]

Although Isaac does not offer a commentary on the Offertory, he describes the sacrifice which ought to be offered to God. Our lives crushed by vicissitudes, mixed with the tears of remorse and devotion, and cooked in the oven of a contrite and humble heart ought to make up the bread of our first offering to God.[36]

Isaac divides the Canon into three principal actions.[37] Allegorically, these actions correspond to the three altars of the tabernacle in the desert.[38] On the first altar of bronze, animal sacrifices were offered; on the second altar of gold, incense was offered; while the third altar, the Holy of Holies, remained hidden behind the wings of the cherubim.[39]

Anagogically, this allegory corresponds to the stages by which a person becomes united to God. The bronze altar represents the contrite heart upon which the spirit of remorse offers the sacrifice of penitence. The gold altar represents the pure heart upon which the spirit of devotion offers the sacrifice of justice. The Holy of Holies represents the great heart upon which the spirit of contemplation offers the sacrifice of intelligence.[40] These three sacrifices, in turn, free us from the devil, unite us to God, and allow us to delight in God.[41]

The three actions of the Canon follow this same movement of humans towards God. The first action of the Canon, the offering of the bread and wine, represents the action of servants offering their whole life, represented by the means of their sustenance, in order to reconcile themselves to their Lord.[42] This offering is, however, insufficient to accomplish our reconciliation with God.[43] Therefore, we beg God to accomplish what we cannot do and, in the second action of the Canon, through the words of consecration our earthly offerings become the spiritual offering of Christ, the new priest who offers his Body and Blood on the heavenly altar, accomplishing our reconciliation and uniting us to God.[44] Because, however, Body and Blood of themselves produce nothing, we hope for even greater things.[45] With this hope we proceed to the third action of the Canon, praying that in our reception of the species of bread and wine on our earthly altar, we might accept the true Body and Blood on the second heavenly altar, and through the power of this sacrament, be united with God.[46]

Isaac's allegory bases itself on the monastic ascent of the soul from *compunctio*, to *devotio*, to *contemplatio*.[47] The purpose of the liturgy lies in its ability to assist this process. The act of consecration and the Real Presence do not hold the central position here. The reception of the bread and wine take place on one level *(de primo altari)*, and the reception of the Body and Blood on another *(de secundo ultra velum)*, but the purpose of both is spiritual union with God.[48] The individual in his or her relationship to God through Christ forms the basic movement of the Mass, which is, it should be noted, directed from the People to God.

The very different approaches to the Eucharistic Liturgy taken by John Beleth and Isaac of Étoile are symptomatic of the latitude of eucharistic teaching in the twelfth century. A similar diversity continues to present itself throughout this century and well into the thirteenth century.

Richardus Praemonstratensis

Another commentary on the Canon of the Mass, written in the third quarter of the twelfth century, appears to be a sermon delivered at Clairvaux by an Augustinian canon named Richard.[49] Too little is known of Richard and his work to judge the influence of his commentary, although at least thirty-one manuscripts of his work are known to exist.[50] His basic approach consists of a rather artificial allegory based on the seven dimensions of the Cross and the seven virtues and vices which he aligns with the seven *ordines* of the Canon which extend from the first prayer of the Canon to the *Agnus Dei*.

Richard, like Isaac, lays great stress on the moral regeneration of the individual. The effect of both the holy Cross and the sacrament of the altar is the same: evil is removed and the Church is renewed.[51] For Richard, this means that we must first discipline ourselves to drive out evil, before we can accept the newness of Christ.[52] In great detail, he lists the vices of the mind and body which must be removed, and which of the corresponding virtues must replace each of the vices. He sees this regeneration as the major virtue not only of the Mass, but of the redemptive act itself.[53]

Richard's description of the movement of the Eucharistic Liturgy has affinities to Isaac's, but a much different theology. In the first *ordo*, we pray that the gifts we offer, bread, wine, and water, might be blessed.[54] In the second and third *ordines*, we pray that they might become the Body and Blood of Christ.[55] In the fourth *ordo*, we pray that Christ, now present, might present our petitions to the Father in heaven.[56] In the fifth *ordo*, we praise the Father, Son, and Spirit, that our petitions might be fulfilled,[57] and in the sixth *ordo*, we honor and glorify the Father through Christ.[58] Finally, in the seventh *ordo*, we pray for the peace of God.[59]

The movement of the liturgy as understood by Richard is very simple. Our gifts are transformed into the Body and Blood of Christ, who now being present, provides us with both the spiritual assistance we need, and with an opportunity for petitioning God the Father. The entire movement depends upon and centers around the Real Presence.

There is no doubt about Richard's belief in the Real Presence. In discussing the reasons why Christ is present under the species of bread and wine, he explains that the glory of Christ unveiled would be beyond the strength of humans to bear. He illustrates his point with a remarkable story from a contemporary Augustinian house in Viviers. One of the canons, in extreme devotion during Mass, saw the glory of Christ revealed above the altar, and was struck blind.[60] The story exemplifies in a graphic way the combination of individual piety and the strong belief in the Real Presence which Richard presents.

Despite Richard's emphasis on the Real Presence, the presence itself has spiritual value in terms of the moral regeneration of the individual. As different as Richard's theology might be from Isaac of Étoile's, the purpose of the eucharistic action remains the same: not the mere presence of Christ on the altar, but the possibilities which that presence presents for the moral regeneration of the individual.

Speculum de mysteriis ecclesiae

An anonymous work from the same period, entitled *Speculum de mysteriis ecclesiae*, comes from the hand of a person familiar with the liberal arts, and with the School of St. Victor in Paris.[61] The *Speculum* appears to have been a well-read book in the twelfth century and forms one of the important sources for Simon of Tournai's theological summa, *Institutiones in sacram paginam*.[62] Although it is difficult to date this work with accuracy, it appears to have been written ca. 1160–75.[63]

The *Speculum* describes the offering of the gifts as twofold. The offering of the people, in the form of money *(munera)* corresponds to the offerings made by the Jewish people at the dedication of the Temple of Solomon, and more importantly stands as a symbol of their offering of themselves to God.[64] The Gospel, Creed, and Offertory follow one another because hearing the Gospel precedes belief, and belief makes possible an acceptable sacrifice.[65] The author of the *Speculum* stresses the inner state of believers as essential in offering themselves and their gift to God. The offering of the priest is the bread and wine, prefigured by the offering of Melchisedech, and the offering of Christ at the Last Supper.[66] The introduction of this offering leads the author into a long discussion of theological issues concerning the Eucharist, to which I shall return after following the author's general allegory on the Mass.

In each of the prayers said over the gifts, the *Speculum* explains the type of the sacrifice in the Holy of Holies of the Old Testament which pertains to the prayer, the corresponding action of Christ in the redemptive act, and the appropriate action in the present liturgy. For instance, the commentary on the first of these prayers reads:

"The high priest formerly entered the holy of holies once a year with blood, and Christ through his own blood once for all entered the sanctuary, having won an eternal redemption for us (Heb 9:12). Thus the minister of the church enters the holy of holies with blood, as often as he bears in mind the victory of the blood of Christ."[67]

This section of the liturgy is the most sacred, for it contains the words of consecration and the Sign of the Cross by means of which the Body and Blood of the Lord are made present, although how this comes about surpasses the understanding of men and angels.[68] Food for the body becomes food for the soul in order that the person who receives worthily might receive eternal life.[69] The prayers over the gifts, too, have a meaning especially for the inner person. The priest shares in holy sacrifice when he "bears in mind" the sacrifice of Christ. The presence of the Body and Blood brought about by the prayers of consecration only become food for the soul of the person who receives worthily.

The commentary on the Communion simply reads: "The communion, which is sung after this, signifies all of the faithful in communion with the body of Christ, which the minister receives sacramentally in behalf of all, that both he and they might receive spiritually."[70] The author certainly understands the reception of the Body and Blood to be important only in the personal spiritual realm.

By returning to the theology of the Eucharist discussed earlier by the author, this emphasis throughout the commentary on the personal spiritual state can be explained. Following the teaching of Hugh of St. Victor, the *Speculum* argues that a sacramental reception of the Eucharist alone accomplishes nothing, only a spiritual reception gives the grace of salvation.[71] The spiritual reception consists, however, in uniting, consecrating and conforming ourselves to Christ in faith and love.[72] He goes so far as to argue that spiritual reception alone suffices for salvation when not in contempt of the ritual.[73] In short, the author describes the entire liturgical action and even the Real Presence as a commemorative aid, and not an absolutely necessary aid, for the spiritual life of a person dedicating his or her life to Christ. The individual and his or her attitude and response to the liturgy determine its efficacy, despite the author's strong belief in a Real Presence.

The author of the *Speculum* also provides a classification of the human faculties. The senses *(sensus)* correspond to the first level of awareness, the imagination *(imaginatio)* to the second level, reason *(ratio)* to the third level and faith *(fides)* to the fourth level. Dialectic belongs to the third level, and the mystery of the Body and Blood of Christ can only be grasped on the level of faith.[74] Thus the author attacks those who treat the Eucharist through dialectic, i.e., on the wrong level. This classification offers two important insights into the theology presented here. First, he does not see faith as an entirely separate realm, apart from the natural attributes of humans. Faith forms the highest region within the psychological realm of the human, not a separate realm above human grasp. Indeed intellect surpasses faith in those cases where the saints are allowed to grasp the secrets of heaven.[75] Secondly, the author rejects any discussion of a "metaphysical" presence in the Eucharist. The presence exists on the level of faith and is grasped by faith. This emphasis on psychology rather than metaphysics is extremely important in understanding the approach taken to the Eucharistic Liturgy in the second half of the twelfth century.

Robert Paululus

A fifth commentary, probably written ca. 1175–80, is that of a secular priest of Amiens, Robert Paululus.[76] Paululus' work treats of all of the Church, and includes a complete commentary on the Mass.

The commentary on the Offertory expresses the joy of the believer as he sees the mystery of his salvation being prepared before him when the deacon, subdeacon, and priest prepare the bread and wine.[77] Robert's commentary on the Canon copies almost verbatim the commentary of Isaac of Étoile which he conscientiously intersperses with material from other commentaries.[78] In fact, he provides nearly two complete commentaries on the Canon.[79]

Fortunately, Robert provides summaries of the movement he envisions in the liturgy. At one point, he describes the order of the liturgical action:

"Notice the order: first God creates the bread and wine according to nature. He sanctifies these same offerings according to grace, through the words of the first action. Thus they have been sanctified before sanctification and set apart from common uses. Then God gives life to these gifts, which have been sanctified by setting them apart, through the sacred words of the second action, when he transubstantiates them into the body and blood of Christ, and blesses them when he gives them the effect of that highest blessing, which is the unity of head and members, which the third action commemorates."[80]

Despite the fact that Robert copies most of Isaac's commentary, he lacks Isaac's subtle mysticism. For Robert, the presence of Christ is the central action necessary to bring about the union of God and man. Robert makes a similar relationship here between nature and faith as that found in the *Speculum*. The natural gifts of God are raised to the status of gifts of faith. Indeed Robert insists that this most holy sacrifice can only be perceived by faith, only profits in faith, and is accepted only by the merit of faith.[81]

Robert offers another summary, however, which shows his interest in the devotional stance of the believer. In the first action, we ought to conform ourselves to Christ's passion. We ought to conform ourselves to his resurrection in the second action by offering the mystery of faith with the gift of devotion, and conform ourselves to his ascension in the third action by contemplating Christ crowned in glory and honor on the right hand of the Father.[82]

Robert refers several times to the devotion which the believer must offer to God, and in which the believer must daily grow. Our hearts must be celestial to receive celestial food.[83] The priest extending his hands in the Canon shows externally that he has crucified himself with Christ in his heart.[84] The fire of the Spirit calls forth the tears first of remorse, and then of devotion.[85] The more we tend toward devotion to God, the more we know we are unable to comprehend him.[86] It is with the eyes of the heart that the priest sees the angels who are standing around the altar.[87] That the sacrifice is taken up by the hand of the angel means nothing else than that the angel has joined us in our devotion.[88] The priest raises the gifts and makes the cross over them in order that he might show how the glory of the Trinity might be acquired by the minds of the faithful through Christ.[89] Finally, Robert offers a commentary on the Lord's Prayer that we might be excited to devotion.[90] Again and again, he expresses his concern for the heart of the believer, the mind of the believer, the faith of the believer, the devotion of the believer.

Robert offers little original material, but for that very reason, he may be seen as a trustworthy witness to the general mood of this time. The mood he expresses is one of personal devotion to Christ as present in the Eucharist, but present in faith. If he would not deny the Real Presence, he would, as the commentators before him, see the presence as important only insofar as it relates to the psychological state of the believer.

Stephen of Autun

Stephen, the second bishop of that name to hold the see of Autun in the twelfth century, probably wrote the *Tractatus de sacramento altaris* during his episcopacy, 1170–89.[91] The *Tractatus* offers a commentary on the offices of the Church, the sacred vestments, and the Mass.

Stephen's commentary on the Offertory (like most of his predecessors') admonishes the believer to offer not only the gifts, but a humble and contrite heart.[92] For Stephen, this commonplace becomes a central theme. No prayer, no mediation, no work will be acceptable to God, unless it is offered in a spirit of humility.[93] The person who renders himself or herself acceptable by good works, rightly gives thanks to God.[94] To pray without charity is unfruitful.[95] Stephen compares our offering with the offering of the saints. We offer with things, they with faith and devotion; we offer by completing the sacraments, they offer by doing God's will; we offer wine and they offer a holy and devout mind.[96]

In two lengthy passages, Stephen compares our sacrifice with the sacrifices of the Old Testament. First, he speaks of the sacrifice of Cain and Abel. Like Abel, we must offer a contrite and pure heart with our sacrifice. If our sacrifice contains our heart with it, it will lead to our salvation; if not, it will lead to our damnation.[97] Speaking of the sacrifices of Abel, Abraham, and Melchisedech, he argues that if we wish to imitate the patriarchs, we must offer our hearts to God, that we might be found pleasing to him by sober, pious, and just living.[98] For

Stephen there are only two possibilities: to offer a true sacrifice of one's whole self to God, and thus gain salvation, or to offer an external sacrifice alone, and merit damnation. Probably for this reason, he rejects the possibility of purgatory.[99]

Stephen's interpretation of the movement of the liturgy differs little from Richard, or Robert Paululus. We pray to God to change the bread and wine into the Body and Blood of Christ in order that he might intercede for us before the divine throne.[100] Here he adds that we remember the passion of Christ, not that the memory might be lost from our hearts, but that we might crucify ourselves with our vices and thus rise renewed with Christ.[101]

In his discussion of the Real Presence, Stephen speaks of the presence as understood—known in the realm of faith, above the senses, above the intellect, and beyond dialectic.[102] As one might expect, he speaks of the reception of the Eucharist as either unto redemption or damnation, depending on the faith and love of the believer.[103] There is no need to belabor the point that Stephen exhibits the same interest in the believer's individual devotion that is so apparent in these commentaries. At times, he breaks into emotional exclamations of devotion that leave no doubt of the reverential piety which he wishes to instill: "Who can despise, like a wretched servant unmindful of his benefits, while holding the Lord in his hands who was crucified and died for him, that testament enacted by His death?"[104] Stephen, like Robert Paululus, is important, not for his originality, but for his expression of the common current of thought that he transmits.

Sicard of Cremona

Sicard, the bishop of Cremona, famous for his teaching in canon law, produced an extensive treatment of the offices of the Church in his *Mitrale*, written ca. 1185–95.[105] The third book of this work contains a complete commentary on the Mass.

Sicard's commentary on the Offertory contains an interesting discussion arising out of the question of the use of leavened bread by the Greeks. Following the opinion of Rupert of Deutz, Sicard claims that only two things are necessary for transubstantiation, the repetition of the words and faith. Whoever says the words and does not believe is like an ass lifting up his ears to the lyre, but not understanding the melody of the song. Whoever visibly eats the Body of Christ, but invisibly rejects it through unbelief, kills Christ. The life present to us is spiritual life, not animal life.[106] This passage is interesting for two reasons. First, because Sicard insists on the necessity of faith, both in the act of consecration and in the act of Communion. Secondly, he quotes precisely those passages of Rupert which William of St. Thierry had criticized earlier in the century for not insisting strongly enough on the change of substance which takes place in the Eucharist.[107] Probably Sicard had not known of William's criticism, but the point remains that Sicard chose those passages of Rupert which insist most strongly on a spiritual understanding of the presence of Christ in the Eucharist. Like the other commentators of this period, Sicard insists that this change must be understood by faith, and he offers the same analysis of human understanding as the *Speculum* to explain it.[108]

In several passages, Sicard refers to the devotion which different actions and signs in the liturgy ought to inspire. Some Mass books contain a representation of the crucifixion at the beginning of the text of the Canon in order to place the passion before the eyes of our heart.[109] The same impression is made by the letter *T* of the *Te igitur,* the first words of the Canon.[110] We offer gifts *(dona)* when we offer ourselves to God. We offer tribute *(munera)* when we are mindful of our benefits from God. We offer a spotless sacrifice *(sacrificia illibata)* when we devote our humility and praise to God.[111] Morally, we offer a pure, holy, and immaculate offering when we offer our sacrifice with a pure heart, a good conscience, and a true faith.[112] Like Stephen of Autun, Sicard also offers a long allegory on the gifts of the patriarchs. He concludes by urging the believer to imitate the patriarchs by offering the sacrifices of innocence, obedience, and justice.[113]

An overall understanding of the movement of the liturgy appears only vaguely in Sicard's work. He sees the purpose of the liturgy as the union of Christ with the members of the Church, which makes it possible for an earthly person to rise to heaven.[114] He describes the liturgy as centering around the act of transubstantiation, whereby Christ is made present to mediate our petitions to the Father.[115]

Despite the eclectic nature of Sicard's work, the same general interest appears in the relationship in faith between the believer and Christ achieved in the liturgy.

Innocent III

The longest commentary on the Mass from this period is the *De missarum mysteriis* of Innocent III, written ca. 1190–97, when he was cardinal deacon of SS. Sergius and Bacchus.[116] The commentary, which describes the ceremony of a papal high Mass, covers six books and includes extensive allegorical and theological material. An entire book is dedicated to discussing the words of consecration, a discussion which comprises a compendium of the scholastic debates concerning the Eucharist in the twelfth century. The work was extremely popular, and was used by most of the later commentators.[117] As with the other commentators, our concern here will be with the general approach to the movement of the Eucharistic Liturgy which Innocent presents, and less with his formal theological discussions.

Innocent offers less moral allegory than his predecessors in relation to the size of his work. Several passages, however, reveal that he was not immune to his contemporaries' interest in the heart and mind of the believer. In his commentary on the Offertory, Innocent relates the Creed, the Offertory Antiphon, and the offering itself as expressions first of the faith of the heart, second of the praise of the mouth, and third of the fruit of works.[118] At the beginning of the Canon, Innocent urges the priest to enter into the chamber of his heart (in cubiculum cordis) and there to close himself away from any distraction, that the Holy Spirit might nourish his mind.[119] The repetition of the words used to describe the offering (haec dona, haec munera, haec sacrificia) is the expression of pious devotion and praise of this sacrament.[120] In a lengthy allegory on the three sacrifices of the Church, Innocent describes the spiritual state which each of the sacrifices represents. In the sacrifice of penance, we offer the wine of sorrow and remorse, the water of grief and lamentation, and the bread of toil and adversity. In the sacrifice of justice, we offer the bread of fortitude and constancy, the wine of rectitude and prudence, and the water of gentleness and temperance. In the sacrifice of the Eucharist, we offer the bread of unity, the wine of charity and the water of fidelity.[121] In speaking of the Mass as a commemoration of the death of Christ, Innocent offers an example to explain why Christ left us this memorial. It is like a man, who, planning to travel abroad, leaves a token with a good friend of his. If the man who receives the gift really is a true friend, he will never be able to look at the gift without remembering their friendship with great lamenting and longing. So when Christ left this world, he left the Mass as a memorial for us.[122] In fact, Innocent gives as one of the reasons why Christ instituted this sacrament the desire of Christ to be with us not only through the indwelling of grace, but also through his corporeal presence.[123] Innocent gives vivid expression here to that attitude which the commentators express so often regarding the believer's sympathetic relationship with Christ, of rapport in mind and heart with the suffering of Christ. The same interest and sympathy prompts Innocent's description of the sufferings of Christ as not only physical, but mental and emotional.[124]

Like Sicard, Innocent gives only hints at a comprehensive understanding of the liturgical movement. Certainly, he considers the consecration the focal point of the Mass.[125] He appears to adopt the approach, not uncommon among the commentators, that the presence of Christ, once achieved, provides the merits of grace and intercessions, and the purpose of the Mass is to achieve this presence.[126] Despite the compendium of theological information which Innocent provides, he is very firm in asserting that the sacrament of the Eucharist and the Real Presence are matters for faith, and not for reason.[127] Like the author of the *Speculum,* he argues that if a person does not receive the Eucharist spiritually, that is in faith *(in fide cordis),* he or she receives unto his or her damnation.[128]

Innocent's work offers no change from his predecessors. Although perhaps more insistent on the Real Presence as an end in itself, he also insists on the importance of the liturgy for the spiritual progress of the believer, both in offering the sacrifice of the Mass, and in the reception of Communion.[129] Certainly, he shows the same interest in the relationship established in devotion between the believer and Christ, and remains firm in asserting the role of faith over reason in the understanding of the Eucharist.

ANALYSIS OF THE COMMENTARIES

Why were the allegorical commentaries written? In many cases, the authors were seeking to instill in their readers a deeper awareness of the moral demand which the liturgy places on the Christian. The means by which this was accomplished no longer appeals. We have lost much of the art of eliciting truth through symbols. Our own mistrust of this method of fathoming the psychological and spiritual depths of both the liturgy and Scripture has severely limited our appreciation of medieval allegory.[130] This, I would suggest, witnesses more to our own loss of symbolic sensitivity than to any theological difference between the allegorists and present views on the Eucharist. The means of expression may be strange to us, but the message of the allegorists is clear. The Eucharist makes moral demands upon a participant, and to take part in the rite while ignoring those demands is the worst sort of blasphemy.

156

Nor were the medieval commentators merely mouthing pious plati-
tudes when they urged conscientious participation in the eucharistic
celebration. Church law and practice encouraged and enforced such
participation. Reception of the Eucharist in the twelfth and thirteenth
centuries was generally limited to thrice-yearly, or after the Council of
Lateran IV in 1215, annual reception.[131] At least in the thirteenth century, special permission was required to receive the sacrament apart
from the Easter duty.[132] The reason for this reluctance to receive was
not indifference, but reverence and in some cases, fear of damnation
through unworthily approaching the Lord's table. Prospective recipients were expected to fast and abstain from conjugal relations during
the days preceding receptions, and confession (at least in theory) was
considered essential for worthy reception.[133] Beginning in the twelfth
century, confessors and popular writers like the allegorists began to
demand not just a formal cleansing from sin, but a true longing for
union with Christ demonstrated by acts of penance and charity. Some
theologians actively discouraged frequent receptions on the grounds
that this kind of familiarity with the sacrament would breed indifference.[134] Sicard expressed the view of many of his contemporaries
when he exclaimed: "[I]t has been instituted that (the people) communicate three times a year, Christmas, Easter and Pentecost, but if only
they would communicate once worthily!"[135] This viewpoint may at
least partially underlie the legislation of Lateran IV which limited
reception to an annual event.

The medievals adopted a definite ecclesiastical stance to the moral
demands which they saw as implicit in the Eucharist. Every effort
was made to insure that reception was made only under the most favorable conditions, and those known publicly to eschew the teaching
or practice of the Church faced the social ostracization of excommunication. Excommunication in the Middle Ages entailed many social
and legal consequences, but in essence remained "ex-communication,"
the inability to participate in the sacrament of the Eucharist.[136] Despite
the difficulty involved in preparation, great social pressure was
brought to bear on the individual to receive on the high feast days.
Not to receive was a public admission of serious sin and public re-
fusal of Communion could easily arouse suspicion, even of heresy.[137]
Odo of Ourscamp, a theologian at Paris and contemporary of Peter
Lombard, argued that a priest ought not publicly to deny the sacrament except to those who were declared excommunicates, because he
might thereby cause false accusations. Stephen Langton, himself a

well-respected Parisian theologian before becoming the archbishop of Canterbury famous for supporting the Magna Carta, similarly stated that a priest should not publicly refuse anyone the sacrament, even if he knew him privately to be in serious sin: "not only because of scandal, but especially that his crime not be made public."[138]

The medieval Church, both laity and clergy, so closely linked the sign of participation in the life of Christ and the living out of that life, that not to participate in the sign was proof of not living the life of a Christian. Participation in the Eucharist was an extremely important moral and social act, establishing oneself publicly as a member in good standing in the Christian community. It was an act not undertaken lightly, and one which was seen as committing the participant to a life of Christian morality.

CONCLUSION

In conclusion, then, the commentaries on the Eucharistic Liturgy in the second half of the twelfth century offer a special kind of eucharistic piety: a devotion to Christ in the species, but not an adoration of the species; a great compassion and sympathy for Christ in the passion that went beyond ritual actions to make demands in the believer's moral life; and a fresh and alarmingly personal veneration that challenges the standard histories of liturgy and devotion in the Middle Ages.

Of course, what the treatises offer is an ideal. They explain what their authors felt the liturgy ought to be at its very best, not what it too often was. In reality, the lives of peasants and priests, nobles and bishops, popes and kings, all fell short of the devotion described in the commentaries, and sometime those lives even flatly contradicted those ideals. And yet to study the ideals of a people, and to study them in the form in which they themselves delighted to express them, takes one deep into the medieval mind. In this, I submit, lies the importance of these neglected little treatises.

---

1. Originally published in *Medieval Liturgy: A Book of Essays,* Lizette Larson-Miller, ed. (New York and London: Garland Press, 1997) 25–59.

2. The best overview of the history of liturgical commentaries is that of Roger Reynolds, "Liturgy, Treatises on," *DMA* 7:624–33.

3. On the rise of eucharistic devotion in the twelfth century, see Gary Macy, *Theologies of the Eucharist in the Early Scholastic Period* (Oxford: Claren-

don Press, 1984) 86–93; Miri Rubin, *Corpus Christi: The Eucharist in Late Medieval Culture* (Cambridge: Cambridge University Press, 1991) 83–163; Cheslyn Jones, Geoffrey Wainwright, Edward Yarnold, and Paul Bradshaw, eds., *The Study of the Liturgy*, rev. ed. (Oxford: Oxford University Press, 1992) 281–82; and Joseph Powers, *The Eucharistic Mystery* (N.Y.: Cambridge University Press, 1992) 185–95. On the first use of the term "transubstantiation," see Joseph Goering, "The Invention of Transubstantiation," *Traditio* 46 (1991) 147–70.

4. *Toward an Understanding of Eucharistic Acclamation: An Examination of the Sanctus, Great Amen and Agnus Dei Especially as Treated in Select Expositiones Missae.* (Ph.D. Dissertation, Pontifical Liturgical Institute, Athaenaeum of Sant'Anselmo, Rome, 1973).

5. *A Medieval Commentary on the Mass: Particulae 2–3 and 5–6 of the De missarum mysteriis (ca. 1195) of Cardinal Lother of Segni (Pope Innocent III).* (Ph.D. Dissertation, University of Notre Dame, 1977).

6. *The Sententia Ivonis Carnotensis Episcopi de Divinis Officiis: Text and Study* (Ph.D. Dissertation, Toronto, 1982).

7. *Twelfth-century Latin Commentaries on the Mass.* (Ph.D. Dissertation, University of Notre Dame, 1983).

8. *Allegorical Liturgical Interpretations in the West from 800 A.D. to 1200 A.D.* (Ph.D. Dissertation, Toronto, 1985).

9. Adolf Franz, *Die Messe im deutschen Mittelalter: Beiträge zur Geschichte der Liturgie und des religiösen Volksleben* (Freiburg: Herder, 1902; rpt. Darmstadt: Wissenschaftliche Buchgesellschaft, 1963) ix. On the allegorical commentaries, see especially 407–58.

10. "L'intérêt de ces petites sommes n'est pas dans leur exégèse, où l'imagination donne libre cours aux interprétations les plus fantaisistes, symbolisme naif qui séduisait les contemporains, mais qui déconcerte aujourd'hui l'esprit le mieux préparé a goûter ces pieuses allégories." "La 'Summa de officiis ecclesiasticis' de Guillaume d'Auxerre," *Études d'histoire littéraire et doctrinale du XIIIe siécle*, 2éme serie 2 (1932) 25. A discussion of other modern authors who speak of the commentaries may be found in Wright, *A Medieval Commentary on the Mass*, 5–43.

11. (N.Y.: Simon and Schuster, 1950) 50, 59.

12. To mention just a few modern authors who describe the effect of commentaries as detrimental to a true understanding of the Eucharist: J. Bauer, *Liturgical Handbook for Holy Mass* (Westminster, Md.: Newman Press, 1961) 10; Theodor Klauser, *A Short History of the Western Liturgy; An Account and Some Reflections* (London: Oxford University Press, 1969) 94; Joseph Powers, *Eucharistic Theology* (N.Y.: Herder and Herder, 1968) 22; Louis Boyer, *Eucharist* (Notre Dame, Ind.: University of Notre Dame Press, 1968) 366; and Powers, *The Eucharistic Mystery*, 195.

13. A list of some thirty manuscripts appears in Gary Macy, "A Bibliographical Note on Richardus Praemonstratensis," *Analecta Praemonstratensia*

52 (1976) 64–69. Since this article was written I have discovered references to some further thirty manuscripts.

14. Heribert Douteil in his edition of Beleth's work, *Iohannis Beleth Summa de ecclesiasticis officiis*, Corpus christianorum, continuatio mediaevalis 41 (Turnhout: Brepols, 1976) 1:75–271, lists 149 manuscripts of this work, while Wright, *A Medieval Commentary*, 50, mentions that there are 194 known manuscripts of Innocent's commentary.

15. Odo describes the intention of his work in the preface (*PL* 160: 1053D–1054D). Fulgentius was abbot of Affligem from 1088–1122, see U. Berliere, "Afflighem" *DHGE* 1:672–74.

16. The letter can be dated from the appeal Isaac makes to the bishop for assistance against the attacks of a kinsman of the bishop, Hugh of Chauvigny (*PL* 194: 1896A–B). A ruling was made on this dispute by the bishop in 1167 (cf. G. Raciti, "Isaac de l'Étoile," *Cîteaux* 13 (1962) 209, n. 268), thus providing a *terminus ante quem*. Raciti, in his article in *DSAM* (cf. n. 29), gives 1165 as a *terminus post quem*, but offers no explanation for this date. John Bellesmains became bishop of Poitiers in 1162. Cf. P. Pouzet, *L'Anglais Jean dit Bellesmains (1122–1204?): evêque de Poitiers, puis archevêque de Lyons (1162–1182, 1182–1193)* (Lyons: M. Camus & Carnet, 1927) 20, and so I have used this date as a *terminus post quem*.

17. See the introductory letters to Honorius' *Gemma animae* (*PL* 172: 541–544) and the *prologus* to Gerhoh's *Expositio super canonem*, Damien and Odulf Van den Eynde and Angelinus Rijmersdael, eds., *Gerhohi praepositi Reichersbergensis Opera inedita*, 2 vols. Spicilegium Pontificium Athenaeum Antonianum 8–10 (Rome: Pontificium Athenaeum Antonianum, 1955–6) 1:3.

18. Ivo, in *Sermo I* of his *Sermones de ecclesiasticis sacramentis et officiis* appears to be addressing clergy: "Quoniam populus ad fidem vocatus, visibilibus sacramentis instruendus est, ut per exhibitionem visibilem, pertingere possit ad intellectum invisibilium, nosse oportet, Domini, sacerdotes, qui haec sacramenta contrectant, modum et ordinem sacramentorum, et veritatem rerum significatarum . . ." *PL* 162: 505C. It would seem reasonable to assume that this series of sermons was addressed to his own clergy at Chartres. This is the opinion of E. Amann and L. Guizard, *DTC* 15:3633–34. On the sermon of Richard at Clairvaux, see Macy, "A Bibliographical Note."

19. On the life of Beleth, his work, the manuscript tradition and influence of the *Summa de ecclesiasticis officiis*, see Heribert Douteil, *Iohannis Beleth Summa de ecclesiasticis officiis*, praefatio cum appendice.

20. Beleth explains his purpose in his preface: "Quid autem in temporibus nostris est agendum, ubi nullus vel rarus qui invenitur legens vel audiens qui intelligat, videns vel agens qui animaduertat? . . . Sed, *ne claudantur ora canentium: Ad te, Domine, Deus meus*, Deo auxiliante contra hoc dampnum triplicis lectionis adhibeamus remedium . . ." Douteil, *ibid.*, 41a, 2.

21. In a passage on the Canon of the Mass, Beleth deliberately leaves out those sections which he feels should be discussed only by priests, indicating that he was addressing an audience which included those other than priests: "Secuntur postea multa ut de nominibus apostolorum, martirum, pontificum, militum, medicorum, uirginum, qui omnes per Christo nostro sacrificio morti se exposuerunt, et quedam alia, que nobis non licet exponere nisi forte solis sacerdotibus et ideo de isto tacebimus." Douteil, ibid., 82. Jean-François Maurel, "Jean Beleth et la 'Summa de ecclesiasticis officiis,'" *Positions de thèses de l'École des chartres* (1953) 77, notes: "Du texte de la *Summa,* on peut conclue que Beleth n'était pas moine, mais probablement prêtre, qu'il écrivait surtout pour des clercs, mais non spécialement pour les prêtres."

22. According to Maurel, 79, Beleth used the scholastic method of argument: "*formules nota quod,* . . . *queritur;* . . . appel à plusieurs autorités entre lesquelles l'auteur se réserve de choisir." His pupils continued to add marginal notes, which later became incorporated into the text. According to Maurel, 80: "Ces notes sont, d'ailleurs, très vite apparues, puisqu'on les trouve déjà presque toutes trente ans après le rédaction." It would be extremely interesting if Beleth actually lectured on the liturgy, or if his book were used in the university. It is worth noting that, although Beleth presumably taught theology at Paris, the only work of his that survives, or that medieval authors quote (cf. Maurel, 78), is the *Summa de ecclesiasticis officiis.*

23. Franz, 444; Joseph Jungmann, *The Mass of the Roman Rite: Its Origin and Development (Missarum Sollemnia),* trans. Francis Brunner, 2 vols. (N.Y.: Benziger, 1951–55) 1:109.

24. Cf. Douteil, 361–64, where the dependency of Beleth on Honorius is amply displayed in tabular form.

25. The closest Beleth comes to an outline of this kind is in his description of the Mass as a battle against the devil, c. 32–33 (Douteil, 61–64).

26. Douteil, 75–76.

27. Ibid., 77.

28. Ibid., 64.

29. For this text, cf. n. 21 above.

30. "Secreta dicitur, quia secreto pronunciatur, cum olim tamen alta uoce diceretur, unde et ab hominibus laicis sciebatur. Contingit ergo ut quadam die pastores super lapidem quendam ponerent panem, qui ad horum uerborum prolationem in carnem conversus est, forsan transsubstantiatur est panis in corpus Christi, in quos diuinitus facta est acerrima uindicta. Nam percussi sunt diuino iudicio celitus misso." Douteil, 78. This story appears in many of the commentators of this period. According to Franz, 627, the first commentator to use this story was Albinus (wrongly identified by Franz as Remigius of Auxerre), (*PL* 101: 1256), although the story itself is older (cf. Franz 627–28). Of the commentators discussed here, the story is repeated by John Beleth, the *Speculum de mysteriis ecclesiae, PL* 177: 368; Sicard of Cremona, *PL* 213: 125A,

and Innocent III, *PL* 217: 840C–D. [The story originally appeared in the sixth-century *Pratum spirituale* of John Moschius, for details see n. 3 in "The Eucharist and Popular Religiosity," the last essay in this volume.]

31. Douteil, 82.

32. Ibid., 85. On the substitution of these practices for reception, see Macy, *Theologies of the Eucharist*, 93–95, and Rubin, *Corpus Christi*, 73–77.

33. A great deal of research has been done on Isaac of Étoile in recent years. The most valuable account of his life is contained in Gaetano Raciti, "Isaac de l'Étoile et son siècle," *Cîteaux* 12 (1961) 281–306; 13 (1962) 18–34, 133–45, and 205–16. This work has been corrected and criticized by Anselm Hoste, in the introduction to *Isaac de l'Étoile, Sermons* 1, Sources Chrétiennes 130 (Paris: Editions du Cerf, 1967) 7–25, and by Raciti himself in his article, "Isaac de l'Étoile," *DSAM* 7:2011–38. This last-mentioned article also contains a useful bibliography. Bernard McGinn summarizes this scholarship in *The Golden Chain, A Study of the Theological Anthropology of Isaac of Stella*, Cistercian Studies Series 15 (Washington, D.C.: Cistercian Publications, 1972).

34. See n. 16 above.

35. Although the list is not complete, twenty-three manuscripts of Isaac's letter have been found, at least seven of which date from the twelfth century. They are listed by Raymond Milcamps, "Bibliographie d'Isaac de l'Étoile," *Collectanea ordinis cisterciensium reformatorum* 20 (1958) 180–82. Additions to this list have been made in a note by A. Hoste, *Cîteaux in de Nederlanden* 9 (1958) 302, and by G. Raciti, "Isaac de l'Étoile," *Cîteaux* 13 (1962) 216. Isaac's work was used by Robert Paululus and Innocent III in their commentaries on the Mass. For the dependence of Robert Paululus on Isaac, see Franz, *Die Messe*, 441–42. Innocent seems to have borrowed from Isaac in discussing the different aspects of sacrifice necessary to offer worthily. Compare the text given in Wright, *A Medieval Commentary*, 192–93, with the text from Isaac given in n. 34 below. According to Raciti, "Isaac de l'Étoile," *DSAM* 7:2020, both the edition by Tissier (printed *PL* 194: 1889–1896) and that of Luc d'Achery (*Spicilegium*, 3rd ed., Paris: 1723, 1:449–51) are faulty. I have referred to the text in the *PL* simply because it is the most widely available, but there is clearly a need for a new edition of this work.

36. *PL* 194: 1889D–1890B.

37. Ibid., 1890D.

38. Ibid.

39. Ibid., 1891D–1892A.

40. Ibid., 1892A–B.

41. Ibid.

42. Ibid., 1893A–B.

43. Ibid., 1894B.

44. Ibid., 1894A–B.

45. Ibid., 1894C.

46. Ibid., 1894D–1895A.

47. See n. 40 above.

48. See n. 46 above.

49. This work has long been misattributed, on the few facts known about this work and its author, see Gary Macy, "A Bibliographical Note."

50. See n. 13 above.

51. *PL* 177: 455D. Once again for the sake of simplicity, I have used the text of this work edited by the canons of St. Victor in 1648 and reprinted *PL* 177: 455–470.

52. Ibid., 457A.

53. Ibid., 458A–B.

54. Ibid., 461D.

55. Ibid., 462B–C.

56. Ibid., 463A.

57. Ibid., 465A.

58. Ibid.

59. Ibid., 467A.

60. "Unde miraculum istud contigit in Vivariensi ecclesia Praemonstratensis ordinis. Cum celebraretur missa in praefata ecclesia, quidam frater respiciens de choro ad altare uidit super illud circulum claritatis immense; et columbam miri candoris super calicem in eadem claritate. Coepit igitur admirari, et admirando intueri: et subito stupefactus et territus amisso uisu cecidit in choro prostratus. Quem fratres ad manus deducentes, et euentus veritatem perquirentes; tamdiu precibus institerunt donec ei Deus uisum restitueret." Ibid., 461B–C. The church at Viviers was one of the oldest Augustinian houses, the canons having replaced the secular clergy in 1124–26 (cf. Norbert Backmund, *Monasticon Praemonstratense* 2 (Straubing, 1952) 537.

61. For a discussion of the original mistaken attribution of this work to Hugh of St. Victor, cf. Barthélemy Hauréau, *Les oeuvres de Hugues de Saint-Victor. Essai critique*, 2nd ed. (Paris: Hachette et cie., 1886, rpt. Frankfurt: Minerva, 1963) 199–203. Heinrich Weisweiler, "Zur Einflussphäre der 'Vorlesungen' Hugos von St. Victor," *Mélanges Joseph de Ghellinck, S.J.*, Museum Lessianum, Section historique 13–4 (Gembloux: Éditions J. Duculot, 1951) 534–70, offers the best discussion of the work, demonstrating its dependence on the lectures of Hugh of St. Victor as preserved in the *reportatio* of Laurentius (Oxford, Bodleian Library MS. Laud. 344), on the *De sacramentis,* and on the *Summa sententiarum,* thus placing it clearly within the influence of the Victorine School. The author of the *Speculum* describes himself as more familiar with logic than theology: "Cum autem libentius, quia facilius et audentius, logicas quam theologas, jure consuetudinis, revolvam sententias: dubitare coepi, an contradicere, an potius scribere mallem." *PL* 177: 335A.

62. The influence of the *Speculum* on Simon of Tournai has been traced by Damien Van den Eynde, "Deux sources de la somme théologique de Simon

de Tournai," *Antonianum* 24 (1949) 19–42. The *Speculum* was also used by another commentary on the Mass, the *Tractatus de sacramento altaris* of Stephen of Autun (cf. n. 91 below). Barthélemy Hauréau, *Les oeuvres de Hugues de Saint-Victor*, 201–02, lists fifteen manuscripts of this work. For references to research on this work, including a list of English manuscripts unknown to Hauréau, see Macy, *Theologies of the Eucharist*, 65 and n. 120 of ch. 3.

62. Damien Van den Eynde, "Deux sources de la somme théologique de Simon de Tournai," 41, and "Le Tractatus de sacramento altaris faussement attribué à Étienne de Baugé," *Recherches de Théologie ancienne et médiévale* 19 (1952) 241, dates this work ca. 1160. He takes as his *terminus post quem* the publication of the sentences of Peter Lombard (1153–58) which the *Speculum* uses. Since the *Speculum* does not use John Beleth, nor any of the other later commentators, and since Beleth was such a popular work, Van den Eynde argues that the *Speculum* was written before the appearance of Beleth's work (1160–64). It would be safer, however, to date this work between the publication of Peter Lombard's work and that of Simon of Tournai, roughly 1160–75. Again for simplicity, I have used the text printed in *PL* 177: 335–380.

64. *PL* 177: 361C.

65. Ibid.

66. Ibid., 361C–D.

67. "Pontifex olim intrabat in sancta sanctorum cum sanguinem semel in anno; et *Christus, per proprium sanguinem introiuit semel in sancta, aeterna redemptione inuenta.* Sic minister ecclesiae intrat cum sanguine in sancta sanctorum, quoties in mente memoriam sanguinis Christi gerens, . . ." Ibid., 369B.

68. Ibid., 370A–C.

69. Ibid., 370C–371A.

70. "Communio, quae post cantatur, innuit omnes fideles corpori Christi communicare, quod pro omnibus minister assumit sacramentaliter, ut sibi et omnibus sumatur spiritualiter." Ibid., 373C.

71. "Sacramentalis autem communio est communis bonis et malis, quae sine spirituali non prodest." *Ibid.*, 366A–B. Cf. Hugh of St. Victor, *De sacramentis christianae fidei*, l. 2, pars 8, c. 5 and c. 7, *PL* 176: 465B–C, 467C–D. On spiritual communion in the twelfth century, see Macy, *Theologies of the Eucharist*, 73–105.

72. *PL* 177, 365D.

73. "Spiritualis autem sumptio, quae vera fide percipitur, sine sacramentali, ubi non est contemptus religionis, sufficit." Ibid., 366B.

74. Ibid., 362A–B.

75. Ibid., 362B.

76. Although printed among the works of Hugh of St. Victor (*PL* 177: 381–456), this work has long been identified as a work of Master Robert Paululus, a priest at Amiens. The identification was made by Jean Mabillon and Luc d'Archéry, *Acta sanctorum ordinis S. Benedicti*, saeculum 3, pars prima

(Paris: Billaine, 1672) 1v. They refer to a manuscript of Corbie (now Paris, Bibliothèque Nationale MS. latin 11579) which attributes this work to Robert Paululus. They also refer to three charters of Corbie bearing the signature *Magister Robertus Paululus, minister Episcopi Ambianensi*, and dated 1174, 1179, and 1184. Robert refers to his own profession as that of a secular priest (l. 1., c. 32; *PL* 177: 399C–D). The only extant manuscript of this work to which I have seen reference is Bibliothèque Nationale latin 11579, and I know of no other author who borrows from Robert. E. Amann, "Robert Paululus," *DTC* 13:2753, contains references to the few modern scholars who mention Paululus. To this list should be added Barthélemy Hauréau, *Les oeuvres de Hughes de Saint-Victor*, 203–04. I have used the text printed in *PL* 177.

77. *PL* 177: 424D.

78. Franz, *Die Messe*, 441–42, was the first to notice the dependence of Robert on Isaac.

79. *PL* 177: 425D–430A and 430A–435C.

80. "Vide ordinem: primo Deus panem et vinum creat per naturam. Eadem in altari oblata sanctificat per gratiam, per verba Actionis primae. Jam tunc enim ante sanctificationem sanctificata sunt et a communibus usibus separata. Deinde per sacra verba secundae Actionis sanctificata promovendo vivificat, dum ea in corpus et sanguinem Christi transubstantiat, et benedicit, dum eis summae benedictionis effectum tribuit, quae est in unitate capitis et membrorum, de qua tertia Actio meminit." Ibid., 433D–434A.

81. Ibid., 429A.

82. Ibid., 432A.

83. Ibid., 425B.

84. Ibid., 426C.

85. Ibid., 429B.

86. Ibid., 429D.

87. Ibid.

88. Ibid., 433A.

89. Ibid., 435A.

90. Ibid., 435B.

91. This work has received close textual study from Damien Van den Eynde, "On the attribution of the *Tractatus de sacramento altaris* to Stephen of Baugé," *Franciscan Studies* 10 (1950) 33–45, and "Le *Tractatus de sacramento altaris* faussement attribué à Étienne de Baugé," 225–43. Van den Eynde dates this work from internal evidence ca. 1180. I have found no references to known manuscripts of this work and have used the text printed in *PL* 172: 1274–1308.

92. *PL* 172: 1284C–D. As Van den Eynde has pointed out in "Le Tractatus de sacramento altaris," 225–37, the *Tractatus* depends heavily on the *Speculum* for his allegorical and doctrinal material.

93. *PL* 172: 1285C–D.

94. Ibid., 1286C.

95. Ibid., 1288A.

96. Ibid., 1288D.

97. Ibid., 1292B–C. Stephen's source here is Odo of Cambrai, *Expositio in canonem missae*, PL 160: 1060D–1061B.

98. PL 172: 1298C. For the entire passage on the offerings of the patriarchs, cf. ibid., 1298B–C.

99. "Non est medium inter infernum ubi est damnatio, et coelum ubi est beatitudo et salus. Qui enim non damnantur, omnes salvari non dubitantur." Ibid., 1291A.

100. Ibid., 1287C–D and 1291C.

101. Ibid., 1297B–C.

102. Ibid., 1293A; cf. also 1294D.

103. Ibid., 1296D.

104. ". . . quis tenens in manibus Dominum suam pro se crucifixum et mortuum, quasi servus nequam et imemor beneficiorum contemnat quod morte sua conscripsit testamentum?" Ibid., 1295B.

105. The best study of the life and work of Sicard, bishop of Cremona, 1185–1215, is that of Ercole Brocchieri, "Sicard di Cremona e la sua opera letteraria," *Annali della bibliotheca governativa e libreria vivica di Cremona* 11 (1958) fasc. 1. He dates the work within the first ten years of Sicard's episcopate. The *Mitrale* was certainly written after Sicard's *Summa Decretum*, written between 1179 and 1181, cf. Charles Lefebvre, "Sicard de Cremone," DDC 7:1009. Brocchieri, 72, argues that the *Mitrale* was written before the introduction by Sicard of the cult of St. Himerius (1196) and of St. Omnebonus (canonized in 1199), as the *Mitrale* makes no mention of these saints during Sicard's treatment of the feast days of the Church year. Charles Lefebvre, ibid., and Leonard Boyle, "Sicard of Cremona," NCE 13:190, give the date of the composition of the *Mitrale* as 1200, but offer no support for this dating. Although no list of manuscripts exists for this work, Brocchieri, 73, mentions four manuscripts to which he has seen references. The only text available to me was that printed in PL 213: 14–434.

106. Cf. PL 213: 118B with Rupert of Deutz, *De divinis officiis*, edited by Rhaban Haacke, *Ruperti Tjuitiensis Liber de divinis officiis*, Corpus christianorum, continuatio medievalis 7 (Turnhout: Brepols, 1967) l. 2, c. 22, p. 54; l. 2, c. 9, pp. 41–42 and 44.

107. William wrote a short letter to Rupert criticizing the Eucharistic theology of the *De diuinis officiis* (printed in PL 180: 341–44). The two passages he takes issue with are both from l. II, c. 9, and are quoted in part by Sicard. William insists that only the substance of the Body and Blood remain after the consecration, and rejects Rupert's distinction between *uita spiritualis* and *uita animalis* as applied to the Real Presence. For an overview of this conflict, see Macy, *Theologies of the Eucharist*, 66–67. A more complete discussion occurs in

John Van Engen, *Rupert of Deutz* (Berkeley: University of California Press, 1983).

108. *PL* 213: 129B–C. For the text in the *Speculum,* cf. nn. 74 and 75 above.

109. Ibid., 124C.

110. Ibid., 125B.

111. Ibid., 127B.

112. Ibid., 131A.

113. Ibid., 131C–D. Sicard's source here is probably Odo of Cambrai, not Stephen of Autun, cf. n. 92.

114. Ibid., 130C. Sicard copies Rupert of Deutz, l. II, c. 11 (Haacke 45–46).

115. Ibid., 131B.

116. The best discussions of this work are Giuseppe Barbéro, *La dottrina eucharistica negli scritti di a papa Innocenzo III* (Rome: Ponficia universitas Gregoriana, 1953); Michele Maccarone, "Innocenzo III teologo dell'Eucharistia," *Studi su Innocenzo III,* Italia sacra: Studi e documenti di storia ecclesiastica 17 (Padua: Editrice Antenore, 1972) 340–431, and Wright, *A Medieval Commentary.* The title printed in Migne, *De sacro altaris mysterio,* is incorrect. Both Barbéro, 16, n. 26, and Maccarone, 334 and 371, describe the text as printed in *PL* 217: 765–916 as inadequate and Wright did not edit the section commenting on the Mass. I have provided references to this text, however, as the only printed edition currently available.

117. See n. 14 above.

118. *PL* 217: 831A.

119. Ibid., 839D–840C.

120. Ibid., 842A.

121. Ibid., 842D–843A. Innocent appears to have copied Isaac of Étoile, *PL* 194: 1892A–B, but changes *sacrificia intelligentiae* to *sacrificia eucharistiae.* Cf. n. 40 above.

122. Ibid., 883C–D.

123. Ibid., 885C.

124. Ibid., 894D.

125. Ibid., 851D.

126. Ibid., 893D–894A and 885A–B.

127. Ibid., 861C–D. On Innocent's basic approach to this issue, cf. Maccarone, 366–70.

128. Ibid., 866C; 867C and 883A.

129. Ibid., 889C. This conclusion follows a long allegory explaining the sacrifices of Abel, Abraham and Melchisedech as symbols of the offering of our lives to God. Innocent's source here is Sicard of Cremona, cf. n. 113, above.

130. Henri de Lubac in his monumental work, *Exégèse médiévale: Les quatre sens de l'écriture* (Paris: Aubier, 1954–64) and his later work, *The Sources of Revelation,* trans. Luke O'Neill (N.Y.: Herder and Herder, 1968) has urged the importance of spiritual exegesis in the Christian tradition: "Finally—and here

again we have an important point—the spiritual meaning, understood as figurative or mystical meaning, is the meaning which, objectively, leads us to the realities of the spiritual life, and which, subjectively, can only be the fruit of a spiritual life." *The Sources of Revelation,* 20. Père de Lubac's insights have yet gone largely unheeded.

131. On the whole question of the frequency of lay reception in the Middle Ages, see Peter Browe, *Die häufige Kommunion in Mittelalter* (Münster: Regensbergsche Verlagsbuchhandlung, 1938) 19–32; idem, *Die Pflichtkommunion in Mittelalter* (Münster: Regensbergsche Verlagsbuchhandlung, 1940) 34–40; Walter Durig, "Die Scholastiker und *die communio sub una specie," Kyriakon. Festschrift Johannes Quasten,* Patrick Granfield and Josef A. Jungmann, eds., (Münster: Aschendorff, 1970) 2:867–68, and Rubin, *Corpus Christi,* 147–55.

132. For references to primary and secondary literature dealing with the general attitude discouraging frequent reception, see Macy, *The Theologies of the Eucharist,* 118–21, and Rubin, *Corpus Christi,* 63–66.

133. Macy, *The Theologies of the Eucharist,* 120.

134. Macy, *The Theologies of the Eucharist,* 188–89, n. 149.

135. ". . . institutum est ut ter in anno communicent: Natali, Pascha, Pentecoste, et utinam semel digne communicent! *Mitrale,* l. 3, c. 8, *PL* 213: 144B.

136. On the question of excommunication in the Middle Ages, see F. Donald Logan, *Excommunication and the Secular Arm in Medieval England,* Studies and Texts 15 (Toronto: Pontifical Institute of Mediaeval Studies, 1968) and Elizabeth Vodola, *Excommunication in the Middle Ages* (Berkeley: University of California Press, 1986).

137. See Browe, *Pflichtkommunion,* 14. See, for instance, c. 13 of the Council of Toulouse, 1229: "Nam si quis a communione, nisi de consilio proprii sacerdotis, abstinuerit, suspectus de haeresi habeatur." G. D. Mansi, ed., *Sacrorum conciliorum nova, et amplissima collectio* 23 (Florence: Antonius Zatta Veneti, 1759) col. 197C.

138. The text is given, and the issue discussed in Macy, *Theologies of the Eucharist,* 120–21.

APPENDIX:
A TENTATIVE LIST OF COMMENTARIES
ON THE MASS WRITTEN 1060–1225

The following list of commentaries is certainly not exhaustive and excludes commentaries on the liturgy from this period which do not discuss the Mass. Since at present no similar guide exists, the following list is offered merely as a general aid for further research.

1. John of Avranches, *Liber de officiis ecclesiasticis,* written 1060–68. Printed *PL* 147: 27-62; critical edition by R. Delamare, *Le De officiis ecclesiasticis de Jean*

d'Avranches archevêque de Rouen (1067–79): étude liturgique et publication du texte inédit du manuscrit H. 304 de la bibliothèque de la faculté de Montpellier (Paris: A. Picard, 1923) with an introduction by P. Battifol. See J. Rjjousee, *Catholisme* 6 (1967) 527, and Guy Oury, *DSAM* 8 (1974) 283.

2. Bernold of Constance, *Micrologus de ecclesiasticis observationibus*, written ca. 1073–85. Printed *PL* 151: 979–95. See Fernand Cabrol, *DACL* 2 (1912) 817–20; Johanne Autenrieth, *Die Domschule von Konstanz zur Zeit des Investiturstreits: Die wissenschaftliche Arbeitsweise Bernolds von Konstanz und zweiter Kleriker dargestelt auf Grund von Handschriften-studien*, Forschungen zur Dirchen-und Geistesgeschichte, n.f., 3 (Stuttgart: W. Kohlhammer, 1956); S. Robinson, "Zur Arbeitsweise Bernolds von Constance und seines Kreises," *Deutsches Archiv für Erforschung des Mittelalters* 34 (1978), and idem, *DMA* 2 (1983) 197.

3. Bonizo of Sutri, *Libellus de sacramentis*, written ca. 1084–99. Printed *PL* 150: 857–866. L. Jadin, *DHGE* 9 (1937) 994–98, and T. Schieffer, *LThK* 2 (1958) 597.

4. Ivo of Chartres, *Sermo de convenientia veteris et novi sacrificii*, written ca. 1090–1115. Printed *PL* 162: 535–562. See E. Amann and L. Guizard, *DTC* 15 (1950) 3633–34; R. Sprandel, *Ivo von Chartres und seine Stellung in der Kirchengeschichte* (Stuttgart: A. Hiersemann, 1962), and Roger E. Reynolds, "Ivonian *Opuscula* on the Ecclesiastical Officers," *Studia Gratiana, Mélanges Gérard Fransen II* 20 (1976) 309–22.

5. *De sacrificio missae*, wrongly attributed to Alger of Liège. Edited Ronald J. Zawilla, *The Sentenia Ivonis Carnontensis Episcopi de Divinis Officiis: Text and Study* (Ph.D. Dissertation, Toronto, 1982). Older editions exist in *PL* 180: 853–56 and H. Hurter, *Sanctorum patrum opuscula selecta* (Innsbruck: Libraria Academica Wagneriana, 1872) 23:371–77. See *DTC* 1:828, *DHGE* 2:423f., *DMA* 7 (1986) 631.

6. Odo of Cambrai, *Expositio in canomen missae*, written ca. 1095–1113. Printed *PL* 160: 1053D–1054D. See E. Amman, *DTC* 11 (1931) 932–35 and Tullio Gregory, *Platismo medievale: Studi e richerche*, Studi storici 26–27 (Rome: Istituto storico italiano per il medio evo, 1958) 31–51.

7. Rupert of Deutz, *De divinis officiis*, written in 1111. Critically edited by Rhaban Haacke, *Ruperti Tjuitiensis Liber de divinis officiis*, Corpus christianorum, continuatio medievalis 7 (Turnhout: Brepols, 1967). See Wolfgang Beinert, *Die Kirche, Gottes Heil in der Welt: Die Lehre von der Kirche nach den Schriften des Rupert von Deutz, Honorius Augustodunensis und Gerhoh von Reichersberg. Ein Beitrag zur Ekklesiologie des 12. Jahrhunderts*, Beiträge zur Geschichte der Philosophie und Theologie des Mittelalters, Texte und Untersuchungen 13 (Münster: Aschendorff, 1973), John Van Engen, *Rupert of Deutz* (Berkeley: University of California Press, 1983), and Michael McCormick, *DMA* 10 (1988) 570–71.

8. Hildebert of Lavardin, *De mysterio misse*, written ca. 1100–15. Critical edition and discussion of Hildebert's work occurs in A. B. Scott, *A Critical*

Edition of the Poems of Hildebert of Lavardin (Oxford, Bodleian Library, MS. D. Phil. d. 2403). See W.T.H. Jackson, *DMA* 6 (1985) 225–27.

9. Petrus Pictor, *De sacra eucharistia*, written ca. 1110–30. Printed *PL* 171: 1198–1212 and *PL* 207: 1135–1154. See E. Amann, *DTC* 12 (1935) 2036–37, and B. J. Comasky, *NCE* 11:226–27.

10. Honorius Augustodunensis, *Gemma anima*, written ca. 1102–33. Printed *PL* 172: 541–738. Idem, *Sacramentarius*, written ca. 1102–33. Printed *PL* 172: 737–806. See Gary Macy, *The Theologies of the Eucharist*, 65, 223–24, and Janice L. Schulte, *DMA* 6 (1985) 285–86.

11. Gerhoh of Reichersberg, *Expositio super canonem*, written ca. 1135–40. Critical edition by Damian and Odulf Van den Eynde and Angelino Rijmerdael, *Gerhohij praepositi Reichersbergensis Opera inedita* 1, Tractatus et libelli, Spicilegium Pontificii Athenaei Antoniani 8 (Rome: Pontificium Athenaeum Antonianum, 1955) 3–61. See Peter Classen, *Gerhoh von Reichersberg. Eine Biographie mit einem Anhang über die Quellen, ihre handschriftliche Überlieferung und ihre Chronologie* (Wiesbaden: F. Steiner, 1960) and Josef Szövérfly, *DMA* 5 (1985) 424–25.

12. William of Malmesbury, *Abbrevatio* of Amalarius' *De ecclesiasticis officiis*, written before 1143. Unpublished. Mentioned in Dom Hugh Farmer, "William of Malmesbury's Life and Works," *Journal of Ecclesiastical History* 13 (1962) 50–51. On William, see Mary Lynn Rampolla, *DMA* 12 (1989) 639–40.

13. Hervé de Bourg-dieu, *Expositio missae*, written before 1153. Unpublished. Mentioned by B. Hauréau, *Histoire littéraire du Maine*, 10 vols. (Paris: Dumoulin, 1870–7) 6:106–116. See Guy Oury, *DSAM* 7 (1969) 373–75.

14. Gilbert of La Porrée, *Instructiones circa divinum officium*, written before 1154. Unpublished. Mentioned by H. C. Van Elswijk, *Gilbert Porreta. Sa vie, son oeuvre, sa pensée*, Études et documents 33 (Louvain: Spicilegium sacrum Lovaniensis, 1966) 44. On Gilbert, see Joseph R. Stayer, *DMA* 5 (1985) 528.

15. Richard the Premonstratensian, *Sermo in canone misse*, written ca. 1150–75. Printed *PL* 177: 455–70. See Gary Macy, "A Bibliographical Note on Richardus Premonstratensia," *Analecta premonstratensia* 52 (1976) 64–69.

16. John Beleth, *Summa de ecclesiasticis officiis*, written ca. 1160–65. Critically edited and discussed by Heribert Douteil, *Iohannis Beleth Summa de ecclesiasticis officiis*, Corpus christianorum, continuatio mediaevalis 41 (Turnhout: Brepols, 1976).

17. Isaac of Stella, *De officio missae*, ca. 1162–67. Printed *PL* 194: 1889–1896. Gaetano Raciti, "Isaac de l'Étoile et son siècle," *Cîteaux* 12 (1961) 281–306; 13 (1962) 18–34, 133–45, and 205–16; Anselm Hoste, *Isaac de l'Étoile, Sermons* 1, Sources Chrétiennes 130 (Paris: Editions du Cerf, 1967) 7–25; Raciti, "Isaac de l'Étoile," *DSAM* 7 (1971) 2011–38; and Bernard McGinn, *The Golden Chain, A Study of the Theological Anthropology of Isaac of Stella*, Cistercian Studies Series 15 (Washington, D.C.: Cistercian Publications, 1972). The *De officio missae* has

been translated by C. W. Boyle, *De officio Missae. The Epistle of Isaac of Stella to John Bishop of Poitiers. Translation and Commentary* (Washington, D.C., 1963).

18. *Speculum ecclesiae*, written ca. 1160–75. Printed *PL* 177: 335–80. For references to research on this work, including a list of known English manuscripts, see Macy, *Theologies of the Eucharist*, 65 and n. 120 of ch. 3.

19. Stephen II of Autun, *Tractatus de sacramento altaris*, written ca. 1170–89. Printed *PL* 172: 1274–1308. Damien Van den Eynde, "On the attribution of the *Tractatus de sacramento altaris* to Stephen of Baugé," *Franciscan Studies* 10 (1950) 33–45, and idem, "Le *Tractatus de sacramento altaris* faussement attribué à Étienne de Baugé," *Recherches de Théologie ancienne et médiévale* 19 (1952) 225–43.

20. Robert Paululus, *De officiis ecclesiasticis*, written ca. 1175–80. Printed *PL* 177: 381–456. See E. Amann, *DTC* 13 (1937) 2753, and B. Hauréau, *Les oeuvres de Hughes de Saint-Victor. Essai critique*, 2nd ed. (Paris: Hachette et cie., 1886, rpt. Frankfurt: Minerva, 1963) 203–04.

21. Sicard of Cremona, *Mitrale*, written ca. 1185–95. Edited *PL* 213: 14–434. Ercole Brocchieri, "Sicard di Cremona e la sua opera letteraria," *Annali della bibliotheca governativa e libreria vivica di Cremona* 11 (1958) fasc. 1; Charles Lefebvre, "Sicard de Cremone," *DDC* 7 (1965) 1009, and Leonard Boyle, "Sicard of Cremona," *NCE* 13 (1967) 190.

22. Innocent III (Lothar of Segni), *De missarum mysteriis*, written ca. 1195. Critical edition of the majority of this work plus a critical discussion in David Frank Wright, *A Medieval Commentary on the Mass: Particulae 2–3 and 5–6 of the De missarum mysteriis (ca. 1195) of Cardinal Lother of Segni (Pope Innocent III)* (Ph.D. Dissertation, University of Notre Dame, 1977). On Innocent, see S. C. Ferruolo, *DMA* 6 (1985) 464–65.

23. Peter of Roissy, *Manuale de mysteriis ecclesiae*, written ca. 1208–13. Unpublished. See V. L. Kennedy, "The Handbook of Master Peter Chancellor of Chartres," *Mediaeval Studies* 5 (1943) 1–38.

24. William of Auxerre, *De officiis ecclesiasticis*, written ca. 1215–25. Unpublished. See R. M. Martineau, "La 'Summa de officiis ecclesiasticis' de Guillaume d'Auxerre," *Études d'histoire littéraire et doctrinale du XIIIe siècle*, 2ème série 2 (1932) 25–58.

Chapter 8

The Eucharist and Popular Religiosity[1]

Teaching in Paris in the early 1160s, the liturgist John Beleth described the secret of the Mass in the following terms:

"The secret is so-called because it is recited secretly, although in the past it was said aloud so that it was known by lay people. It happened, therefore, that one day shepherds placed bread on a rock which, at the recitation of those words, was changed into flesh, perhaps the bread was transubstantiated into the body of Christ since vengeance was most rapidly taken against them by divine agency. For they were struck down by a divine judgement sent from heaven. Hence it was decreed that in the future it be said silently. . . ."[2]

The story originally appeared as a cautionary tale in the sixth century *Pratum spirituale* of John Moschius and was repeated in several medieval commentaries on the Mass, including the *Speculum ecclesiae* attributed to the twelfth-century School of St. Victor and the *De missarum mysteriis* of Cardinal Lothar Segni, the future Pope Innocent III.[3]

The intriguing part about this story lies in its presumption that the words of consecration, or at least the words of the canon, consecrate by themselves regardless of the celebrant. Nor were the liturgists of the time alone in so teaching. The famous twelfth-century theologian and reprobate, Peter Abelard, related in his *Theologia christiana* that he knew of two brothers, counted among the greatest masters, who taught that the divine words confected the sacrament whoever might recite the words even if they were not ordained or even if they were a woman. The brothers have been identified by modern scholarship as Bernard and Thierry of Chartres, the leaders of the famous school located in that city.[4]

In the middle of the twelfth century, then, respectable theological opinion could hold that there was no necessary connection between consecration and sacramental ordination. The fact that such a theological opinion existed raises the yet more intriguing question of who exactly did lead liturgies in the early Middle Ages, since ordination was not seen as necessary, as least by some theologians, to effect the presence of the risen Lord. The assumption of modern liturgists and historians has been that possibly from the fourth century and certainly from the Carolingian reforms of the eighth century, liturgies could only be celebrated by ritually ordained ministers. A new reading of the evidence, however, at least suggests the possibility that no absolute distinction between laity and the ritually ordained existed before the late twelfth and early thirteenth centuries. Yves Congar, in an article written in 1984, pointed out that the Latin words *ordinare* and *ordinatio* could, and often did, refer merely to an assignment to a particular role or rank in society or more simply to an appointment to the administration of a particular locale. Thus, kings, popes, archdeacons, and abbots were equally spoken of as "ordained" when they took on their particular assignments.[5] Especially given this more limited meaning, ordination was not seen as irreversible until the thirteenth century. Before that time, deposed clergy were considered laity and even reordained when recanting from heresy.[6]

Further, persons understood as laity in later centuries did exercise functions that would later be reserved to ritually ordained clergy. Roberto Rusconi has demonstrated that later Franciscan legends felt it necessary to change their early records to posthumously ordain early members of the order who clearly acted as confessors.[7] Abbesses as well still retained the practice of confessing their own nuns through the late twelfth and early thirteenth centuries.[8] Extensive study has been done on the major dispute of the late twelfth and early thirteenth centuries over episcopal control of lay preaching.[9] Many laity of that period clearly felt that preaching was not the exclusive preserve of the clergy. It is possible, then, that the celebrants of the eucharistic liturgy were "ordained" only in the sense that they were assigned for this purpose to a particular community, without any understanding of entering some permanent clerical state. Certainly, groups considered heretical by the late twelfth century held eucharistic liturgies celebrated by what their enemies deemed to be laity, most notably the Waldensians. It may well be these groups were continuing the older practice of ordination as assignment, a practice which had become heretical by the time of their condemnation.[10]

Evidence for liturgies lead by nonsacramentally ordained clergy, apart from that of the heretical Waldensians, would naturally be extremely rare. Once the clerical state had been clearly defined and set apart by sacramental ordination, there would be no need to go through the great expense of copying liturgical manuscripts which indicate a nonritually ordained celebrant since they would no longer be of any use. Yet just such evidence may be contained in a set of *ordines* for the distribution of Communion from the tenth and eleventh centuries. Since one of the *ordines* has the prayers in the feminine, it is clear that the women officiated at these services and they surely constituted a group later deemed to be mere laity.[11] Although described as Communion services by Jean Leclercq, he admits that "nevertheless, in their ensemble they really constitute a long eucharistic prayer."[12] While modern liturgists would understand these Communion services as a form of *missa sicca* (that is, Mass without a consecration) it is not altogether clear that they were so understood by the participants. Given that neither the moment of consecration nor the clerical state itself had yet been closely defined, these rituals may represent the last vestiges of liturgies lead by women for their own communities.[13]

An added difficulty to historical research into the status of liturgical celebrants in the Middle Ages is, obviously, that documents that speak of "ordained" clergy may be referring only to the commissioning of individuals to a particular post or function rather than to a permanent clerical state. Even laws demanding that only the "ordained" may perform certain functions may have a far different meaning than that which such proscriptions would have from the thirteenth century on. The word "priest" in Old English, for instance, presents a similar problem since the word *preost* meant any cleric while the liturgical celebrant was further specified by the term *mass-preost*.[14]

In fact, the first official ecclesiastical document specifically linking ritual ordination with consecration occurred in the decrees of the Fourth Lateran Council in 1215. Here, too, the wording is suggestive. "And certainly no one is able to confect the sacrament except priests who have been ritually ordained according to the keys of the Church which Jesus Christ himself entrusted to the apostles and their successors."[15] Did Innocent III have in mind priests who were not ritually ordained; a practice which he meant to condemn?[16] In 1210, the pope had written to the bishop of Burgos and abbot of Morimundo complaining about women in that diocese usurping clerical functions[17] and John Hilary Martin has suggested that the first clear theological argument against women's ordination, that of John Fishacre ca. 1240, "might be the result of some actual case, or concrete agitation on the matter."[18]

The first point, therefore, that I would like to make in this paper would be that the question of who celebrated liturgies in the early Middle Ages deserves much closer scrutiny. Historians and theologians should not assume that references to the "ordained" or even to priests earlier than the late twelfth century always refer to a permanently and ritually ordained group of males. Much more research is needed before any firm conclusions can be reached, but at the very least, we need to take great care not to read back into earlier centuries an institution which seems to have appeared only in the thirteenth.

By the middle of the thirteenth century all such ambiguities had been removed, however, and theologians and canonists had clearly established the connection between ordination and consecration. Only a validly ordained priest reciting the words of consecration with the intention of the Church could perform the miracle of transubstantiation. Interestingly enough, just at the time when consecration was being claimed as an exclusively clerical preserve, laity were claiming reception as their own through the use of popular devotions known as spiritual communion.

It is in the mid-twelfth century that specific references to the practice first appear. Theologians ca. 1140 debated the validity of the peculiar practice knights had of taking three blades of grass in place of viaticum on the battlefield. The School of Gilbert of La Porrée argued that the full benefits of sacramental reception were effected by the practice.[19] Stephen Langton, teaching in Paris between 1187 and 1193, asked whether a sick person seeking the Eucharist ought to be given unconsecrated bread as a substitute if the priest had no consecrated bread at hand. Yes, Langton replied, and although such a reception has not all the graces of regular communion, it has the same value for eternal life.[20] William of Auxerre, writing in the early thirteenth century, was the first writer to encourage the laity to offer their petitions at the elevation of the Mass, and urged spiritual communion for the laity during the sacramental Communion of the priest.[21] By the middle of the thirteenth century the practice of spiritual communion could and did take many forms. Commentaries on the liturgy, in fact, urged spiritual communion as the common form of reception, replacing sacramental Communion which ordinarily occurred only once a year following the legislation of the Fourth Lateran Council.

The theology of the Eucharist developed in the late twelfth and early thirteenth centuries reflected this practice and emphasized the quintessentially symbolic nature of both the liturgy and even of the Real Presence itself. First elaborated by the School of St. Victor at Paris in the mid-twelfth century, this theology would find its major exponent in the first Franciscan master, Alexander of Hales. Basing himself on earlier writers, and especially Pope Innocent III, Alexander argued that reception depended upon the recognition of the sign value of the symbols (in Latin, *sacramentum*) by the recipient.[22] In Alexander's commentary on Peter Lombard's *Sentences*, written ca. 1222–23,[23] he explained that since the Body of Christ is spiritual food, only an intellectual nature is capable of receiving it. As Augustine had pointed out, the outward sign leads to the inner reality and only the intellect can so reach beyond the sign to the reality behind it. Animals then receive simply the outer forms, the taste of bread and wine, whereas humans can understand symbols. Therefore only humans can access the presence of the Lord underlying the symbol *(sacramentum)* of bread and wine.[24]

Writing between 1220 and 1236 in a work now known as the *Quaestiones disputatae 'Antequam esset frater,'* Alexander suggested that there are three kinds of union possible in the Eucharist. One can be united in thought, in love and in nature to Christ. Those who existed before the coming of Christ could be united in thought and love, but not in nature. Angels, too, having a different nature than Christ, cannot receive him naturally. Then, too, Christ can be received with more or less love, and more or less understanding. This means there are different degrees of reception of Christ. Perfect reception would take place only in heaven, Alexander intimated. Those who receive the sign alone, like Jews and pagans, are united only to the sign, as if it were mere bread. Again there is a union of those who both believe and understand the reason for the sign. Finally, there is the greater union of those who believe and love, and this is spiritual reception.[25]

Alexander discussed the question of whether only rational creatures have the ability to receive this sacrament. It would seem that irrational creatures must be able to receive, since once transubstantiation takes place, the Body of Christ remains as long as the species of bread and wine remain. If an animal receives the species of bread, it ought as well to receive the Body of Christ. If, however, by sacramental reception is meant that the recipient touches or accesses the reality behind the sign as well as the sign alone, then neither animals, nor Jews, nor pagans can be said to receive symbolically *(sacramentaliter)*. True to the principles established earlier, Alexander asserted that to receive symbolically, properly speaking, is to be united either in nature or faith or charity with Christ. Certainly animals cannot then receive. Even Jews and pagans, however they might share in the same human nature as Christ, do not receive symbolically since they do not understand the reality underlying the signs.[26]

Alexander's discussion of reception is extremely important. Not only do I know of no earlier medieval author who had so explicitly argued that reception was dependent on the intentionality of the receiver, but Alexander's theology would be very influential. It was adopted by the majority of thirteenth- and fourteenth-century theologians and canonists, making it far more influential during those centuries than that of Thomas Aquinas, who was one of the few theologians who at least partially disagreed with Alexander.[27]

One important example of a theologian who followed the teaching of Alexander is Nicholas of Lyra, the Franciscan exegete who became a master at the University of Paris in 1309. He wrote his famous commentary on Scripture between 1322 and 1339, and died while teaching at Paris in 1349. The commentaries are not his only works, however. Among his other writings is a short work entitled *Dicta de sacramento* which was later published in Cologne in 1480, and then reprinted in 1485, 1490, 1495, and a final time in Paris in 1513. Although widely read in the fifteenth and sixteenth centuries, modern scholars have virtually ignored this work.[28]

The treatise is a discussion of the conditions necessary for worthy reception of the Eucharist, in which Nicholas suggests twelve requirements for a worthy reception. One must be a human, a viator (that is still in this life), a believer, an adult, mentally competent, fasting devoutly, without awareness of mortal sin, not guilty of notorious crimes, having a clean body, not prohibited by the appearance of a miracle, having a proper minister, and finally having a right intention.[29]

Fascinating as some of these requirements might be, my discussion will be limited to the two conditions most interesting for this study, that the recipient be a human and that he or she must be a believer. The first condition, according to Nicholas, immediately excludes both animals and angels. If one asks what an animal receives when it eats the sacrament, Nicholas responded that some argue that the Body of

Christ ceases to be here. This is the opinion of St. Bonaventure, although Nicholas does not name him. Nicholas rejects this opinion, however, both on the grounds of authority, and because God has made a special pact with the Church that as long as the species exist after consecration the Body of Christ will remain united to them. Nicholas then posited that animals receive really but not sacramentally.[30]

Nicholas explained further when he discussed why the recipient must be a believer. If one asks what unbelievers receive in the sacrament, Nicholas responded that they receive as animals do. Nicholas argued that there is a difference between receiving the symbol *(sacramentum)*, and receiving symbolically *(sacramentaliter)*. To receive symbolically, one must understand the signified reality under the sign, and this neither unbelievers nor animals can do.[31] They can, however, receive the bare symbol of bread and wine under which the Body and Blood lie. The connection between the bread and the Body of Christ and between the wine and the Blood of Christ continue to exist in such a reception. There is, however, no connection between the recipients and the Body and Blood since the bread and wine are not recognized as the signs they are. There are two separate relationships here: the relationship between the Real Presence and the symbols which remains as long as the symbols are recognizable as such, and a quite separate relationship between the Real Presence and the recipient. This second relationship exists only when and if the recipient recognizes the symbol as pointing to the Real Presence.

Nicholas is consistent in his use of these distinctions. Children before the age of reason can receive really, but not symbolically, just like animals and infidels. In the same way, those who are mentally incompetent should only receive if they are capable of giving some sign of devotion, or if they were recently capable of such a sign. In short, there must be some evidence that these people are capable of understanding the signification of the symbols. If not, they are not capable of symbolic reception.[32]

Nicholas stated the importance of asserting the continued presence of the Body and Blood of the Lord in the Eucharist somewhat more strongly than Alexander. As long as the species exist, so does the Body and Blood, despite what happens to the symbols of bread and wine. He equally strongly asserts, however, that the presence is only there for those capable of understanding both that the species of bread and wine are a sign, and of what they are signs. Neither animals, nor infidels, nor children, nor the mentally incompetent can understand the sign value of this ritual, and therefore they do not have access to the Real Presence. For them, this might as well be ordinary food.

Nicholas' treatise is a thoughtful presentation of the theologically important insight of Alexander that since the Eucharist is a sign, only those capable of understanding this sign are capable of any form of relationship with the Body of Christ really present under the symbols of bread and wine. It is this relationship that is central.

For most medieval theologians, however, a mere recognition of the Real Presence in the ritual of the Eucharist did not itself offer any aid in salvation. The Real Presence alone, in fact, had no spiritual effect. In the language of the School of St. Victor, the Real Presence was the *res et sacramentum*, but not the *res* of the ritual. That is to say that the whole point of the ritual, which the Latin word *res* implies, resided not in the Real Presence. That presence itself was a symbol pointing beyond itself to another far more important reality, the *res*, the thing itself, the point of the entire exercise. Theologians from the twelfth century on were nearly unanimous in their agreement that the *res*, the end result of the Eucharist, was spiritual communion and that this form of communion could and did take place apart from the sacramental reception. Most commonly, this *res* was described as living a life of faith and charity.[33] In effect, the predominant theology of the Eucharist in the late Middle Ages understood the liturgy as intimately and intrinsically tied to the moral life. The liturgy celebrated and strengthened an active Christian life, a purpose for which the Real Presence was in fact incidental.

Again, one example will have to suffice. An anonymous work entitled *Speculum de mysteriis ecclesiae,* came from the hand of a person familiar with the liberal arts and with the school of St. Victor in Paris.[34] The *Speculum* appears to have been a well-read book in the twelfth century and forms one of the important sources for Simon of Tournai's theological summa, *Institutiones in sacram paginam.*[35] Although it is difficult to date this work with accuracy, it appears to have been written ca. 1160–75.[36]

The commentary on the Communion simply reads: "The communion, which is sung after this, signifies all of the faithful in communion with the body of Christ, which the minister receives sacramentally in behalf of all, that both he and they might receive spiritually."[37] The author certainly understands the reception of the Body and Blood to be important only in the personal spiritual realm.

Following the teaching of Hugh of St. Victor, the *Speculum* argues that a sacramental reception of the Eucharist alone accomplishes nothing, only a spiritual reception gives the grace of salvation.[38] The spiritual reception consists, however, in uniting, consecrating and conforming ourselves to Christ in faith and love.[39] The author goes so far as to argue that spiritual reception alone suffices for salvation when not in contempt of the ritual.[40] In short, the author describes the entire liturgical action and even the Real Presence as a commemorative aid, and not an absolutely necessary aid, for the spiritual life of a person dedicating his or her life to Christ. The individual and his or her attitude and response to the liturgy determine its efficacy, despite the author's strong belief in a Real Presence.

This brings me to the second point of my paper. To argue either that reception of the Eucharist in the later Middle Ages was infrequent, or that eucharistic devotion in the Middle Ages centered on the Real Presence is not quite accurate. Spiritual reception, which from a medieval perception was true reception, took place at least in every liturgy for all the devout whether they received sacramentally or not. Devotion centered not only around the Real Presence, but equally if not more strongly around spiritual reception. The Real Presence alone could not aid in salvation; this was the role of spiritual reception. Indeed, unworthy sacramental reception could lead to damnation, something which could never occur in spiritual reception. Late medieval eucharistic theology clearly and emphatically described the liturgy as the embodiment and celebration of an active life of faith and charity and this emphasis plays a far more important role in eucharistic theology than does transubstantiation.

I believe it no accident that poverty was considered no shame in the Middle Ages and that, according to Brian Tierney in his study of charity in medieval England, "taken all in all, the poor were better looked after in England in the thirteenth century than in any subsequent century until the present one."[41] People were expected to live the Eucharist in a very real way and evidence exists to show that to some extent at least, they succeeded.

Medieval eucharistic theology has gotten a bum rap. Far too often, the extensive and often moving treatises of this period are mined merely for their discussions of transubstantiation (our obsession, not theirs) or the opinions of hundreds of medieval writers are reduced to the final work of one hefty Dominican. Thomas's work, interesting as it remains, was an idiosyncratic voice in thirteenth-century eucharistic theology and by the end of that century, a voice which ceased to convince. If historians and theologians are to fairly represent the theology of the Middle Ages, they simply must get beyond Thomas and I strongly recommend the far more interesting and influential theology of symbol developed by Hugh of St. Victor and Alexander of Hales.

Does my defense of medieval eucharistic theology imply that I disagree with Dr. Mary Collins in her approval of Fr. Edward Kilmartin's claim that the scholastic synthesis has no future?[42] Not at all. In fact, I would argue that the "scholastic synthesis" not only has no future; it had no real past. The "scholastic synthesis" was (or is) a construct of the nineteenth century based on sixteenth-century commentaries on Aquinas. It bears little relationship to the rambunctious, daring, and contentious diversity of the real thirteenth-century theologians. Advocates of the "scholastic synthesis" conveniently forget that using Aristotle as the basis for one theology in 1260 was just as controversial then as using Marx as the basis for ones theology in 1960 and got people in just as much ecclesiastical hot water.

The scholastics were confident (some contemporaries argued even reckless) in their belief that anything true must come from God, even if it came from "the pagan Aristotle [or] the Saracen Averroes."[43] The true heirs of the real thirteenth-century theologians are not those who desperately wrap themselves in Aristotle's musty toga, but those who are trying on the more modern raiment of Marx and Gramsci. The real heritage of true scholastic theology ought to be their intended boldness and their perhaps unintended but very real diversity.[44]

But let us return to the medieval theology of reception to make one final historical observation. The most interesting aspect of their theology, at least for me, is the centrality of spiritual communion, for spiritual communion was entirely a lay matter. No minister was necessary to make a spiritual communion, since even the miracle of transubstantiation was unnecessary for this devotion. The lay practice of spiritual communion and the theology of spiritual reception effectively removed the priest as the exclusive mediator of the presence of the risen Lord just as the theology and practice of ordination were attributing the power of consecration solely to the ordained. Spiritual communion could even occur as an admonition to clergy not to deny sacramental communion to those who so desired it. I need not rehearse here the miracles recounted by Caroline Walker Bynum in which Jesus himself gave devout lay women the sacrament when it was withheld by the clergy.[45] These incidents were merely the most dramatic forms of spiritual communion without, and in fact, despite the benefit of clergy.

This is the third point that I would like to make concerning the eucharistic theology and practice of the late twelfth and early thirteenth centuries. What occurred during this period, I would suggest, was what Catherine Bell describes as a "negotiation" between the ordained and the nonordained participants in the eucharistic ritual for control of the means of access to the divine. Put into the language of modern social science, this negotiation would be a struggle for access to the processes of objectification and embodiment of the social whole.[46] In other words, if ritualization within a social group is one means, and perhaps the major means, by which a society creates and maintains its structures, then in the late twelfth and early thirteenth centuries, a new society was slowly being invented. Liturgies which clearly separated clergy and laity mirrored and also created a society with two clearly separated realms. Here the ever more fervent devotion to the Real Presence in the Eucharist, witnessed by eucharistic miracles, tabernacle lights, the removal of the chalice from the laity, and the elevation of the host would serve to reinforce the miraculous power of the priest to make the risen Lord present.[47] Eventually the two realms of priesthood and laity were understood as metaphysically different; the clergy eternally differentiated from the laity by the indelible mark received by ritual ordination.[48]

This "clericalization" of Western society, which began with the Gregorian reform movement in the eleventh century, was complete by the mid-thirteenth century and continued unabated, despite major revision during the Reformation, until the present day, more particularly, of course, in the Roman Catholic community. It is important to note that given Bell's analysis of the ritual nature of society, this new society created in the late twelfth and early thirteenth centuries continued to exist only because the participants, both ordained and nonordained, continued to ritually recreate that society.

In the renegotiation of ritual power which took place during that period, the clergy, as specialists, allocated to themselves the sole right to make the risen Lord present in the Eucharist. This particular aspect of the change has been studied by scholars (and either praised or lamented depending on the author's particular theological stance).[49] It is very important to point out, however, the other side of the coin. By allocating to themselves control over popular devotions, especially spiritual communion, the laity "negotiated" or redefined the understanding of the Eucharist to allow for a form of immediate access to the divine by which the laity bypassed the power of the clergy without denying or confronting the clergy's exclusive power to consecrate.[50] This particular aspect of the renegotiation deserves much more careful study by scholars than it has yet received. In this sense, the laity, too, were celebrants, but celebrants of "unofficial" rituals as opposed to the celebrants of "official" liturgies. Ritual specialists would exist, then, in both the clerical and lay worlds and both would provide access to the divine without challenging the authority of the other. Here I am indebted to the seminal work of Orlando Espín which points out the intricacies of the parallel access to the divine provided by "popular" and "official" Roman Catholicism in the Latino experience.[51]

If Bell is correct in her analysis of ritual, and I believe she is, some such sort of renegotiation was inevitable. To quote Bell, "The criteria for authentication (of a ritual) are nothing less than a satisfying sense of adherence to precedent in addition to a close resonance with lived experience—in other words, a collective confidence in the continued well-being of the society along with an individual sense of participation in a process of redemptive activity."[52] If clergy were to claim control over the Eucharist as well as the other "official" rituals of the Church, then some other means had to be found for the laity to continue to find an individual sense of participation in redemption. As Espín has pointed out, popular devotions not only clearly play this role, but they also provide a close and personal connection with the lived experience of individual communities. Popular devotions are necessarily grounded in the local community—this statue which is in our town, this procession, these clothes; now, here, and for us. Popular devotions provide the "close resonance with lived experience" which can be lacking in a liturgy formed under the tight control of an international or even a national magisterium. A balance was struck in the late twelfth and early thirteenth centuries between official rituals with their specialists and unofficial rituals which could also have their specialists. Clergy obtained official access to the divine by means of tightly controlled universally undifferentiated liturgies. Laity retained direct access to the divine by means of widely diverse, locally grounded and largely unregulated popular devotions.

This renegotiation of the roles of the clergy and of the laity in the late twelfth and early thirteenth centuries was one of the most momentous such shifts in the history of the Eucharist. The shift was so successful that the settlement reached by the end of the thirteenth century has been and often still is read back into all of earlier Christian history. From this point of view, this paper is clearly a call for further research into the diversity of both practice and theory concerning the Eucharist during that half of Christian history misleadingly lumped into the single epithet, or perhaps more accurately, epitaph, "the Middle Ages." We have allies back then, subversive memories that remind us that the way it is now is not necessarily always the way it was then. Things have changed substantially before, and we certainly need not fear them changing substantially in the future. To paraphrase that great historian and former president of this august body, Walter Principe, history is freedom from the tyranny of the present.[53] I would never advocate a return to the Church of the tenth and eleventh centuries, but the fact that they were substantially different from the Church of the thirteenth century allows us the freedom to dream of a Church substantially different from that of the early twentieth century.

My concerns, however, are not just historical. My sense is that Roman Catholics in the United States are in the midst of another momentous "renegotiation" of the ritual power of the Eucharist. Of course, for many Catholics and particularly for Hispanic Catholics, the old allocation of "official" and "unofficial" ritual power still remains in force. But for many others, a striking shift in the allocation of ritual power has already occurred. According to the Notre Dame Study of Catholic Life, laity, and particularly women, have taken over many important liturgical roles, even roles previously reserved for ordained men.[54] I won't bore you with the statistics; most of you know them far better than I. I would only point out that, from an historical perspective, the clear and careful separation between clergy and laity established in the thirteenth century is quietly disappearing from parish life. To give but one example. The results of the Notre Dame Study's analysis of confession today led the researchers to conclude that "We suspect these figures [on attendance at penance rituals] reflect some misunderstandings among parishioners about the relationships among private confession to a priest and the resultant absolution, private confession directly in prayer to God or another person, public confession in the Confiteor during Mass, and mixed public/private confession in the communal penance service."[55] In short, when asked about their participation in the sacrament of penance, those questioned saw all of the above described actions as equally fitting the definition of the ritual of penance. The situation described in the study closely parallels the practice of penance as it existed in the Middle Ages before the clergy claimed the sole right to the power of the keys in the thirteenth century. Parishioners today are no longer distinguishing clearly between those rituals performed by the permanently ordained clergy and those rituals performed by laity. In parishes where the laity already celebrate the Liturgy of the Word, distribute Communion, and even lead the congregation in communion services in the absence of official clergy, it will hardly be surprising that the demarcation between those officially and permanently ordained, and those "ordained" in the older sense of being ritually appointed to a particular role will be largely lost on the younger generation of Catholics. I am not a liturgist, nor do I study modern parish life, but I suggest, as an historian, to those that do, that despite the protests of the magisterium, a new negotiation of ritual power is taking place in the pews as I speak, and it is a renegotiation which minimizes the difference between permanent and temporary forms of "ordination."

Again to use the analysis of Catherine Bell, the rituals that now constitute parish life in the United States are creating and mirroring a very new Church, indeed a new form of Catholicism, every time a liturgy is said, or a parish group meets. As a product of the 1950s and 1960s, I must admit that it is difficult for me to quite imagine the shape that new form of Catholicism will take, but I do know that it is already happening, that it cannot be stopped and that a new and wonderfully exciting Church is appearing all around us. And fortunately for the Church, perhaps, I very much doubt that either the magisterium or we theologians can do much to stop it. At best we can be participants in the new negotiation of ritual power.

To close, let me make one further observation. As I look out at this crowd of distinguished theologians, I see a group for whom the great Vatican Council of thirty years ago was *the* defining moment. One of the most important tasks of this generation has been to implement the insights of that council most often in the context of, and often in opposition to, that preconciliar Catholic life which makes up our shared heritage. Thirty years from now, there will not be one person at the CTSA convention who will have had any meaningful experience of Catholicism as it existed before Vatican II.[56] If present trends continue, the majority of that audience will be laity and the majority of the laity will be women. They will have grown up in parishes where leadership, liturgy, and social action are, for the most part, organized and celebrated by laity, and again, mostly lay women. As Dr. Bernard Cooke points out in his new book on the Eucharist, this is a sign of great hope for eucharistic celebration, and I share his optimism for the future.[57] For the first time in seven hundred years, something really new and wonderful is stirring and I, for one, am thrilled to be part of it.

---

1. Originally published in *Proceedings of the Catholic Theological Society of America* 52, Judith A. Dwyer, ed. (Macon, Ga.: Mercer University Press, 1997) 39–58. Without the assistance, support, and criticisms of the Department of Theological and Religious Studies at the University of San Diego, I would not have been able to produce this paper. I would like to particularly thank my colleagues, Dr. Orlando Espín and Fr. Dennis Krouse for their insights and suggestions.

2. "Secreta dicitur, quia secreto pronuntiatur, cum olim tamen alta uoce diceretur, unde et ab hominibus laicis sciebatur. Contingit ergo, ut quadam die pastores super lapidem quendam ponerent panem, qui ad horum uerborum prolationem in carnem conuersus est, forsan transsubstantiatus est panis in corpus Christi, in quos diuinitus factus est acerrima uindicta. Nam percussi sunt diuino iuditio celitus misso. Vnde statutum fuit, ut de cetero sub silentio diceretur, . . ." *De ecclesiasticis officiis,* c. 44, Heribert Douteil, ed., *Iohannes Beleth, Summa de ecclesiasticis officiis,* Corpus christianorum, continuatio medievalis 41A (Turnhout: Brepols, 1976) 78.

3. *Pratum spirituale,* c. 196, *PL* 74: 225C–226D; Pseudo-Albinus, *De divinis officiis,* c. 40, *PL* 101:1256D; *Speculum ecclesiae,* c. 7, *PL* 177: 368C-D and Lothar of Segni, *De missarum mysteriis,* l. 1, c. 1, *PL* 217: 840C-D. On the dating of these commentaries on the Mass, see Roger Reynolds, "Liturgy, Treatises on," *DMA* 7:624–33, and Gary Macy, "Commentaries on the Mass During the Early Scholastic Period" included as the seventh essay in this volume.

4. "Nouimus et duos fratres qui se inter summos connumerant magistros, quorum alter tantum uim diuinus uerbis in confidiendis sacramentis tribuit, ut a quibusdam ipsa proferantur aeque suam habeat efficaciam, ut etiam mulier et quislibet cuiuscumque sit ordinis uel conditionis per uerba dominica sacramentum altaris conficere queat." *Petri Abaelardi opera theologica,* E. Buytaert, ed., Corpus christianorum, continuatio medievalis 12 (Turnhout: Brepols, 1969) 302. On the identification of these brothers as Bernard and Thierry, see Buytaert, ibid., and M.-D. Chenu, "Un cas de platonisme grammatical au XIIe siècle," *Revue des sciences philosophiques et théologiques* 31 (1967) 666–68.

5. Yves Congar, "Note sur une valeur des termes «ordinare, ordinatio»," *Revue des sciences religieuses* 58 (1984) 7–14.

6. Paul F. Bradshaw, "Medieval Ordination," *The Study of Liturgy,* C. Jones, G. Wainwright, and others, eds. (N.Y.: Oxford University Press, 1992) 377–78.

7. "I Francescani e la confessione nel secolo XIII," *Francesconesimo e Vita Religiosa dei Laici nel '200* (Assisi: Università degli studi di Perugia, 1981) 251–309. On the whole question of the laity hearing confessions in the Middle Ages, see A. Teetaert, *La confession aux laïques dans l'Église latine depuis le VIII jusq'au XIV siècle* (Paris: Universitas Catholica Louvaniensis, 1926).

8. For a discussion of the powers exercised by abbesses in the Middle Ages, see Joan Morris, *The Lady Was a Bishop* (Cambridge: Cambridge University Press, 1978).

9. For an exhaustive discussion of this dispute, see Rolf Zerfaß, *Der Streit zum die Laienpredigt. Eine pastoral-geschichtliche Untersuchung zum Verständnis des Predigtamtes und zu seinen Entwicklung im 12. und 13. Jahrhundert* (Frieberg, Basel, Wien: Herder, 1974).

10. On the fundamentally conservative nature of the Waldensian liturgy, see Gary Macy, *Theologies of the Eucharist in the Early Scholastic Period* (Oxford: Clarendon Press, 1984) 56–57.

11. E.g., "[E]xaudi, quaeso domine, gemitum mei *famulae tuae indignae et peccatricis supplicantis*, et, quae de meritorum qualitate diffido, non iudicium, sed misericordiam consequi merear. Per d<ominum>." Italics mine. The entire text of this *Oratio ad accipiendum eucharistiam* has been published by Jean Leclercq, "Prières médiévales pour recevoir l'eucharistie pour saluer et pour bénir la croix," *Ephemerides liturgicae* 97 (1965) 329–31.

12. Jean Leclercq, "Eucharistic Celebrations Without Priests in the Middle Ages," *Worship* 55 (1981) 160–68.

13. Medieval theologians speculated that the Sign of the Cross, or the entire Canon, or perhaps even the Lord's Prayer, could consecrate, see Macy, *Theologies of the Eucharist*, 57. On the gradual clarification of the clerical state and of the sacrament of ordination, see Bradshaw, "Medieval Ordinations," 377–79, and the still excellent articles by P.-M. Gy, "Notes on the Early Terminology of Christian Priesthood," in *The Sacrament of Holy Orders* (Collegeville: The Liturgical Press, 1962) 98–115, and by G. Fransen, "The Tradition in Medieval Canon Law," ibid., 202–18.

14. Christopher N. L. Brooke, "Priest, Deacon and Layman, from St. Peter Damien to St. Francis," *The Ministry: Clerical and Lay*, W. J. Sheils and Diana Wood, eds. (Oxford: Basil Blackwell, 1989) 65–85, mentions this point as part of his excellent discussion of the gradual separation of the laity and clergy during the eleventh, twelfth, and thirteenth centuries.

15. "Et hoc utique sacramentum nemo potest conficere, nisi sacerdos, qui rite fuerit ordinatus, secundum claves ecclesiae, quas ipse concessit apostolic eorumque successoribus Iesus Christus." *Constitutiones Concilii quarti Lateranensis una cum commentariis glossatorum*, Antonio García y García, ed., Series A: Corpus glossatorum 2 (Vatican City, 1981) 42. The passage occurs in the opening creed against the Cathars and the Waldensians and García y García believes that the wording may well be that of Innocent III himself (ibid., 6–8).

16. In 1208, Innocent used even more emphatic wording in a profession of faith to be demanded of the Waldensians: "Unde firmiter credimus et confitemur, quod quantumcumque quilibet honestus, religiosus, sanctus et prudens sit, non potest nec debet eucharistiam consecrare nec altaris sacrificium conficere, nisi sit presbyter ab episcopo, ut praediximus, ad illud proprie officium constitutus, et illa sollemnia verba, quae a sancta Patribus in canone sunt expressa, et fidelis intentio proferentis; ideoque firmiter credimus et fatemur, quod quicumque sine se posse sacrificium eucharistiae facere, haereticus est et perditionis core et suorum complicum est particeps et consors, et ab omni sancta Romana ecclesia segregandus." *Professio Valdesii,* A. Dondaine, ed., *Archivum Fratrum Praedictorum* 16 (1946) 231.

17. "Nova quaedam nuper, de quibus miramur non modicum, nostris sunt auribus intimata, quod abbatissae videlicet, in Bugensi et in Palentinensi dioecesibus constitutae, moniales proprias benedicunt, ipsarum quoque confessiones in criminibus audiunt, et legentes evangelium praesumunt publice praedicare. Quum igitur id absenum sit pariter et absurdum, [nec a nobis aliquatenus sustinendum,] discretioni vestrae per apostolica scripta mandamus, quatenus, ne id de cetero fiat, auctoritate curetis apostolica firmiter inhibere, quia, licet beatissima virgo Maria dignior et excellentior fuerit Apostolis universis, non tamen illi, sed istis Dominus claves regni coelorum commisit." *Corpus Iuris Canonici, Decretales* l. 5, t. 38, c. 10, E. Friedberg ed. (Graz: Akademische Druck- u. Verlagsanstalt, 1959) 2, cols. 886–87.

18. "The Ordination of Women and the Theologians in the Middle Ages," *Escritos del Vedat* 36 (1986) 145. Fr. Martin's study is an excellent and thorough study of the medieval discussion of women's ordination and is contained in *Escritos del Vedat* 36 (1986) 115–77 and 38 (1988) 88–143. For an exhaustive discussion of the canonists' position on the ordination of women, see Ida Raming, *The Exclusion of Women from the Priesthood: Divine Law or Sex Discrimination?* Norman R. Adams, trans. (Metuchen, N. J.: The Scarecrow Press, 1976).

19. For the references to this practice, see Macy, *Theologies,* 101.

20. "Item infirmus petit eucharistiam. Sacerdos non habet. Queritur an debeat dare purum panem. Quod videtur quia nonne prodest ei tantum illa voluntas quantum si reciperet eucharistiam cum nullus subsit ibi error. Ad hoc dicimus non tantum valet purus panis quantum ad cumulum gratie sed tantum valet ad vitam eternam." Stephen Langton, *Questiones,* Cambridge, St. John's College, MS C.7 (57), fol. 255v1.

21. "Et notandum tamen quia sub utraque specie est totus Christus quo facto sacerdos elevat corpus Christi ut omnis fideles videant et petant quod prosit ad salutem vel ad ostendendum quia non est aliud dignus sacrificium." William of Auxerre, *Summa de officiis ecclesiasticis,* Paris, Bibliothèque nationale, latin MS 15168, fol. 88r2. "Postea sacerdos communicat sacramentaliter ut ipse et populus spiritualiter et sicut dictum est aliis dat duas partes, scilicet, dyacono et subdiacono vel ipse comedit." Ibid., fol. 89v2.

22. Ideas similar to those espoused by Alexander exist in late twelfth- and early thirteenth-century writers. Cf., for instance, Innocent III, *De sacro altaris mysterio* l. 4, c. 16 : "Nam in quo similitudo deficeret, in eo sacramentum non esset, sed ibi se proderet, et fidei locum aufferret, neque jam crederetur quod ita fieri non oportet. Itaque quantum ad nos servat per omnia corruptibilis cibi similitudinem, sed quantum ad se non amittit inviolabilis corporis veritatem." *PL* 215: 867D. See also Peter of Capua, *Summa "Uetustissima ueterum"* (ca. 1201–02): "Et potest dici quod etiam in ipso sumente manet materiale corpus donec in eo est aliqua forma ipsius panis. Non tamen incorporatur ei quia cibus est anime non corporis ut dicit Augustinus." Vatican City, Biblioteca Vaticana, Vaticana latina MS 4296, fol. 70r1, and Jacques de Vitry, *Historia occidentalis* (ca. 1219–25): "Forma igitur gustatur, sentitur, dentibus atteritur. Corpus autem non in uentrem descendit, sed ob ore ad cor transit. Comeditur sed non consumitur." J. F. Hinnebusch, ed., *The Historia Occidentalis of Jacques de Vitry,* Spicilegium Friburgense, Texts Concerning the History of Christian Life 17 (Fribourg: The University Press, 1972) 231.

23. On the dating of Alexander's works, see Alexander of Hales, *Quaestiones disputatae 'Antequam Esset Frater,'* Collegium S. Bonaventurae, eds., Bibliotheca franciscana scholastica medii aevi 19–21 (Florence: Quaracchi, 1960) 34*–36*.

24. E.g., "Quaestio est propter quid, si corpus Christ ibi est, non sumitur a brutis animalibus.—Responsio est ad hoc, quod differt sensus in brutis et in nobis. Est enim in nobis ordinatus ad rationem, in brutis vero non. Quia ergo corpus Christi sub sacramento non dicit tantum quod ad sensum pertinet, sed quod ad rationem, quod sensus est a brutis sumitur, scilicet species panis; quod in ordine ad rationem est non sumitur, scilicet corpus Christi." Alexander of Hales, *Glossa in quatuor libros sententiarum,* Collegium S. Bonaventurae, eds., Bibliotheca franciscana scholastica medii aevi 15 (Florence: Quaracchi, 1957) 204. Cf. also 161–62.

25. *Quaestiones disputatae,* 966–67, no. 199, esp. p. 967: "Item, alia est unio speciei tantum, ut in iis qui manducant secundum quod est sacramentum solum, sicut panem aliquem, ut Iudaei vel pagani.—Item est unio secundum rationem signi, ut in eo qui credit et intelligit; et maior adhuc est eo qui credit et diligit, ut in iis qui spiritualiter accipiunt; et sic secundum quod maior unio, maior manducatio."

26. Ibid., 699–700, nos. 205–10. E.g.: "Respondeo: manducare sacramentaliter, ut proprie dicitur, est attingere rem sub sacramento; ergo ubi nullo modo attingitur, nec per modum crediti, nec per modum cogniti, nullo modo est manducatio sacramentalis vel sacramentaliter; sed est quodam modo manducatio carnalis, et adhuc, proprie non est ibi manducatio carnalis, quia non est ibi divisio substantiae, cum non sit ibi nisi divisio accidentium solum . . . Ad hoc quod obicitur de Iudaeo vel pagano, dico quod plus est in hac manducatione quam in manducatione irrationalis creaturae, quia unio est ibi in natura. Tamen quia non est ibi cognitio rei sub specie, et cum manducatio sacramen-

talis importet accipere species et attingere rem quae est sub sacramento fide, non manducant sacramentaliter."

27. For a further discussion of this issue, see Gary Macy, "Reception of the Eucharist According to the Theologians: A Case of Diversity in the 13th and 14th Centuries," included as the third essay in this volume, and idem, "A Re-evaluation of the Contribution of Thomas Aquinas to Thirteenth-Century Theology of the Eucharist." *The Early Universities,* by Nancy Van Dusen, ed., Studies in Medieval Culture 39 (Kalamazoo, Mich.: Medieval Institute Publications, 1997) 53–72. On the influence of Alexander's theology, see Victorin Doucet, *Doctor Irrefragabilis Alexandri de Hales ordinis minorum Summa Theologica . . .* vol. 4, liber 3 *(Prologomena).* (Florence: Quaracchi, 1948).

28. For a recent summary of what is known about Nicholas' life and works, see *DMA* 9:126.

29. "He sunt conditiones necessaria requisite ad idoneum susceptorem sacramenti eucharistie per quas potest responderi ad plures questiones consuetas fieri. Requiritur enim quod sit homo, viator, fidelis, adultus, mente preditus, ieiunus deuotus, sine conscientia peccati mortalis, crimine non notatus, corpore mundus, apparitione miraculosa non prohibitus, a ministro ydoneo tempore debito, intentione recta." Nicholas of Lyra, *Dicta de sacramentis* (Cologne, 1495). The edition is unfoliated.

30. "Prima conditio est quod sit (homo) per quod statim excluditur omne brutum animal et angelis siue bonus siue malus. Sed si queratur Numquid brutum animal suscipit sacramentum. Dixeratur aliqui quod immediate quando brutum suscepit sacramentum desinit ibi esse corpus Christi. Sed hoc reprobatur a magistro sententiarum in quarto de consecratione. Et similiter in decretis de conse. di.ii.ca. Qui bene non custodierit. Et ideo dicitur ab aliis aliter et melius ut videtur quod quamdiu species ille sacramentales mutare non fuerint per calorem naturalem stomachi: tamdiu remanet ibi corpus Christi. Vnde sicut habemus ex speciali facto diuino quod ad vltimam dispositionem corporis humani deus infundit creando ipsam animam et eam tenet in corpore durante tali dispositionem: sic etiam deus statuit pactum cum ecclesia quod tamdiu esset ipsum corpus Christi sub sacramento quamdiu permanent ille species quam prius afficiebantur et aspiciebant panem sicut subiectum a quo postea miraculose separantur et manu tenentur et propter illud est ut redderet deus ecclesiam certam quando ibi esset corpus Christi et quando non. Recipit ergo brutum realiter et non sacramentaliter et hoc exponam inferius in tercia conditione." Ibid.

31. "Tertio dixi (fidelis) et intelligo non illum qui de fide solum instructum est sed illum qui iam accepit sacramentum baptismi et factus est per hoc de familia Christi. Ex quo statim patet quod cathecumino quamtamcumque habenti fidem perfectam non debet hoc sacramentum administrari. Sed si queratur Numquid infidelis recipiendo sacramentum recipit corpus Christi dicendum de ipso sicut de bruto supra tactum est quod sumit realiter sed

nullo modo sacramentaliter inquantum infidelis. Si queras Numquid idem est sumere sacramentum et sacramentaliter sumere. Dico quod non quia sumere sacramentaliter addit supra sumere sacramentum modum sumendi videlicet quod referat signum in signatum suum credendo et si opus est confidendo ore quod sub illis speciebus veraciter contineatur corpus Christi quod non facit infidelis nec etiam brutum." Ibid.

32. "Nunc autem pueri ante annos discretionis et si possunt eucharistiam realiter sicut quemcumque alium cibum comedere, non tamen possunt hoc sacramentum sacramentaliter manducare nec eo uti ut sacro signo, referendo significandum in signatum sed ut communio signo, et sic propter carentiam discretionis non percipiunt ibi veraciter continere corpus Christi." Ibid. See also: "Si autem sit amentes sic quod non fit furiosus sed tantummodo loquens inania et a vero sensu alienatus. Adhuc distinguendum est, quia vel pretendit actus et signa deuotionis tunc potest ei ministrari, si vero nullum actum aut signum deuotionis pretendit, recurredum est ad tempus precedens passionem quia si tunc petierit et deuotionem pretenderit et obstet aliquid aliud periculum, licite potest sibi dari." Ibid.

33. Peter the Lombard, Thomas Aquinas, Albert the Great, Bonaventure, and Duns Scotus all describe the *res sacramenti* in this fashion. Since these texts are readily available to scholars, I will include here a sample of texts less often consulted.

"Unde: 'Quid paras dentem et ventrem? Crede et manducasti.' Qui credit in Deum , comedit ipsum; qui incorporatur Christo per fidem, id est membrum ejus efficitur, vel unitate corporis ejus firmius solidatur." Innocent III, *De missarum mysteriis*, PL 217: 866D.

"Modus sumendi duplex est, sacramentalis et spiritualis: Sacramentaliter sumunt boni et mali; nam sacramentaliter sumere est ipsam carnem veram Christi sumere, sive inde percipiatur fructus, id est ecclesiastica pax, sive non. Spiritualiter sumunt soli boni: spiritualiter sumere est fructum provenientem ex carne Domini sumere; id est esse de unitate Ecclesiae, sive sumatur corpus Christi sive non." Peter of Poitiers, *Sententiarum libri quinque*, PL 211: 1252D–1253A.

"Quidam spiritualiter tantum ut boni eremite. Unde Augustinus, 'ut quid paras dentum et ventrem? Crede et manducasti.' Quidam spiritualiter et sacramentaliter ut boni sacerdotes." Prepositinus of Cremona, *Summa Theologicae*, ed. Daniel Edward Pilarczyk, *Praepositini Cancellarii de Sacramentis et de Novissimis [Summa Theologicae Pars Quarta]*, Collectio Urbaniana, Textus ac documenta 7 (Rome: Editiones Urbanianae, 1964) 93.

"Item dicit Augustinus in libro de remedio penitentie anime, 'Ut quid paras dentem et ventrem? Crede et manducasti.' Ergo si habet quis fidem huius articuli et aliorum qui neccesarii sunt ad salutem, fidem dico virtutem, sufficet ei ad salutem etsi numquid sumat sacramentaliter carnem Christi. Ergo semper possumus non sumere hoc sacramentum sine detrimento virtutis."

Magister Martinus, *Questiones*, Cambridge, St. John's College, MS C.7 (57), fol. 123v1.

"*Nam prostrati sunt in deserto sicut enim in bonis ulto melius id quod per figuram significatur quam ipsa figura* spes enim melior est quam sacramentum ipsius rei. Unde corpus Christi quod traxit de virgine sit sacramentum unitatis ecclesiatice. Magna apparet eius excellentia non tamen dicimus quod unitas ecclesie sit melior vel dignior quam corpus Christi." Stephen Langton, *Glossa in glossam Petri Lombardi*, Cambridge University, University Library MS Ii.4.23, fol. 205v2.

"In sacramento isto duplex est caro Christi: unas naturalis, quam assumpsit de Virgine, et quantum ad illam, manducamus corpus Christi; et ibi est etiam caro Christi mystica, id est unitas ecclesiastica, quae est per compaginem caritatis, et quantum ad istam revera manducamur, id est Christo incorporamur. Sed quia prima caro est causa secundae, id est naturalis causa mysticae, potius dicimur manducare quam manducari." Gui of Orchelles, eds. Damian and Odulph Van den Eynde, *Tractatus de sacramentis, Guidonis de Orchellis, Tractatus de sacramentis ex eius Summa de sacramentis et officiis ecclesiae*, Franciscan Institute Publications, text series 4 (St. Bonaventure, N.Y.: The Franciscan Institute, 1953) 76.

"Alii corpus Christi tantum spiritualiter manducant. De quibus dicit beatus Augustinus: «Vt quid paras dentum et uentrem? crede et manducasti.» Hoc modo qui credit in Christum fide per caritatem operante manducat ipsum, licet sub forma sacramenti ipsum non recipiat. Incorporatur enim Christo per fidem et eius membrum efficitur et, in unitate ecclesie Christo capitis uinculo caritatis adherens, unus spiritus efficitur cum eo." Jacques de Vitry, *Historia Occidentalis*, 214.

"Huius et hoc modi soluta sunt iam per distinctionem predicatam tamen notandum quod primus modus dupliciter distinguntur; secundum duos modos manducandi corpus Christi. Unde consistit in solo sacramento quo manducant tam boni quam mali; illius consistit in virtute sacramenti et hoc modo sumit corpus Christi qui manet in unitate ecclesie. Unde Augustinus de verbis evangelii ait 'Quid est Christum manducare? Non est hoc solum in sacramento corpus eius accipere, sed in Christo manere et habere ipsum in se manentem.' Spiritualiter enim manducat qui in unitate Christi et ecclesie quam ipsum sacramentum signat manet. Nam qui discordat a Christo nec carnem Christi manducat nec s[anguinem] bibit etsi tante rei sacramentum ad iudicium cotidie accipiat. De hac spirituali manducatione ait Augustinus 'Ut quid paras ventrem et dentum; crede et manducasti.' Robert of Courçon, *Summa*, British Library Royal MS 9.E.14, fol. 65r2.

"*In sacramentorum* . . . Continentur autem tria in hoc sacramento: forma visibilis panis et vini: veritas corporis et sanguinis Christi et virtus spiritualis. id est. virtus unitatis et charitatis .id est. eterna coniunctio et dilectio Christi ad ecclesiam." *Glossa ordinaria* on the *Decretum*, *De consecratione*, dist. II, c. 1

(In sacramentorum), *Decretum Gratiani Nouissime* (Venice: n.p., 1525) fol. 598v1–2.

34. For a discussion of the original mistaken attribution of this work to Hugh of St. Victor, cf. Barthélemy Hauréau, *Les oeuvres de Hugues de Saint-Victor. Essai critique* (Paris: Hachette et cie, 1886; rpt. Frankfurt: Minerva, 1963) 199–203. Heinrich Weisweiler, "Zur Einflusssphäre der 'Vorlesungen' Hugos von St. Victor," *Mélanges Joseph de Ghellinck, S.J.* Museum Lessianum, Section historique 13–14 (Gembloux: Éditions J. Duclot, 1951) 534–70, offers the best discussion of the work, demonstrating its dependence on the lectures of Hugh of St. Victor as preserved in the *reportatio* of Laurentius (Oxford, Bodleian Library MS. Laud. 344), on the *De Sacramentis*, and on the *Summa Sententiarum*, thus placing it clearly within the influence of the Victorine School. The author of the *Speculum* describes himself as more familiar with logic than theology: "Cum autem libentius, quia facilius et audentius, logicas quam theologas, jure consuetudinis, revolvam sententias: dubitare coepi, an contradicere, an potius scribere mallem." *PL* 177: 335A.

35. The influence of the *Speculum* on Simon of Tournai has been traced by Damien Van den Eynde, "Deux sources de la Somme théologique de Simon de Tournai," *Antonianum* 24 (1949) 19–42. The *Speculum* was also used by another commentary on the Mass, the *Tractatus de sacramento altaris* of Stephen of Autun. Barthélemy Hauréau, *Les oeuvres de Hugues de Saint-Victor*, 201–02, lists fifteen manuscripts of this work. For references to research on this work, including a list of English manuscripts unknown to Hauréau, see Macy, *Theologies of the Eucharist*, 65 and note 120 of ch. 3.

36. Damien Van den Eynde, "Deux sources de la somme théologique de Simon de Tournai," 41, and "Le Tractatus de sacramento altaris faussement attribué à Étienne de Baugé," *Recherches de théologie ancienne et médiévale* 19 (1952) 241, dates this work ca. 1160. He takes as his *terminus post quem* the publication of the sentences of Peter Lombard (1153–58) which the *Speculum* uses. Since the *Speculum* does not use John Beleth, nor any of the other later commentators, and since Beleth was such a popular work, Van den Eynde argues that the *Speculum* was written before the appearance of Beleth's work (1160–64). It would be safer, however, to date this work between the publication of Peter Lombard's work and that of Simon of Tournai, roughly 1160–75.

37. "Communio, quae post cantatur, innuit omnes fideles corpori Christi communicare, quod pro omnibus minister assumit sacramentaliter, ut sibi et omnibus sumatur spiritualiter." *PL* 176: 373C. A similar opinion is offered by the thirteenth-century *Glossa ordinaria* on the *Decretum*: Dist. II, c. 56 *(Non iste panis)* "*Accipere* si sit sacerdos; si laicus tempore constituto, vel potius mystice spiritualem notat sumptionem: unde glossa ibi *accipere quotidie*, id est, quotidie te preparas habilem ad suscipiendum." *Decretum Gratiani Nouissime*, fol. 607v1.

38. "Sacramentalis autem communio est communis bonis et malis, quae sine spirituali non prodest." *PL* 176: 366A–B. Cf. Hugh of St. Victor, *De sacramentis christianae fidei* l.II, pars 8, c. 5 and c. 7, *PL* 176: 465B–C, 467C–D.

39. *PL* 177: 365D.

40. "Spiritualis autem sumptio, quae vera fide percipitur, sine sacramentali, ubi non est contemptus religionis, sufficit." Ibid., 366B.

41. Brian Tierney, *Medieval Poor Law: A Sketch of Canonical Theory and its Application in England* (Berkeley: University of California Press, 1959) 109. For a summary of the medieval attitudes toward poverty, see Bernard Hamilton, *Religion in the Medieval West* (London: Edward Arnold, 1986) 132–41, esp. 141: "Consequently, it was not considered socially acceptable to adopt a patronizing attitude toward the poor and destitute, for that would have been taken as evidence of retarded spiritual growth. This, perhaps, is the best measure of the church's success in making people understand what the virtuous life, as conceived in Christian terms, was about."

42. Mary Collins, "The Church and the Eucharist," Judith Dwyer, ed., *Proceedings of the Catholic Theological Society of America* 52 (Macon, Ga.: Mercer University Press, 1997) 21.

43. "I curse the fact that the pagan Aristotle, the Saracen Averroes and certain other infidel philosophers are held in such great esteem, veneration and authority by certain scholars, especially in the study of sacred theology." Thus the Franciscan theologian, John Peter Olivi, writing in 1285. The quote is contained in David Burr, "Quantity and Eucharistic Presence: The Debate from Olivi through Ockham," *Collectanea Franciscana* 44 (1974) 7.

44. For discussion of the diverse opinions about transubstantiation in the thirteenth and fourteenth centuries, see David Burr, *Eucharistic Presence and Conversion in Late Thirteenth-Century Franciscan Thought*, Transactions of the American Philosophical Society 74 (Philadelphia: The American Philosophical Society, 1984) and Gary Macy, "The Dogma of Transubstantiation in the Middle Ages," included as the fifth essay in this volume.

45. *Holy Feast and Holy Fast: The Religious Significance of Food to Medieval Women* (Berkeley: University of California Press, 1987) 116–19, 127–29, 130–32, 140–42, 236–37.

46. *Ritual Theory, Ritual Practice* (N.Y.: Oxford University Press, 1992) 197–223.

47. This connection is made by Brooke, "Priest, Deacon and Laity," 68, where he ascribes the idea to me! I honestly did not see this connection until it first was pointed out to me by Fr. Dennis Krouse. Only later did I read Brooke's article where he too connected the increasing separation of the clergy from the laity with the rise in eucharistic devotion.

48. According to Nathan Mitchell, "Not until the fifteenth and sixteenth centuries did the church's official teaching, expressed in ecumenical councils, directly affirm the view that order is a sacrament which is permanently effec-

tive and 'imprints character.'" *Mission and Ministry: History and Theology in the Sacrament of Order* (Wilmington, Del.: Michael Glazier, Inc., 1982) 254.

49. See, for instance, the excellent discussion of this issue in Bernard Cooke, *The Distancing of God: The Ambiguity of Symbol in History and Theology* (Minneapolis: Fortress Press, 1990). A more standard discussion occurs in *The Study of the Liturgy*, section IV, "Ordination."

50. Bell, 197–223.

51. See especially his *The Faith of the People: Theological Reflections on Popular Catholicism* (Maryknoll, N.Y.: Orbis Press, 1997).

52. Bell, 213.

53. An excellent summary of Fr. Principe's position is contained in his presidential address to the Catholic Theological Society of America, "The History of Theology: Fortress or Launching Pad," John P. Boyle and George Kilcourse, eds., *The Proceedings of the Catholic Theological Society of America* 43 (Macon, Ga.: Mercer University Press, 1988) 19–40.

54. The results are summarized in Joseph Gremillion and Jim Castelli, *The Emerging Parish: The Notre Dame Study of Catholic Life Since Vatican II* (San Francisco: Harper and Row, 1987) esp. 30–76 and 119–43. Again, I am indebted to Fr. Dennis Krouse for pointing out the importance of this study for my own research.

55. This passage is not included in Gremillion and Castelli, but does occur in the original study by David Legge and Thomas Trozzolo, "Participation in Catholic Parish Life: Religious Rites and Parish Activities in the 1980s," *Notre Dame Study of Catholic Parish Life* 3 (April, 1985) 4.

56. Even those young Catholics being trained in the older devotions and theology will not have experienced the pre-Vatican Church since such moves now are clearly reactionary and nostalgic in nature, something the same devotions and theology could not have been before Vatican II. The entire cultural framework for such devotions and theology has shifted, thus changing their very meaning.

57. *The Future of the Eucharist* (Mahwah, N.J.: Paulist Press, 1997). Dr. Cooke does, however, assume a continued role in the liturgy for the permanently ordained clergy. I would disagree with his analysis on this point.

Index